EGYPT

SPIRALGUIDE

AA Publishing

Contents

Written by Anthony Sattin and Sylvie Franquet
Revised and updated by Sylvie Franquet

Project Editor Linda Miles
Project Designer Alison Fenton
Series Editor Karen Rigden
Series Designer Catherine Murray

Published by AA Publishing, a trading name of AA Media Limited,
whose registered office is Fanum House, Basing View, Basingstoke,
Hampshire, RG21 4EA. Registered number 06112600.

ISBN: 978-0-7495-6241-0

A CIP catalogue record for this book is available from the
British Library.

Cover design and binding style by permission of AA Publishing
Colour separation by Keenes, Andover
Printed and bound in China by Leo Paper Products

Find out more about AA Publishing and the wide range of travel
publications and services the AA provides by visiting our website at
www.theAA.com/bookshop

A03805
Maps in this title produced from mapping © Freytag-Berndt u.
Artaria KG, 1231 Vienna-Austria
(except pp81 & 182-183)

The Magazine

A great holiday is more than just lying on a beach or shopping till you drop — to really get the most from your trip you need to know what makes the place tick. The Magazine provides an entertaining overview to some of the social, cultural and natural elements that make up the unique character of this engaging country.

THE DESERT
& THE SOWN

There is a delicate balance between the fertile and the barren in Egypt. Thin strips of agricultural land line the ribbon of the Nile, and fan out into the delta. Beyond are the great deserts that form 90 per cent of the country.

Because of this stark contrast and the low rainfall, few countries are as dominated by their geography as Egypt. The welcoming fertility of the Nile valley and the awesome wilderness of the all-encompassing deserts have had a huge influence on Egypt's history and culture. And one of ancient Egypt's most popular and enduring myths – the ongoing clash between desert and sown – is still relevant today.

Order and Chaos

The ancient god Osiris (▶ 12–15) brought order and civilisation to the Nile valley, making laws and teaching the Egyptians how to cultivate crops and produce wine. Along this generous if confined strip of land, the Egyptians thrived for thousands of years. It seemed such a wonderful place that ancient Egyptians hoped for its equal in their afterlife. Their idea of the perfect valley is echoed in many religions – in the Garden of Eden, for example, and in the Islamic shaded paradise cut through by running water, with food and drink in abundant supply.

Osiris's evil brother Seth, on the other hand, was associated with the desert, which was a constant threat to the sown. Perhaps not by chance the myth ties in with Egypt's early history, when global warming destroyed the forests on which the people of the Nile depended and the desert closed in on the river. Communities used to hunting and gathering then became reliant on the annual flooding of the Nile to irrigate their crops.

The desert is never far away in Egypt and its people have long struggled to tame it

The Desert Resource

The desert wasn't seen in solely negative terms: Ancient Egyptians used the desert as a place to escape; it was where Moses and his people were tested and purified, and where Christianity's first monastic orders were founded in the 4th century. It was also a place of wealth, for in spite of the challenging climate and landscape, some of the pharaohs' gold was mined from the Red Sea mountains, while turquoise and lapis lazuli were found in Sinai. The desert acted as a buffer against the wild Berber tribes of the Libyan Desert and the ambitious Bedouin Arabs to the west.

Shifting Sands

Thebes was eulogised as "The Hundred Gated" by the Greek poet Homer and it was the epitome of the an ancient city. Alexandria was the model of the classical city and Cairo was extolled as "the Mother of the World" in the Thousand and One Nights. But despite this, Egyptian society has always been predominantly rural, until now.

Throughout history most Egyptians were farmers, tending their plots and bartering their produce. At the beginning of the 19th century Cairo was still mostly confined within its medieval walls and Alexandria was smaller than the Greek and Roman city from which it had grown. But since then, and particularly since the 1970s, when the Aswan High Dam stopped the annual flooding of the Nile, people have been expanding the villages and towns on agricultural land. A huge exodus took place from the countryside to the cities, particularly to Cairo. And there have been similarly dramatic changes in the desert.

> "New satellite cities have been established in the desert to ease the population squeeze"

The Desert Solution

As the limited land along the Nile valley is becoming overpopulated, the solutions are being sought in the desert. The Suez Canal, cut across the desert between the Mediterranean and Red seas in 1869, is currently the country's second-largest earner of foreign currency. Elsewhere in the desert, significant reserves of gas, oil, phosphates and fresh water boost Egypt's economy. New satellite cities have been established in the desert to ease the population squeeze in Cairo. In the Libyan Desert work continues on a project to divert water from the Nile along the new Toshka Canal and into a desert depression to create an alternative valley, a mirror image of the Nile. These developments herald the start of a new era in the stormy yet inseparable relationship between the desert and the sown.

Intense farming occurs on the thin strip of fertile land along the Nile

Slow boat from Cairo –
NILE CRUISING

A cruise on the Nile is many people's idea of a romantic holiday, and it's easy to see why. Its banks are lined with some of the world's oldest and most intriguing monuments, ultra-green fields and desert, all bathed in beautiful light.

Pharaohs were cruising the Nile in ancient times for spiritual reasons, but now more than ever travelling slowly in our fast moving world has become the attraction.

Ancient Ways of Cruising

The earliest boats in ancient Egypt were most probably made of bundles of papyrus reeds, and used to travel short distances, or to go hunting and fishing. Later on, more eleborate wooden boats appeared, with several oars and a narrow sail, as on display in the Solar Boat Museum (► 66), and these were used for longer trips. The ancients took the deceased by boat across the river from the East Bank of the living to the West Bank of the dead. On wall paintings in pharaonic tombs (► 91, Valley of the Kings) the sun god Ra is seen travelling on a boat through the skies every night, and the pharaoh travels on a barque through the underworld.

A mural in the tomb of Sennefer, Valley of the Nobles, depicts boatmen on the Nile

The *Egypt*, one of the paddle steamers operated by Thomas Cook for Nile cruising

Cruising for the Elite

During the Middle Ages a traveller wrote that there were more than 35,000 ships on the Nile, most of them cargo boats or *lateens*. The pashas and rulers had luxurious riverboats, *dahabeyyas*, to make pleasure trips on the Nile. As part of their Grand Tour, 19th-century travellers rented a *dahabeyya*, or golden boat, in Cairo, kitted it out and sailed for two months past the monuments to Abu Simbel. This was the only way to travel until the 1850s when steamers made their first appearance on the river.

The Art of Going Slowly

In 1869 Thomas Cook equipped one of these steamers and brought the first group of tourists to Egypt, marking the beginning of mass tourism and the end of *dahabeyya* travel. Today a trip on a cruise ship is often part of a package tour to Egypt, and there are hundreds of large cruisers on the Nile. Cruise boats come in all sizes and to suit all budgets, but the experience is no longer as romantic as it used to be because they often have to moor next to each other, so the view from your window may well be of another boat rather than the Nile. Budget travellers prefer to travel from Aswan to Esna by *felucca*, a simple sailing boat without facilities, where the captain cooks fish from the river and you sleep on deck. In recent years *dahabeyyas* have reappeared on the scene, either restored or new, as small luxury boats with four to ten cabins, travelling slowly from Esna to Aswan and stopping at sites where the big boats are not allowed. They are the ultimate travelling experience in Egypt now.

VITAL STATISTICS

- The Nile is the world's longest river, 6,680km (4,150 miles) long.
- The Nile basin covers 3.35 million sq km (1.29 million sq miles), 10 per cent of the African continent, shared by 10 countries.
- The White Nile rises in Lake Victoria in Uganda, the Blue Nile in Lake Tana in Ethiopia, and the two meet in Khartoum (Sudan) from where the river flows more than 1,000km (620 miles) farther north to the Mediterranean, fed by only one tributary and hardly any rain.

DEATH
ON THE NILE

It's hard to get away from death in Egypt with so many monuments associated with the cult of the dead. But ancient Egyptians were not obsessed with death: Pharaohs and the noblemen enjoyed life so much they wanted it to last forever.

Osiris, God of the Underworld

Osiris was the archetypal good king and is credited with bringing civilisation to his people, teaching them how to farm and to honour their gods. Although he lived as a man, Osiris was born a god – the son of Geb, god of the earth, and Nut, the sky goddess. In true ancient Egyptian style, he married his sister Isis, while his brother Seth married their other sister Nephthys. But Seth was jealous of Osiris's success and, after inviting him to a feast, Seth presented Osiris with a beautiful box. Suddenly, Osiris was bundled into it, thrown into the Nile and drowned.

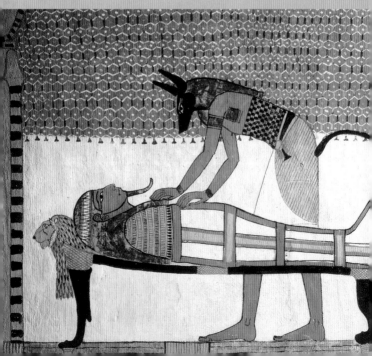

According to the Greek writer Plutarch (c46–120), Isis found Osiris's body in Lebanon. She returned her husband's corpse to Egypt, using magic to revive him for long enough to conceive a child: the falcon-headed god Horus. Later, Seth again found Osiris and this time cut him into 14 parts that were thrown into the Nile. The ever-resourceful Isis collected the parts, and bandaged them up before burying them. So Osiris became the first mummy. The tears Isis shed over her husband were believed to have caused the Nile to rise. The night in June when the Nile is seen to rise is known as the Night of the Drop.

A mummy with funerary mask from the Ptolemaic era

Life After Death

Osiris's myth offered the promise of resurrection, so Egyptians began to follow his style of burial by having themselves mummified. Isis kept the location of Osiris's tomb a secret, but it was believed that a part of his corpse was buried in each of Egypt's provinces where temples were dedicated to him. His head was believed to be buried at Abydos on the Nile itself, which Egyptians saw as the gateway to the afterlife (▶ 101). He was also held in reverence at Isis's temple on Philae (▶ 116–117).

Going Prepared

Ancient Egyptians believed that happiness in the afterlife depended on making the right preparations in this one. As well as being well preserved, a dead person needed help from spells and prayers. The Book of the Dead was intended as a map to guide the deceased to the afterlife. The final barrier was Osiris's judgement, when the dead person's heart was weighed against the feather of truth, a common image on tomb walls. If the scales tipped in your favour, you were through to everlasting happiness.

Even if you were lucky enough to get through to paradise, your tomb still had to be kept in order, as it contained all the goods, treasures and models of workers that would be needed to provide for you. These,

Jackal-headed Anubis attends to the mummy of King Sennutem

together with prayers and offerings made at your tomb, gave you a good chance of a sweet eternity.

Islamic Death Rites

Islam, which changed religious rituals, also changed burials. The Prophet Mohammed announced that the best grave was one you could wipe away with your hand – a winding sheet and a hole in the desert were all that you needed. But before long the old ideas began to reassert themselves, especially the ancient cult of the dead and a belief in the ability of spirits to affect the living.

> "Qaytbay's tomb complex in Cairo's City of the Dead is one of the glories of Islamic architecture"

City of the Dead

When the Fatimid caliphs (► 24) established the city of al Qahira (Cairo), they brought the bones of their ancestors. And when the 15th-century sultan Qaytbay built his tomb, he added a school, monastery and *caravanserai* (lodgings). He wanted the tomb to be maintained after his death, and hoped that prayers would still be said for him long after he had gone. His name has certainly lived on – Qaytbay's tomb complex in Cairo's City of the Dead is one of the glories of Islamic architecture (► 179).

Although it was built in a desert, outside the city limits, Cairo has since grown so dramatically that this City of the Dead is now well within the city – a city within the city. It's also where many ancient Egyptian funerary traditions are kept alive, from the regular, sometimes weekly, offerings of the family to the spirit of the deceased and the families of the deceased coming for a meal in or around the tomb, to people living in the cemetery alongside the dead.

Cairo's City of the Dead (left), and the sarcophagus of a rich merchant in Giza (above)

The Land of
BELIEVERS

The Greek historian Herodotus, who visited Egypt in 450 BC, called the Egyptians "religious to excess, beyond any other nation in the world". Much has changed over the past 2,000 years, but religion still plays a key part in everyday life.

The altarpiece in Ben Ezra Synagogue in Cario, Egypt's oldest synagogue

Almost all Egyptians will identify themselves as much by their religion as by their city or region of birth. One reason for this is that Egypt has been important to the development of the region's three main religions: Islam, Christianity and Judaism.

Moses and the Ten Commandments

The formative years of the early Jews were spent in Egypt, with Moses receiving the Ten Commandments on Gebel Musa in Sinai. In the 3rd century BC, the Torah, the Jewish holy book was first translated into Greek in Alexandria, making it accessible to a wider audience. Alexander the Great relocated Jews to his new city of Alexandria soon after it was founded in 331 BC and there's been a community in Egypt ever since.

Most Jews emigrated or were expelled in the mid-20th century as a result of the creation of the State of Israel and the Arab–Israeli wars, although small and mostly elderly groups do survive in Alexandria and Cairo. Consequently, the Jews are now the smallest religious group in Egypt.

The Early Christian Church

Egypt had links with Christanity from the very beginning, because Mary and Jesus are said to have travelled along the Nile with their child Jesus, and many chapels and churches mark places where they stopped and rested. According to legend the Christian Church in Egypt was founded after the evangelist St Mark sailed into Alexandria in the 1st century AD. Egyptians played an important part in establishing the rituals of the early Church, but they refused to accept the dual nature of Jesus as God and man, as for them Jesus was inseparably both in one. They were condemned as heretics in AD 451 and since then, they have been isolated, their rituals and liturgy essentially uncorrupted by outside influences. Some scholars are now looking to the Egyptian Church to provide them with a glimpse of how the early Christian Church must have been.

Detail of an illustrated Coptic papyrus, made using ancient Egyptian techniques

The Coptic Church

At the time of the Arab invasion in AD 639, most Egyptians belonged to the Coptic (Egyptian Christian) Church. Although Copts are now in the minority, making up between 6 and 10 per cent of the population, they still exert a significant influence, particularly in politics and trade, perhaps because they claim to be the true heirs of Egypt's ancient civilisation.

Many aspects of Coptic rites seem to have preserved some of the world of the pharaohs. The Coptic language, still in use in churches, would have been understood by the last of the ancients, while the liturgy and other prayers contain many phrases and images that seem to come from pagan texts. This idea is supported by the Jewish philosopher Philo of Alexandria (c15 BC–AD 50), who noted that Christians merely changed some of words of the ancient prayers. Many ancient gods seem also to find parallels in the new Coptic religion, from the holy mothers Mary and Isis, to Horus the Elder who is often depicted harpooning a hippo in the manner of St George fighting the dragon.

The Coming of Islam

The Prophet Mohammed never visited Egypt, but several of his companions and close family members are buried there. Today, some 94 per cent of Egyptians are Muslims, or followers of Islam. The holy book of Islam, the Quran, is based on a series of revelations received by Mohammed from about AD 610 to 632. The new religion was influenced by earlier religions such as Zoroastrism, Judaism and Christianity, but claimed to have superseded these.

> "One thing Copts and Muslims share is a love of celebrations, in particular the *moulids*"

Islam was brought to Egypt along with an army commanded by the great Arab general Amr ibn al As in AD 641, while the country was under the nominal rule of the Christian emperors of Constantinople (Istanbul). Islam radically abolished the priesthood that had dominated the older religions. In Egypt like in other countries, where the priests had often ruled the lives of its inhabitants, the idea of praying directly to God because all people were regarded as equal in His eyes, must have been especially popular.

Many young Coptic men have become monks

The Rift

After Prophet Mohammed's death in 632, both his friend, Abu Bakr, and his son-in-law, Ali, claimed the title of leader of the faithful. The dispute caused a rift which continues today, with the followers of Ali known as Shi'a (Shi'ite) and the followers of Abu Bakr as Sunni. Most Egyptians are Sunni Muslims.

Religious Tensions

There has always been tension between the different religions in Egypt. In 2nd- and 3rd-century Alexandria there was fighting between Christians, Jews and pagan sects, while medieval Cairo was a battleground for Copts, Sunni and Shi'a Muslims. In the 1950s and 60s, when

The Coptic Church of the Holy Virgin is set within the walls of St Anthony's Monastery

Egypt was at war with Israel, the country's remaining Jewish population was discriminated against. In the decades since then, particularly since the Afghan and Gulf wars (in which Egypt took part) there have been attacks on churches and Christian interests.

This has so embittered some of the Christian community that the Coptic Patriarch, Shenouda III, lifted his ban on Copts emigrating. Recently several young professional Coptic men have retreated to desert monasteries and created a monastic revival.

Common Ground

One thing Copts and Muslims share is a love of celebrations, in particular the annual saints' days, called *moulids*. These festivals often last several days and take place all over the country. Some are small gatherings but others, such as the *moulids* of Sayyidna al Husayn in Cairo and Sayyid al Badawy in Tanta, attract millions. Their mixture of religion, social bonding and trade is similar to celebrations held in ancient Egypt. Whether the saint is Christian or Muslim, *moulids* tend to attract a mixed crowd who go for the saint's blessing and the chance to party.

CONTEMPORARY
EGYPTIAN FICTION

The Egyptian writer Naguib Mahfouz is generally regarded as the father of contemporary Arab writing, but many other writers have found their voice since then, despite serious censorship. None more so perhaps than Alaa al Aswany.

The Beginnings

Many Egyptian writers in the 1940s and 1950s trained themselves in the techniques of western fiction, later finding their own voice. Often using colloquial Egyptian instead of standard modern Arabic, many writers describe and often criticise local political and social trends. The most influential of all was Naguib Mahfouz (1911–2006) who drew most of his inspiration from the streets and cafés of Cairo's old city where he was born. His masterpiece is the *Cairo Trilogy* and his work received the Nobel Prize for Literature in 1988. Yusuf Idris is considered to be the prince of short stories, the Arab Anton Chekhov, while Albert Cossery, an Egyptian who has lived in Paris since 1945, has written beautifully and engagingly

The increasingly prolific output of Egyptian writers is becoming widely available

WESTERN NOVELS SET IN EGYPT

The Alexandria Quartet by Lawrence Durrell
Death on the Nile by Agatha Christie
The English Patient by Michael Ondaatje
City of Gold by Len Deighton
Moon Tiger by Penelope Lively
The Levant Trilogy by Olivia Manning

about the Egyptian underdog particularly in *Proud Beggars*. *Zayni Barakat* by Gamal al Ghitani is another classic novel, set in Mamluk times.

Best-selling author Alaa al Aswany

Egyptian Writers Today

Egyptian literature is more varied and energetic today than it has been in a long time. Most writers are politically engaged, either dealing with domestic situations or with the Arab/Muslim relationship with the West. If you read one Egyptian novel while visiting Egypt, let it be Alaa al Aswany's bleak portrait of contemporary life in an apartment building in downtown Cairo, in the best-ever-selling Arab novel *The Yaqoubian Building*. His second novel *Chicago* is set in the Egyptian expat community in Chicago, where the saga of corruption and state control continues well beyond Egyptian borders. Ibrahim Abdel Meguid's *No One Sleeps in Alexandria* is set in Lawrence Durrell's Alexandria but as seen by two poor Egyptians. The splendid *Taxi* by Khaled al Khamissi gives a portrait of Cairo through semi-fictional stories told by Cairene taxi drivers, and the Arab world's first graphic novel for adults by Magdy al Shafei was a great success.

Women Writers

Egypt has many influential female writers, none more so than Ahdaf Soueif, whose *The Map of Love* was shortlisted for the 1999 Booker Prize. Nawal al Saadawy wrote novels about the difficulties of Egyptian women in a male-dominated society, but was imprisoned for her radical beliefs. Her book *The Fall of the Imam* is still banned. Salwa Bakr's *The Golden Chariot* is set in a women's prison near Cairo, while Bahaa Taher's *Aunt Safiyya and the Monastery* decribes life in an Upper Egyptian village.

Ahdaf Soueif, shortlisted for the Booker Prize

EGYPTIAN
CHRONICLES

Egypt has a chequered history of more than 7,000 years, and many monuments and documents to illustrate it. While most of the world was still hunting and gathering, and living in caves, the Egyptians already had a sophisticated civilisation.

King Menes may have been a composite of several kings

c5000 BC
Neolithic farming communities are already well established in the Nile valley area.

c3000 BC
King Menes (or Narmer) unites the two lands of Upper and Lower Egypt (the Nile delta), establishing its capital at Memphis. Menes is regarded as the first pharaoh of the 1st Dynasty in Egypt.

c2600 BC
Imhotep, architect to the 3rd-Dynasty King Zoser (2667–2648 BC), creates the world's first pyramid, at Saqqara (▶ 59–61). The ancients were suitably impressed and later deified him. He became the god of medicine, son of the god Ptah and his consort Sekhmet.

1352–1336 BC
The ruling pharaoh Amenhotep IV tries to free his administration from the influence of the priesthood of Thebes by moving the capital to Amarna, some 370km (230 miles) north. To promote the worship of a single god, the sun god Aton,

he changed his own name from "Amun is pleased" to Akhenaton ("Soul of Aton"). Akhenaton is most famous today for being depicted in art with his beautiful wife Nefertiti and his children (➤ 51).

1336–1327 BC

After Amenhotep's death, his nine-year-old son-in-law Tutankhaten becomes ruler. Within a short time, he restores the old order, moves the capital back to Thebes and reinstates Amun as the state god, changing his name to Tutankhamun. He dies at the age of 18 with no heirs, the last male of the 18th Dynasty.

1279–1213 BC

Ramses II rules for more than 60 years – time enough to build grand monuments, marry many wives and father more than 100 children, helping to guarantee his name in posterity. He leaves his mark on almost every significant monument in Egypt, adding huge colossi in his image and decorating temple walls with scenes of his greatest victories. He deifies himself in the eighth year of his reign and the two temples that bear his name, at Abu Simbel and in Thebes, are as monumental as his self-esteem. Many of his 50 sons are buried in KV5, the princely gallery tomb that is now being excavated in the Valley of the Kings (➤ 93).

8th–7th century BC

Egypt is ruled for a time by kings from Nubia, the area which comprises southern Egypt and northern Sudan.

General Alexander the Great

332 BC

Alexander the Great (356–323 BC) conquers Egypt, which passes to a general, Ptolemy, and into the Ptolemaic era.

c270 BC

In Alexandria, the Greek architect Sostratos builds one of the seven wonders of the world – the marble lighthouse on the island of Pharos in the harbour.

The Pharos was said to contain 300 rooms for its mechanics and builders

47–30 BC

At the beginning of her reign, at the age of 21, Cleopatra VII flees Egypt to escape her murderous brother-husband Ptolemy XIII, but is restored to the throne by Julius Caesar. In return she bears his only son, Caesarion. Five years later, with Caesar dead, Cleopatra falls for his successor Mark Antony, by whom she has three more children. But in 30 BC Octavian, the future Emperor Augustus, defeats the lovers' army and captures Alexandria. When Mark Antony commits suicide, Cleopatra causes her own death soon afterwards by the bite of an asp, thus sealing one of the greatest love stories. Cleopatra is the last ruler, until the modern era, of an independent Egypt. The country falls under Roman and Byzantine rule.

AD 251–356

At the age of 18 the future St Anthony, a wealthy young man from the town of Beni Suef, is inspired to become a hermit after hearing the gospel of Matthew. He retreats to an isolated cave on Mount Qalala, where he lives until the age of 105. His followers, settling at the foot of the mountain, founded the world's first monastery (► 164).

639–641

When Amr ibn al As visits Alexandria as a young man he is impressed by the capital's wealth. He returns in 639 accompanied by a 4,000-strong Arab army and meets little opposition from the ruling Byzantines. The Arabs

St Anthony of Egypt lived to the ripe old age of 105

take Heliopolis and then besiege Babylon-in-Egypt. By 641 Egypt is an Arab province. Amr establishes his capital in Fustat (later Cairo), where he builds his mosque and introduces Islam.

973–1171

During the Fatimid Dynasty, al Hakim, who rules from 996 to 1021 is the maddest and most capricious of the caliphs (literally, "Successor to Mohammed"). He persecutes the Jewish and Christian minorities and destroys countless churches. He forbids women to go out, outlawing the manufacture of their shoes. He also hates daylight, decreeing that all work should be done at night. He even declares himself divine just as the pharoahs did before him. After mysteriously disappearing while out riding, he is commonly presumed dead, but according to the Druze, a political and religious Islamic sect for whom he becomes a cult figure, he has actually escaped to Lebanon.

1171–1193

Legacies of the reign of the Kurdish general Salah ad Din (Saladin) include Cairo's Citadel and the ending of the Shi'a caliphate rule. He establishes the Ayyubid Dynasty after becoming sultan, and is also notable for uniting Egyptian Muslims in a common cause. For most of his rule he is away fighting a *jihad* ("holy war") to free the Holy Land from the Crusaders. He recaptures Syria and Jerusalem, but dies in Damascus, where he is buried. His legendary qualities turn him into a hero throughout Europe and the Arab world.

1250–1517

The Mamluks – soldiers who were descended from the slaves who made up the Ayyubid army – overthrow the Ayyubids with their highly professional army, led by amirs. Their subsequent Muslim dynasty lasts more than 250 years until they are conquered by the Ottoman Turks.

1517

Egypt comes under the control of the Ottoman Empire, which had been founded in the 13th century by Osman I, but the Mamluks continue to rule. With increasing trade between the East and Europe, the important route between Alexandria, Cairo and Suez prompts British and French attempts to control it.

Cairo was always an important trading post

1798–1801
Napoleon Bonaparte leads scholars and troops into Egypt to study and to remove antiquities, creating the first systematic record of Egypt's treasures.

1805–1848
Muhammad Ali, an Albanian officer whose army arrived in Egypt with the French, is regarded as the founder of modern Egypt. After the French leave, Ali supports Egypt's rulers against the Mamluks and becomes viceroy. Influenced by advances in Europe, he modernises the country's infrastructure, building roads and Africa's first railway. He reorganises the army, reforms agriculture with improved irrigation and establishes industry. His dynasty rules Egypt under the title of Khedive and later King, until the revolution in 1952.

1869
After 10 years of problematic construction, the Suez Canal is finally opened, linking the Mediterranean at the newly created Port Said with the Red Sea at Suez (► 168–169). The new towns of Port Said and Ismailiya grow as the area becomes wealthy. Port Said is named after Egypt's ruler (although he dies before the project was completed) and Ismailiya receives its name from the subsequent ruler, Khedive Ismail, who opens the canal.

1882
Riots begin after an army faction objects to the British and French control of Egypt's finances. As a result, British troops bombard Alexandria and occupy Egypt under the pretext of restoring peace to the country. They remain as a colonial presence until 1956.

1952
A military coup by the "Free Officers" overthrows King Farouk and declares a republic. The army officer and politician Gamal Abd al Nasser (1918–70), becomes Egypt's prime minister in 1954 and later president (1956–70). His Arab nationalism and socialism makes him popular in Egypt and the Arab world. When he nationalises the Suez Canal in 1956, Britain, France and Israel invade Egypt, but Nasser stands up to them, thus adding to his cult status.

1970s
Both Egypt and Israel claim victory after several Arab–Israeli wars. Anwar al Sadat (1918–81) becomes president in 1970 and sets about restructuring the political system (founding the National Democratic Party) and

Left: Napoleon defeated the Mamluks at the Battle of the Pyramids in 1798
Below: Scottish troops at the Sphinx in 1882

diversifying the economy. After some initial aggression, his work towards peace in the Middle East leads to talks with the Israeli Prime Minister Menachem Begin (1913–92). This culminates in the 1978 Camp David Peace Accord, for which the two leaders share the Nobel Peace Prize. Although Egypt becomes somewhat isolated from other Arab countries, the agreement encourages foreign investment and strengthens the economy. However, only a minority become wealthy and the decade ends in social unrest and a general feeling of dissatisfaction.

1981 to present
On 6 October 1981, President Sadat is assassinated by radical Islamists. Hosni Mubarak (born 1928), the vice-president, succeeds him as president, with the support of the armed forces. Mubarak has continued Sadat's policy of liberalisation of trade. In 2005 Mubarak changed the constitution to allow multi-party presidential elections, but the popular fundamentalist Muslim Brotherhood remained banned. He won the elections in 2006, but there is growing dissent in Egypt, particularly from the opposition party Kifaya, Arabic for Enough. The frail 81-year-old Mubarak would love to see his son Gamal take over from him, but the future will be very uncertain when the last of the Free Officers of the 1952 revolution dies.

Current president, Hosni Mubarak

Kul kul...
yallah kul

The phrase means "eat, eat... come on eat", and you'll hear it often when dining with Egyptians, who love to eat, to talk about food and to share a meal. Some ancient dishes, such as *meloukhia*, are still favourites today.

Modern meals include as many dishes as the host can afford, and the tastiest morsels will be put in your mouth at what can be an alarming rate. In restaurants Egyptians continue the habit of sharing by ordering vast amounts of *mezze,* hot or cold starters, dips and salads.

The Egyptian Staples

Fuul (fava beans) is one of the basics of the national diet and, while some poorer Egyptians live on them, even wealthy Cairenes have them for breakfast. The dried beans are simmered for about six hours, and then sold in the morning from carts on street corners. The stew is often eaten with *taamiya,* fried patties of crushed dried fava beans. Another staple is *koshari,* a delicious carbohydrate galore of rice, macaroni, lentils, chick peas, fried onions and a spicy tomato sauce, which is eaten at all times of the day. *Meloukhia* is a thick green soup made with Jew's mallow, a leafy vegetable similar to spinach, served with chicken or rabbit. On Thursday nights Egyptians eat *qawaria,* a clear cows' feet soup, or sandwiches with lamb testicles, both said to enhance sexual potency.

AUTHENTIC RESTAURANTS

For a taste of real Egyptian food, try one of these:

■ In Alexandria, Hoot Gondol Seafood
   (➤ 147), Qadoura (➤ 148)

■ In Cairo, Abu el-Sid (➤ 74), Felfela
   (➤ 75), Seqouia (➤ 76)

■ In Luxor, Restaurant Mohammed
   (➤ 105), Sofra (➤ 104)

■ In Aswan, Al Masry (➤ 126)

Mint tea is refreshing

A selection of *mezze* is popular as a starter and for sharing

Sweetness Delight

Egypt's numerous *pâtisseries* sell a wide variety of cream-filled Western pastries, and Oriental pastries dripping with honey. The "queen" of Egyptian desserts is *Umm Ali,* a hot dessert of crisp pitta bread soaked in milk, with coconut, cream, nuts, raisins and sugar. Some sources suggest it was introduced into Egypt by an Irish woman, Miss O'Malley, who was mistress of the 19th-century leader, Khedive Ismail.

Absence Makes the Heart Grow Fonder

During the lunar month of Ramadan Muslims abstain from eating, drinking, smoking and making love between sunrise and sunset. Ramadan also brings its social obligations, when people visit friends and relatives for *iftar,* the evening breakfast. They indulge in meat and more luxurious ingredients than usual to celebrate the holy month.

Café Pleasures

The best thirst-quencher in Egypt's hot climate is tea, and there's no shortage of it.Tea is drunk black or with milk and lots of sugar at the local *ahwa* (coffee house). The other ubiquitous drink is syrupy Arabic coffee. Cafés are places to relax or chat while drawing on a *sheesha* (water pipe or hookah), with normal tobacco, *ma'assal* (tobacco sweetened with molasses) or *tuffah* (sweetened with apple). Traditional cafés also serve herbal infusions such as *yansoon* (anis), *helba* (fenugreek), *karkadeh* (hibiscus) and *irfa* (cinnamon). Warm yourself with a custardy *sahlab* – made of arrowroot and cinnamon topped with coconut and other nuts.

Juicy Delights

To ensure you're fit enough to enjoy your stay, avoid tap water and river water – look for bottled mineral water or head for the colourful juice bars behind piles of oranges or strawberries and indulge in seasonal delights.

UNDULATIONS AND **GYRATIONS**

From Salomée's dance of the seven veils, to modern-day sell-out shows at 2am, belly dancing has always pulled the crowds.

Raqs sharqi, as Oriental dance is called in Arabic, is a social phenomenon in Egypt. Originally from the Middle East, it stretches back in time, as can be seen in ancient tomb paintings of women apparently belly dancing, and it cuts through social barriers: Everyone, from the haughtiest society princess to the poorest rag-picker, will try it some time.

Professional dancers claim it's in the genes and that every Egyptian is born with the ability to dance in this way. But it's not all in the belly. The dance also demands great control of the hips, expression of the hands and (if you can afford it) the backing of a 30-piece band.

The older famous Egyptian belly dancers have stopped performing in public, except perhaps at weddings and big family parties. There's a growing social stigma for the Egyptian dancers, linked to increasing religious conservatism, and many have become popular actresses, with their place being taken by European dancers. However, some of the biggest stars, Dina, Lucy and Soraya, remain Egyptian.

Younger couples now often prefer to have a European style DJ rather than a belly dancer. However, these days belly dancing is not confined to the Middle East, as the energy required and effort involved has made belly dancing a popular way of keeping fit in the West.

A belly-dancing show is a riot of colour and sound

Star of the East
UMM KUALTHOUM

In Egypt and the Arab world one voice is heard above all others, that of Umm Kulthoum (1898–1975), often called *Sitt al Kull* (The Lady of All) or *Kawkab ash Sharq* (The Star of the East). Fêted around the world, she was a guru in Egypt.

Umm Kulthoum was born in the village of Tumay al Zahayra in the Egyptian delta. Talented from an early age when she started singing dressed up as a shepherd boy, she stood out for her extraordinary voice. She starred in several films, but she gave up acting in 1947 to concentrate on singing. The best poets and the most talented musicians competed for the pleasure to work with her, and she became a social phenomenon. At a time when Egyptians didn't talk about love, emotions or sexual pleasure, she provided them with a vocabulary to do so, using ambiguous lyrics to avoid offending public morals. In the process she liberated both men and women.

Painting of Diva Umm Kualthoum by Adel al Siwi

BEST LIVE RECORDINGS

- *Alf Layla wa Layla* (The Thousand and One Nights)
- *Enta Omri* (You Are My Life)
- *Al-Atlal* (The Ruins), was voted one of the top 100 songs of the 20th century by French newspaper *Le Monde*.

The singer's life was often controversial. She first sang for King Farouk, and after the 1952 revolution was involved in president Nasser's propaganda machine. Her success aroused the jealousy of other singers, who accused her of stifling younger talent. Her passionate songs also provoked rumours about her love life and she was romantically linked to several men and women, but she married in 1953. Millions of fans attended her funeral in 1975.

The Umm Kulthoum Museum, on Cairo's Rhoda island (Monastirli Palace, tel: 02-362 1467, open daily 10–5), has memorabilia and archive footage.

WHEN IN EGYPT

Egyptians' first response to any calamity, big or small, is often *"inshallah, bukra, maalesh"*...

Inshallah
Step into a taxi and tell the driver where you want to go and he'll invariably reply, *"Inshallah"*. He means "yes" but is actually saying "God willing". To assume that this is just a hackneyed saying is to underestimate the importance of Allah in everyday life, and to dismiss the fundamental belief in divine intervention.

Bukra
"Bukra" (tomorrow) is often the standard reply for whatever service you request, showing that Egyptians have a different perception of time. But times are changing and even Egyptians resort less and less to this line of defence.

Maalesh
"Maalesh" (never mind) has a multitude of applications. You'll hear it after some mishap because even calamities are part of the grand scheme of things. If someone's pestering you to buy a plastic wallet or flashing sunglasses, *"maalesh"* shows you're not interested.

Exchanging Greetings
Wherever they are and whatever pressing business they have, Egyptians always make time for an elaborate exchange of greetings. A simple version might be a rally of blessings such as *sabah al ishta* (morning of cream) and *sabah al yasmin* (morning of jasmine). Between men there's also likely to be handshaking, kissing, hugging and an insistence that they visit the nearest café there and then. Usually there follows a series of questions and answers about each other's family and their health.

Talk Like an Egyptian
If you speak Egyptian Arabic in another Arab country, chances are you'll get a laugh – and not just for your accent. Egyptians are notorious in the Arab world for their irrepressible sense of humour and love of play and drama.

Detail of a colourful cloth with Arabic design, used to wrap a Koran

Finding Your Feet

First Two Hours

Cairo is traditionally the main point of entry for visitors to Egypt, but there are a growing number of international flights direct to Luxor and Alexandria, and also charter flights to Hurghada, Sharm al Sheikh and al Alamein.

Cairo International Airport

- The main airport is **25km (16 miles) from the centre**, or 45 minutes by car.
- Cairo Airport (www.cairo-airport.com) has **two terminals** connected by a free Egypt Air shuttle bus. **Terminal 1** is used by Egyptian and Arab airlines while **Terminal 2** serves all other international flights. A new **Terminal 3** is expected to be fully operational in early 2009 and will double the airport's capacity. For flight information tel: 0900 77777.
- Terminal 1 and Terminal 2 have **24-hour currency exchange** and automatic cash machines accepting Visa, Cirrus and Mastercard.
- **Taxis** are generally cheaper than in Europe and America, but beyond customs you'll be accosted by taxi drivers, some of whom may overcharge. If you've already booked a hotel they may tell you it has closed down and offer to take you to another hotel where they will earn a commission.
- To avoid the hassle you can book a **limousine** in the arrival hall. These are more expensive, but you fix a price, pay before you ride, and tip the driver.
- There is a new comfortable **shuttle bus** (tel: 02-2265 3937; 70-100LE per person, every half an hour) from outside the two airport terminals into town, to Zamalek, Maadi and the pyramids area. Tickets are available from the shuttle bus desk in the arrivals hall of Terminal 1 and Terminal 2. There are very cheap **public buses** (24 hours): Nos 356, 400 and minibus No 27 from Terminals 1 and 2 to the Abd al-Moneem Riyad terminal behind the Egyptian Museum.
- The **tourist office** at Terminal 1 is open 24 hours (tel: tel: 02-2265 3642) and the tourist office at Terminal 2 is open 24 hours (tel: 02-2265 2269).

Luxor International Airport

- The airport is about 10km (6 miles) out of town and there's **no public transport** into town, so try to arrange to be met by a travel agent. Otherwise, you'll have to deal with Luxor's taxi drivers, who are notorious for overcharging; agree the fare before getting in.
- Beyond the airport run, **taxi fares** in Luxor, as elsewhere in Egypt, are generally relatively cheap.
- The airport **tourist office** is open 8am–9pm (tel 095-237 2306).

Hurghada Airport

- There's **no public transport** from the airport into the town centre so independent travellers must rely on taxis, which charge reasonable fares.

Sharm al Sheikh

- Ras Nasrani airport is about 15km (9 miles) north of the tourist centre at Naama Bay, and again there's no public transport. Most visitors are met by a travel agent, but if you're arriving independently you'll have to take a cab.

Tourist Information Offices

- Most tourist offices in Egypt are **rather limited** in the services and brochures they provide. They can be useful for official prices of *calèches* (horse-drawn carriages), taxis and *feluccas* (boats), or for a city map, but they may not be as accurate as maps in this and other guidebooks.
- Tourist offices will rarely help with accommodation, except those at airports.

Cairo Tourist Office
➕ 196 C4 ✉ 5 Sharia Adly, Downtown
☎ 02-2391 3454
🕐 Daily 8:30–7; 9–4 during Ramadan
Good for some dusty brochures, but staff could be more helpful.

Egyptian Tourist Authority, Luxor
➕ 202 C4 ✉ Tourist Bazaar on Corniche, opposite Old Winter Palace
☎ 095-237 2215
🕐 Daily 8–8
Provides a useful list of official rates for *calèches*, taxis, *feluccas* and guides.

Hurghada Tourist Information
➕ 201 E2 ✉ Opposite the Grand Hotel in New Hurghada
☎ 065-344 4420
🕐 Sat–Thu 9–8, Fri 2–10

Aswan Tourist Office
➕ 202 C3 ✉ Beside the train station
☎ 097-231 2811
🕐 Sat–Thu 8–3, 7–9, Fri 9:30–3, 6–8
Helpful staff, who can point you towards the trustworthy *felucca* captains.

Alexandria Tourist Office
➕ 195 C5 ✉ Midan Saad Zaghloul, Downtown
☎ 03-485 1556
🕐 Daily 8:30–6 (also 6–8pm mid-Jul to mid-Aug); 9–4 during Ramadan

Local Issues

In the 1990s anti-Christian and anti-governmental violence coincided with the emergence of the Islamic group, the Gamaiyat al Islamiya, which has carried out attacks not only on governmental institutions but also on tourists in an attempt to force the government to agree to their demands for an Islamic state. Their attacks against trains, cruise boats and tourist buses culminated in 1997 at Deir al Bahari in Luxor, when 58 foreigners and 10 Egyptians were killed. The government responded by arresting many suspects and introducing the death penalty for terrorists. Nothing of this sort has happened in recent years, but tourists are protected by police and soldiers at main sites, and must travel through Upper Egypt in armed convoy.

However, the subsequent discussion of the role of religion in the state has led to a new wave of religious conservatism. The most obvious sign of this trend is the growing number of middle-class women wearing the veil, the ever-greater numbers who spread prayer mats in the street for Friday's midday prayers and men with "raisins" or bruises on their forehead caused by praying.

Visitors should respect the culture when visiting more traditional areas and mosques by dressing modestly (women should cover their hair, upper arms and legs) and behaving discreetly. Men and women should not show affection in public.

Admission Charges
The cost of admission for museums and other sites of interest mentioned in the text is indicated by price categories:

Inexpensive under 30LE   **Moderate** 30–60LE   **Expensive** over 60LE

Getting Around

On the whole the public transport system in Egypt works well, with regular buses and trains to most major destinations, and service taxis *(beejous)* covering the other tourist sights.

Urban Transport
Cairo

- Cairo has a whole fleet of **buses**, but they're usually packed, and women may get hassled. You might be happier sticking to the smaller **mini-** and **microbuses**, which are slightly more expensive but take only as many passengers as there are seats. Minibuses are orange and white, and follow the usual bus routes. Microbuses are more like a shared taxi.
- **Taxis** are cheap and more comfortable than buses.
- The **metro** is clean and easy to use, especially from Downtown Cairo to Coptic Cairo. Tickets are inexpensive (£) and there are special carriages for women only (at the back or front). Women travelling in a mixed carriage alone will be stared at.
- Private **motorboats** (launches) and *feluccas* make excursions on the river; always agree on a price first.

Outside Cairo

- Outside Cairo it's a different story. In most other cities, except perhaps Alexandria, you may prefer to use taxis rather than the **scant public transport** service.

Buses

- **Intercity buses** are inexpensive, faster and usually more reliable than trains, and often serve areas not covered by the rail network, such as Sinai and the oases. Almost all intercity buses now leave from one bus station, the **Turgoman Garage** (Mo'af Turgoman) on Sharia al-Gisr in Bulaq, 600m (650 yards) southwest of Ramses train station. Buses 983 and 984 or minibus 32 go there from the Abd al-Moneim Riyad Terminal in downtown Cairo. Buses, particularly the long-haul air-conditioned services, fill up quickly, so it is advisable to book seats one day in advance.
- The four bus companies listed below all have offices at Turgoman, and all run both **air-conditioned** and **non air-conditioned** services.
- The **West Delta Bus Company** (tel: 02-2432 0049) runs services to Alexandria, Marsa Matruh and the Nile delta.
- The **East Delta Bus Company** (tel: 02-2574 2814) operates to Sinai and the Canal zone. Some buses also stop at the old Sinai Terminal on Sharia Ramses in Abbaseya.
- The **Upper Egypt Bus Company** (tel: 02-2576 0261) serves all cities south of Cairo along the Nile, the Fayoum, the Western Desert oases and the Red Sea coast up to Marsa Alam. There are no direct buses to Siwa from Cairo; you have to take a bus to Mersa Matruh or Alexandria and change there.
- **Superjet** (tel: 02-2290 9017) runs more luxurious air-conditioned buses (with video, snacks and toilet) from Cairo to Alexandria, Luxor, Aswan and Hurghada. There are also five fast buses daily to Sharm al Sheikh.

Taxis

- Taxis in Cairo are **black and white** and tend to be four-seater cars.
- **Taxis** are cheaper than in Europe, but rarely use their old meters.

Even if they do, the amount shown will probably bear little resemblance to the fare charged by the driver.

- Cairenes usually **hail a taxi** by shouting out their destination as it drives past. They don't discuss the fare as they know roughly what to pay, but as a visitor it may be best to agree a fare and ask someone in your hotel for the going rate before you travel. Be prepared to haggle for a reasonable price.
- **Estate-car cabs**, known as **service taxis**, usually charge limousine rates if they're working as normal taxis. These serve everywhere in Egypt and can be the fastest way of getting around. As they're usually Peugeots, they're known as **beejous**. The drivers announce their destination and leave as soon as there are six or seven passengers. The fares charged are similar to buses (again, check that you are not charged tourist rates).
- Due to **travel restrictions** for foreigners, it can be difficult to take a service taxi. Often you have to pay for all seven seats and use the car as a private taxi in an armed convoy.
- Beware: **beejous** have been nicknamed **"flying coffins"** as they tend to be driven fast and recklessly. Accidents are common, especially at night.

Trains

- The government-owned **Egyptian State Railway** operates services through the Nile Valley to Aswan, Alexandria, Suez, Port Said and Marsa Matruh. The line from Safaga on the Red Sea coast to Qena, Kharga and Baris is expected to be connected to the Toshka region in the Western Desert in the coming years.
- Egyptian State Railway tickets are inexpensive and must be **bought in advance** from the railway station.
- The privately owned **Abela Sleeping Trains** operates a rather worn, but good, sleeper train from Cairo to Luxor and Aswan, and several fast and comfortable turbo trains a day to Alexandria (2 hours). In summer there are three sleeper trains a week to Marsa Matruh.
- Abela Sleeping Trains tickets must be booked in advance from **Ramses Station** in Cairo (tel: 02-2574 9274; www.sleepingtrains.com).

Domestic Flights

- **Egypt Air** almost has a monopoly on domestic flights, but the domestic fares have come down in price considerably recently. If you are flying into Egypt with Egypt Air, book your internal flights at the same time to save up to 50 per cent on published fares. Egypt Air flies **daily** from Cairo to most of Egypt's main cities (tel: 02-2392 7680; www.egyptair.com.eg).
- **Book well in advance**, especially during the busy winter season, and be aware that overbooking is unfortunately quite common. To minimise the risk of being "bumped", always reconfirm bookings well in advance, and turn up earlier than the recommended check-in time at the airport.
- All domestic flights leave from **Terminal 1** of Cairo airport, also known as the Old Airport (al matar al qadim).
- You can also book **Air Sinai** flights to Hurghada, Sinai, and Tel Aviv in Israel. Same contact information as Egypt Air.
- **Orascom Aviation** (tel: 02-2305 2401), a private airline, operates regular flights from Cairo and Luxor to Gouna.

Driving

- Driving in Cairo can be nerve-wracking, and in rural areas it's often dangerous, so consider **renting a car with a driver** if you are nervous.
- Since the terrorist attack in Luxor in 1997 **security** is tight along Egypt's roads and it's almost impossible for foreigners to pass the many roadblocks along the Nile without the protection of an armed convoy.

Driving Essentials
- Speed limits on **highways**: 100kph (62mph)
- On other **roads**: 90kph (56mph)
- In **urban centres**: 50kph (31mph)
- **Seat belts** are compulsory.
- Driving is on the **right**-hand side of the road.
- Avoid driving in the **dark** outside cities as most people drive without headlights, saving them for the moment before collision, when they use full beam. In the countryside, remember that villagers walk their animals home just after dusk and that people often sit on the side of the road.
- Many roads have **checkpoints**, where the police may ask for your papers, so be prepared for delays.
- Always carry your passport and driving licence. Failing to do so makes you liable to an instant fine, and onward travelling may be prevented.
- If your car hits someone in a rural area, **report it** immediately at the nearest police station, and be aware that you may be attacked by angry villagers.

Car Rental
- **Car-rental agencies** operate in most major hotels.
- **Credit cards** are accepted.
- Drivers must be at least **25 years old** and hold an International Driving Licence.
- Car-rental contracts must be sold with a **third-party liability insurance**, but check if **accident and damage insurance** is included. If you're involved in an accident, you'll need to provide the insurance company with a written report from the police and from the doctor who first treats the injuries.

Upkeep
- Main towns and cities will have many petrol *(benzene)* **filling stations**, but there are fewer in the countryside. To be safe, always fill the tank to the limit, and clean the oil filter regularly because dust and impurities in the fuel tend to clog up the engine.
- Larger **filling stations** are often open until late at night.
- Fuel is much **less expensive** than in Europe.
- The cheapest petrol is **normal** *(tamaneen)*, but **super** *(tisaeen)* is better quality. Lead-free fuel is available only from a few filling stations in more affluent areas of Cairo and Alexandria.
- Egyptian car **mechanics** are often masters of invention and can usually fix a breakdown.
- Most large garages stock a good range of **spare parts**.
- If you run into trouble, **people will often gladly help** you push your car to the next garage or to the side of the road.

Motoring Club
Automobile and Touring Club of Egypt
10 Sharia Qasr al Nil, Downtown Cairo
✚ 197 D4 ☎ 02-2574 3355 (Sat–Thu 9am–1:30pm)

Travel Restrictions
- Incidences of terrorist violence against tourists have led to **tight security** and travel restrictions for visitors on certain overland routes, notably between cities along the Nile, with travel possible only in armed convoys.
- Officially, tourists are also allowed only on two guarded air-conditioned **trains** between Cairo, Luxor and Aswan.
- The **situation changes frequently** so check with the tourist office before travelling, or use river transport where possible.

Accommodation

There's a large choice of accommodation in Egypt's main tourist centres, but elsewhere it's often down to the very basic. This guide includes a cross-section of places to stay, from luxury hotels in palaces to good inexpensive pensions.

Hotels

- Hotels are rated from **deluxe to budget**, with a few unclassified hotels geared mainly towards backpackers and Egyptian families.
- **Deluxe** hotels, almost always part of international chains, usually have international facilities, but although service is getting better it may not always be up to international standards.
- **Mid-range hotels** include some characterful old hotels, such as the Cecil in Alexandria, and also modern concrete resort hotels on the Red Sea.
- **Budget hotels** are rarely air-conditioned, but some will have cooling fans. A few are real gems, old art-deco buildings with high ceilings, old-fashioned furniture and unreliable plumbing. The less said about others, the better.

Pensions

Pensions are similar to budget hotels but, as they're often run by one family, the atmosphere tends to be much friendlier and relaxed, and the rooms better maintained.

Hostels

- Egypt has **15 cheap hostels** in the main towns, recognised by Hostelling International. Rooms are cheaper if you have a HI membership, but it is not strictly necessary.
- Information is available from **Egyptian Youth Hostel Association**, 1 Sharia Ibrahimy, Garden City, Cairo (tel: 02-2794 0527).

Camping

- Camping is **not popular** in Egypt and the country's few campsites are mostly along the coast and in the oases. They are generally a long way from the sights and poorly equipped. Campsites attached to hotels are usually better.
- Camping outside designated sites along the coast is not advisable as some empty beaches are still **mined**. This is less of a problem in the desert.

Booking Accommodation

- Rooms at more expensive hotels are often cheaper when booked either through the chain's international reservation system or when bought as part of a package. Other places recommended here should preferably be **booked in advance**, particularly in high season when hotels fill up fast.
- Check the website **www.egyptreservation.com** for hotels, reservation services, travel agents and other related services.

Accommodation Prices

In many hotels, it is possible to bargain over the advertised room rate, particularly in off-peak periods and if you are staying for a few days. The set price of accommodation featured in the guide is indicated below. The prices are for a double room per night.

£ under 450LE   **££** 450–1000LE   **£££** over 1000LE

Food and Drink

You can eat well in Egypt, but don't expect to find a variety of gourmet food.
Egyptian cuisine is peasant food, a lot less sophisticated, for instance, than its
Lebanese neighbour (➤ 28–29).

The Egyptian Way of Eating

- **Lunch** is usually served from 12:30 to 3pm and dinner from 8 to 10:30pm,
  but many places in tourist areas stay open all day.
- At a **restaurant**, Egyptians tend to start a meal with a good selection of cold
  and/or hot *mezze* (small dishes) with drinks. If the spread is big enough,
  this can sometimes make a whole meal.
- **Flat pitta bread** is often used in place of a fork to scoop up food.
- An important point of etiquette to remember: only use the **right hand** while
  eating this way, because the left hand is traditionally used for ablutions.

On the Street

Everywhere in Egypt you will come across street vendors selling everything
from cheese sandwiches and delicious *shawarma* to cow's-feet soup and
lamb-testicle sandwiches. However tempting these may look and smell,
street food is only recommended for the adventurous or those with a strong
stomach, as hygiene conditions on these stalls can be quite poor and very
few have running water.

International Cuisine

- You can now find most styles of cooking in **Cairo** and, unlike in Europe,
  ethnic restaurants are usually more expensive.
- **Outside Cairo** the choice is more limited. Most international restaurants are
  in the luxury hotels, with prices to match. Hotel food can often be bland,
  especially set menus or open buffets, but some restaurants are excellent.
- International **fast-food** chains are a relatively recent arrival in Egypt, but
  have proved to be immensely popular and just about every tourist resort now
  boasts McDonald's, PizzaExpress and so on.
- In spite of this success, Egyptians have not entirely abandoned their own
  interesting varieties of fast food. Examples include *kushari* (a spicy mix of
  pulses, pasta and rice) and *falafel/taamiya* (deep-fried, spiced, mashed
  chickpeas/ground beans) or *fuul* sandwiches.

Vegetarians

Although most Egyptians can't afford to eat meat more than once a week,
there is little understanding of why a foreigner should choose to live off
vegetables alone. Having said that, there are usually plenty of vegetable
stews or other vegetarian dishes on restaurant menus and fish, usually from
the Nile or the Red Sea, is available for those who eat it. "**Ana nabaati/iya**" is
Arabic for "I'm a vegetarian".

Eating Out

- If you have a **sensitive stomach**, try to avoid raw vegetables, unpeeled fruit,
  ice-cream, open buffets and food that has been cooking for a while, such as
  shawarma.
- Drink plenty of **water and fresh juices** to replace fluids, but avoid heavily
  chilled drinks in the midday sun, particularly alcohol.
- Egyptians love to **dress up** to go to a fancy restaurant, but other places are
  fairly casual about clothes.

Useful Reading

- The *Egypt Today Restaurant Guide*, available from local bookshops, has reviews of a wide selection of restaurants and watering holes.
- The monthly magazine *Egypt Today*, which also has a restaurant selection, reviews new places in Cairo.

Best for Egyptian Food

Abu al Sid, Cairo (➤ 74)
Adrere Amellal, Siwa (➤ 145)
Restaurant Muhammad, West Bank Luxor (➤ 105)
Sequoia, Cairo (➤ 76)
Sofra, East Bank Luxor (➤ 104)

Drinks

- **Tap-water** and ice made from it is chlorinated but can still cause problems.
- **Bottled mineral water** *(maaya maadaniya)* is widely available.
- Most Egyptians drink a lot of tea, coffee, herbal drinks and cold drinks. Everywhere you'll find stalls making inexpensive, **fresh juices** from whatever is in season: orange, pomegranate, strawberry, carrot and mango, as well as bananas in milk. Fresh lime juice is often served with lots of sugar. If you want drinks without sugar, mention it when ordering.

Alcohol

- Egypt is officially a Muslim country and, although alcohol is widely available in tourist centres, it's **prohibited** in some parts of the country, particularly away from the main towns. Even where it is available, show your respect for the culture by drinking it only in moderation.
- Hotels and some restaurants usually sell **local beer and wine**, but imported alcoholic drinks are often only available in the luxury hotels and at hugely inflated prices.
- **Locally made liquors**, with names such as Johnny Talker and Good Gin, are best avoided; there have been several cases of serious illness resulting from bootleg liquor. Zbib, quite similar to Greek ouzo, is the exception.
- Several good **beers**, including Stella and Sakkara, are brewed in Egypt.
- The long-established **Gianaclis Vineyards** in the delta region produce drinkable red, white and rosé wines.
- The other local wine, red, white, rosé and sparkling **Obelisk**, is made in Al Gouna from good-quality grape concentrates from Sicily.

Best Watering Holes

After Eight, Cairo (➤ 78)
Greek Club, Cairo (➤ 76)
Sequoia, Cairo (➤ 76)
Cap d'Or, Alexandria (➤ 147)
Little Buddha Bar, Sharm al Sheik (➤ 172–173)

Restaurant Prices
Below is the price of establishments featured in this guide, based on the amount you should expect to pay per person for a three-course meal, excluding alcoholic drinks and tips.

£ up to 100LE   **££** 100–200LE   **£££** over 200LE

Note that some hotels charge an extra service tax of 22 per cent.

Shopping

Wherever you go in Egypt, there will be no shortage of shopping opportunities. Egyptians are traders at heart and they also love to shop, so it often seems as if most of the country is one big bazaar. Shopping can be a lengthy process involving exchanging greetings, drinking tea, choosing the items you want to buy and then, eventually, bargaining and agreeing on the price.

Shopping Hours

- **Department stores**, often state run, are usually open Monday to Saturday from 9am to 1pm and again from 5 to 8pm, while smaller shops tend to be open all day, and often until 8pm or later in tourist areas.
- Most **bazaars** are closed on Sundays, but some tourist shops might still be open.
- Some Muslim shopkeepers close during the **Friday noon prayers**, but will reopen as soon as they come back from the mosque. At the regular prayer times you may find the shopkeeper performing his prayers behind the counter. Just hang around, as these will not take very long.
- Major **credit cards and travellers' cheques** are now widely accepted in tourist areas, but many smaller shops still accept only cash or will add a surcharge for using credit cards.

Bargaining

Western visitors are often too embarrassed or impatient to haggle over a price, but for Egyptians this is the normal state of affairs: when Egyptians go shopping they expect to bargain for everything. You may prefer the few shops with fixed prices, but they are often more expensive and tourists who cannot read Arabic numerals are still likely to be overcharged. Just remember that bargaining can be fun once you understand the rules. Window-shop at the fixed-price stores to get an idea of prices before venturing into the bazaars, where haggling is the norm. As a general rule, try halving the asking price and watching the trader's reaction. If he's quick to accept, you're still offering too much. If he's not interested, you could offer a little more, or try walking away: if your price was fair he will call you back.

Handicrafts

- The **variety** of Egyptian handicrafts is endless and prices are very good, but the quality of the work has deteriorated as Egyptian tastes have changed; most crafts are now produced for the tourist trade. Typical souvenirs are mostly cheap reproductions of pharaonic art. Papyrus, for example, is often made of banana leaves, painted with scenes copied from original papyri and tomb paintings. Also be on the look out for poorly executed reproductions of ancient statues.
- Several aid organisations are trying hard to revive old crafts, such as embroidery, pottery and weaving, particularly as a way of making the women in rural areas who produce them more financially independent. A sign of their success is the appearance of a few new shops selling better-quality products, such as **Fair Trade Egypt** (➤ 77), a fair-trade shop selling quality products from projects all over Egypt, **Khan Misr Touloun** (➤ 77), **Oum el Dounia** (➤ 77) or **al-Khatoun** (➤ 77).
- The cheapest place to buy crafts is in **Khan al Khalili** in Cairo (➤ 70), or in the bazaars at Luxor and Aswan. The best buys are painted papyrus, hand-blown recycled glass, mother-of-pearl inlay work, brass and copper work, woven tablecloths and alabaster.

Antiques and Antiquities

Genuine pharaonic, Islamic and Coptic antiques can be exported only with a licence from the Department of Antiquities, best obtained by the dealer. Be aware that most antiquities on offer are fakes, although there is still an important and damaging trade in stolen antiquities.

Cotton and Other Fabrics

- Good-quality **Egyptian cotton** is hard to come by in Egypt as most of it is exported, but it's still possible to find inexpensive cotton casual clothes almost everywhere.
- For traditional **Egyptian clothes** it's best to try looking in the markets in the main towns.
- The small towns of **Akhmim** and **Nagada** in Upper Egypt are famous for their superb woven textiles, available from better fabric shops in Cairo and Luxor.
- Bedouin women produce beautifully **embroidered shawls** and clothes.
- Cairo is probably the best and the cheapest place to buy **belly dance outfits**. You can buy ready made clothes or have them tailored with as much beading, glitter, bells and sequins as your heart desires. The best place is the Haberdashery emporium in Khan al Khalili (➤ 77).

Jewellery

- Many Egyptian women still prefer to put their money into **jewellery**, preferably gold, rather than in a bank, so jewellery is readily available.
- Bedouin and rural women prefer 21-carat gold, but most Western-style jewellery is 18 carat. **Gold and silver jewellery** is sold by the gram, with an additional fee for the workmanship. Bullion prices are printed daily in the *Egyptian Gazette*.
- Jewellery is **relatively inexpensive** in Egypt, as wages are still very low.
- Gold or silver **cartouches** with names written in hieroglyphics are probably the most popular jewellery buy for tourists. These usually take the form of pendants on chains.

Perfumes and Spices

- Cairo has long been the **largest perfume and spice market** in the Middle East. Try the spice market in Khan al Khalili (➤ 71) for the best selection.
- Essences are sold by the **ounce** (28g), to be diluted in alcohol for perfume.
- Take care when buying scents. Egypt produces many pure essences that are used in Western perfumes, and several shops offer close copies of famous brands. Some shops offer the real thing, but overcharging and diluting pure essences is a common scam.
- **Spices** such as black pepper *(filfil)*, cumin *(kammum)*, red pepper *(shatta)* and cinnamon *(irfa)* make inexpensive and welcome souvenirs, useful for recreating Egyptian cuisine back home.
- **Stick to the spices used locally** as more exotic spices such as saffron *(zaafaran)* or green pepper *(filfil akhdar)* may be considerably cheaper than back home, but since they are often artificially dyed and have no taste whatsoever, are of inferior quality.
- In Aswan look out for the red **hibiscus** flower *(karkadeh)*, which makes a delicious hot or cold drink.

Best Markets...

...**souvenirs**: Khan al Khalili, Cairo (➤ 70; 77)
...**antiques and junk**: Attarin Market, Alexandria (➤ 149)
...**camels**: Daraw (➤ 122)
...**spices**: *souk*, Luxor Town (➤ 105), Aswan (➤ 127)
...**Nubian baskets, silk shawls**: *souk*, Aswan (➤ 127)

Entertainment

Most visitors to Egypt have such a full schedule that they have very little energy left for sports or nightlife. But if you have the time and the inclination, you can find information about what's on in the *Egyptian Mail* (Saturday), the daily *Egyptian Gazette*, *Al Ahram Weekly*, and the monthly magazines *Egypt Today* and *Insight*. If you have access to a computer or Internet café, also try the websites www.egypttoday.com, www.cairocafe.com and www.cairotimes.com

Bars and Clubs

- Cairo has a wide variety of bars and clubs, but elsewhere in the country most of the nightlife happens in the hotels. The **music** on offer is partly Western and partly Egyptian, with the occasional Sudanese or Greek song thrown in.
- Some places will refuse you entry if you are dressed too **casually** or in jeans, and others have a couples-only policy to avoid trouble, although single foreign women will invariably be let in.
- **Outdoor cafés** are a great place to watch the world, but this is usually done over tea, coffee or cold drinks and a *sheeshas* (water pipe), as alcohol is rarely served.

Belly Dancing

Belly dancing has become less popular in recent years as many younger Egyptians and Arabs opt for Western-style entertainment. When religious leaders condemned belly dancing as sinful, many Egyptian dancers took early retirement, and their places were filled by foreign dancers. You'll find the best shows in the nightclubs of the luxury hotels, which charge a flat fee for the show and a four-course meal. The dancers to look out for are Lucy, Dina and the British-born Yasmina. Less salubrious clubs can be rather sleazy but fascinating, where beer flows at a price and where men shower dancers with paper money. (See also Undulations and Gyrations, ▶ 30)

Nile-side Entertainment

On hot summer nights many Egyptians like to go down to the Nile to catch the cooler breeze. Many towns have casinos, or café terraces on the banks of the Nile where families come for cold drinks and a snack, and where lovers meet to discuss their future. At almost any time of the year it's possible to rent a *felucca* (sailing boat) or a motorboat to watch the sunset or to spend a pleasant evening with drinks and a picnic.

Spectator Sports

Egyptians are crazy about soccer and the adventurous can attend matches during the season (September–May). Cairo has two premier league teams. Ahli's stadium is in Zamalek and, rather confusingly, Zamalek Club plays at Muhandiseen. The national stadium is in Madinet Nasr. Another popular spectator sport is horse-racing, which is held at Cairo's Gezira Club or Heliopolis hippodromes, between October and May.

Festivals

October: Pharaoh's Rally, a desert 4WD race attracting an international field.
November: Arab Music Festival at Cairo Opera House, featuring classical and traditional Arabic music.
December: Cairo International Film Festival held in several Downtown cinemas.

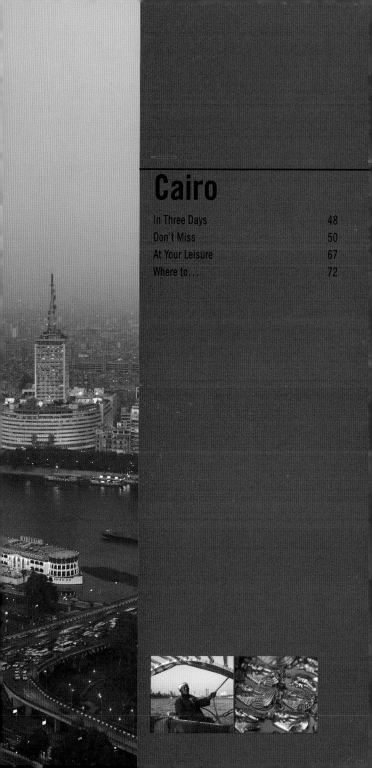

Cairo

Getting Your Bearings

The secret of enjoying Cairo is perhaps to do as the Cairenes and take it as it comes, with humour and heaps of patience. The reward is instant and you'll soon discover one of the most fascinating cities in the world, where history is just another part of everyday life.

In a tale from *The Thousand and One Nights*, a man who is talking of wondrous cities claims:

"He who has not seen Cairo has not seen the World. Its dust is gold; its Nile is a wonder; its women are like the black-eyed virgins of paradise: and how could it not be otherwise, when she is the Mother of the World?"

The Nile still runs like a mirage through the city and some of the women are indeed beauties, but the dust today is more concrete than gold, and the Mother of the World now nurses a population close to 20 million.

Al Qanatir al Khairiya

Al Khanka

Birqash

Bahtim

Warraq al Arab

CAIRO AL QAHIRA

Al Giza

5

Pyramids & Sphinx
Al Ahram & Abu'l Hol

Saqqara 4

Al Maasara

Memphis 4

Nile

Helwan

Al Tabbin

| 0 | 30 km |
| 0 | 20 miles |

Cairo is full of extremes: poverty and wealth, widespread illiteracy and Internet cafés, mudbrick buildings beneath skyscrapers. There's always a surprise around the corner, but somehow the city continues to function, and even to flourish.

Far left: View looking east from Cairo Tower on Gezira Island. Left: One of the herbalists in Khan al Khalili bazaar

At first sight you may think of hell rather than paradise, for the traffic is usually solid, pollution leaves a brownish haze on the horizon and the cacophony of noises produces instant headaches. Less than 200 years of urban and industrial sprawl is now threatening to engulf monuments that have stood for 5,000 years. Yet in the face of turmoil, Cairenes merely go about their business. You may lose patience – some people hate the city, but most are exhilarated by the chaos of humanity, and its unpredictability.

In Three Days

If you're not quite sure where to begin your travels, this itinerary recommends a practical and enjoyable three days in Cairo, taking in some of the best places to see using the Getting Your Bearings map on the previous page. For more information see the main entries.

Day One

Morning
Start with a long morning visit to the ■ Egyptian Museum (left, ▶ 50–53), then stroll over to ⑥ Downtown Cairo (▶ 67) for lunch in one of the numerous restaurants. Try either the stylish Gallenia Food Court (▶ 76) or the less expensive Felfela (▶ 75).

Afternoon
Walk back to Midan Tahrir (Liberation Square), cross the Nile over Qasr al Nil Bridge, passing the modern Opera House and walk to the ⑦ Mr and Mrs Mahmoud Khalil Museum (▶ 67). Walk back towards the Nile and take a *felucca* to watch the sun setting over Cairo.

Day Two

Morning
Start early and take a taxi or the metro to ② Coptic Cairo (▶ 54–55) to visit the Coptic Museum and some of the old churches. Take a taxi to the ⑪ Sultan Hasan Mosque-*Madrasa* (below, ▶ 69) and after a visit, from there another cab to the Al Azhar Park (▶ panel 71) for a stroll and lunch at a restaurant (▶ 74–76).

Afternoon
After lunch, it's a short cab ride to **14 Khan al Khalili** (➤ 71). Stroll through the *souks* towards the Barquq Mausoleum and on to the merchant's house, **Beit al Suhaymi** (➤ 57). Afterwards, walk back along **3 Sharia al Muizz li Din Allah** (➤ 56–58) up to the Tentmakers Bazaar. Return to Khan al Khalili for a restorative cup of mint tea and a water pipe at the al Fishawi café (➤ 75).

Evening
Finish the evening watching a belly dance show at one of the top-quality hotels (➤ 78).

Day Three

Morning
Take a taxi for the day to Memphis, and continue from there to the Step Pyramid and tombs at **4 Saqqara** (➤ 59–61). Have a late lunch at Andrea's (➤ 74) or in the garden of the Mena House Oberoi (➤ 73).

Afternoon
Take another cab or walk over to the **5 Giza Pyramids, the Sphinx** (above) and the **Solar Boat Museum** (➤ 62–66) for a leisurely visit. Head for the stables and rent a horse or camel to go for a sunset trip in the desert.

Evening
Head back into town and join the in-crowd at the bar-restaurant Sequoia (➤ 76) with wonderful views over the Nile.

❶ The Egyptian Museum

The Egyptian Museum in Cairo houses the world's most exquisite and extensive collection of ancient Egyptian artefacts, covering more than 3,000 years, from the Old Kingdom to the Roman period. It's said that if you allowed one minute for each exhibit, it would take nine months to see everything here. But if that's a little too long, take at least a morning (or better still two) to see the museum's many highlights, even though the exhibits are often badly lit and displayed. The ground floor is arranged chronologically, moving clockwise from the entrance hall, while exhibits on the first floor are grouped thematically.

Detail of relief work on a sarcophagus

The imposing frontage of the Egyptian Museum

Ground Floor Highlights

The beginnings of Egyptian art are marked by the **Narmer Palette** in Room 43, which records the unification of Egypt by King Menes (➤ 22), and by the museum's oldest **statues** (Room 48) – that of the seated King Zoser was found near his step pyramid at Saqqara. The smooth black statue of the pyramid builder Khafre is a masterpiece, as is the striking wooden man known as the Sheikh al Balad or Village Chief (both Room 42).

Room 32 is dominated by the striking double statue of the harmonious couple Rahotep and Nofret, which has exceptionally well-preserved colours. Rather more bizarre is the statue of the dwarf Seneb and his wife, with his children placed to hide his short legs. The remarkably colourful chapel of Hathor, with a life-size statue of the cow goddess (Room 12), was found at Hatshepsut's Temple, Deir al Bahari, in Luxor (➤ 94–95).

One of the museum's most fascinating collections, in Room 3, shows the ground-breaking **realistic art** from the time of the rebellious pharaoh Akhenaton (➤ 22–23). In four large statues here Akhneton is shown with a long face, a gorgeous mouth, and oversized hips and belly. He's seen accompanied by his famously beautiful wife Nefertiti, and playing with their children.

Now walk along the eastern wing to the southeast staircase leading to the first floor.

GRAND EGYPTIAN MUSEUM

When the present Egyptian Museum first opened it saw about 500 visitors daily, but the ever-growing collection now attracts some 7,000 visitors a day. A running joke has it that the museum's basement is the last important dig in Egypt. The new 38,000sq m (410,000sq feet) Grand Egyptian Museum is expected to open on a site near the Giza Pyramids in 2012. More than 100,000 objects will be on show, and it will include a museum shop, an Egyptology library, an auditorium and a media centre. The current museum will be about Egyptian Art and the archaeological background of each piece.

The First Floor

The biggest crowd-puller among the museum's many world-class treasures is undoubtedly **Tutankhamun's treasure**. Akhenaton's son-in-law ruled for only nine years, but he became famous when the English archaeologist Howard Carter (1874–1939) discovered his intact tomb in 1922 in the Valley of the Kings, packed to the roof with the dazzling objects that were intended to see him through the afterlife.

By walking up the southeast stairs you encounter the items more or less as they were placed in the tomb. Room 45 starts with two life-size statues of the pharaoh that guarded his burial chamber, and the next galleries show the vast amount of refined furniture, often gold-plated, that was placed in this modest tomb. Rooms 7 and 8 are filled with the gilded wooden shrines that fitted into each other and contained the pharaoh's sarcophagus. You may have to queue in Room 3 to see the biggest treasure of all, Tutankhamun's solid-gold death mask, encrusted with semi-precious stones, his golden sarcophagus and his jewellery.

In Room 4 you'll find more ancient jewellery from all over the country, and Room 2 has the spectacular jewellery found in Tanis tombs. The newly arranged Rooms 53 and 54 have a wonderful collection of animal mummies.

The Royal Mummy Room

Room 56 houses the **mummies** of 11 of Egypt's most illustrious pharaohs, including Seti I, his son Ramses II (► 23) and Tuthmosis II. Former President Sadat had the room closed in 1981, considering it disrespectful to the dead. But since it partly reopened in 1995, visitors are asked to keep respectfully quiet and tour groups are not allowed.

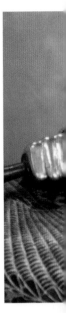

Tutankhamun's mask is made of solid gold with decorations in lapis lazuli, turquoise, carnelian and glass paste
Below: This gold jewel from his tomb is inlaid with semi-precious stones

TAKING A BREAK

The museum cafeteria is rather dull, but the courtyard of the **Nile Hilton** is just a few steps away. Their Abu Ali's terrace café offers snacks and *sheeshas* (water pipes), the Italian **Da Mario** does good pastas and pizzas, or you can stop for coffee and cakes at the coffee shop. The **Semiramis** hotel near by has several excellent restaurants.

➕ 196 C4 ✉ Midan Tahrir, Downtown ☎ 02-2575 4319; www.egyptianmuseum.gov.eg ⏰ Daily 9–6:45 🍴 Museum cafeteria (£); Italian restaurant (££); Abu Ali café terrace (£) at the Nile Hilton 🚇 Sadat station 💵 Moderate; extra charge for the Mummy Room from its first-floor entrance (expensive)

THE EGYPTIAN MUSEUM: INSIDE INFO

Top tips Most tour buses get to the museum around 10am, so avoid the crowds by going earlier, or later in the afternoon.
- The amount of things to see is staggering so try to spread your visit over at least two half days, maybe exploring one floor at a time.

Ones to miss The eastern wing of the ground floor, mostly devoted to the Late Period, is badly labelled and less interesting than the rest, except for the Graeco-Roman art in Room 34.
- You could also skip the western outer galleries of sarcophagi on the first floor and the eastern inner galleries (except Room 14) for the same reasons.

Hidden gems Room 14 on the first floor is rather poorly presented but has a superb collection of Graeco-Roman mummies with beautifully painted face masks, known as the Fayoum portraits.
- Also on the first floor (in Rooms 32 and 27) are some amazingly detailed, lifelike models of fishing boats, butchers, cattle with herdsmen and a villa with garden that give a fascinating insight into life in the Middle Kingdom.

In more depth A digital guide (moderate) is available inside the museum. For more details of the antiquities visit the museum's bookshop. *The Illustrated Guide to the Egyptian Museum in Cairo*, by Zahi Hawass, the secretary-general of Egypt's Supreme Council of Antiquities, is a descriptive guide with pictures of the main exhibits and some useful itineraries (AUC Press). A wonderful illustrated book by Francesco Tiradritti is *The Treasures of the Egyptian Museum in Cairo* (AUC Press).

2 Coptic Cairo

One of the oldest-inhabited parts of the city is Masr al Qadima (Old Cairo), the Coptic neighbourhood that provides a fascinating link between Egypt's pharaonic and Islamic civilisations. In the 6th century BC a garrison known as Babylon-in-Egypt guarded a river crossing here. There are some Roman fortifications, but the area's real attraction is its narrow lanes lined with early churches, and Egypt's oldest synagogue. Cairo's first mosque, built by Amr Ibn al As in AD 642, is near by.

The first thing you'll see when you get here are two Roman towers, which were part of the fortifications built by Emperor Trajan in AD 130, and some fragments of the walls of Babylon-in-Egypt. Behind these lies the fascinating, recently renovated **Coptic Museum**, which gives an overview of Coptic art from the Graeco-Roman period to the early Islamic era (from about AD 300 to 1000). It is clear that some Christian symbols may have evolved from pharaonic ones, including the cross and the image of the Virgin and Child. The Copts were excellent weavers and the upper floor of the museum contains a beautiful collection of early textile fragments.

The elegant towers of the Coptic church of al Muallaqa

A passage near the cafeteria leads to the **al Muallaqa Church** (Hanging Church), built over one of the Roman bastions, visible at the back of the church. The building is reached via a steep staircase and a vestibule where Coptic souvenirs are on sale. The church probably dates from the 7th century, although some Copts claim it's older. Its dark interior is magnificent, with cedar panelling, a wooden Ark-like ceiling, a fine carved marble pulpit supported by 12 pillars representing the Apostles, and superb 13th-century panels inlaid with bone and ivory hiding the three *haikals* (altars).

Probably the oldest church here is the 5th-century **Abu Sarga (St Sergius)**, with an even older crypt where the Holy Family is said to have

THE HOLY FAMILY IN EGYPT

"The angel of the Lord appeared to Joseph in a dream, saying, 'Arise, and take the young child and his mother, and flee into Egypt...for Herod will seek the young child to destroy him'...He took the young child and his mother by night, and departed into Egypt." Matthew 2:13–14. It's believed that the Holy Family – Mary, the infant Jesus and Mary's husband Joseph – spent four years on the move, crossing Sinai and then travelling along the Nile to Asyut. Coptic churches and monasteries were built in many of the places where they are believed to have rested.

rested during their exile in Egypt. In the chapel of the Convent of St George visitors wishing to be blessed can be wrapped in chains by the nuns.

The Jewish community has long gone but the **Ben Ezra Synagogue**, at the other end of the street, has been restored to its former glory. Originally a Coptic church, the building was transformed in the 11th century and the decoration remained very similar to that of the nearby churches. According to Jewish tradition, this is where the prophet Jeremiah preached in the 6th century BC, while the Copts believe that it marks the site where baby Moses was found in a basket.

Above: You may see Coptic monks worshipping at one of the churches

TAKING A BREAK

The **cafeteria** in the museum garden is a peaceful place to relax after exploring Coptic Cairo.

Coptic Museum

➕ 196 C1 ✉ Masr al Qadima (Old Cairo) ☎ 02-2363 9742; www.copticmuseum.gov.eg 🕐 Daily 9–4 🍴 Cafeteria in garden (£) 🚇 Mar Girgis (from Midan Tahrir) 🎫 Moderate

Coptic Churches

➕ 196 C1 ✉ Masr al Qadima (Old Cairo) 🕐 Churches and synagogue daily 9–4 and during services 🚇 Mari Girgis (from Midan Tahrir) 🎫 Free; donations welcome

---

COPTIC CAIRO: INSIDE INFO

Top tip Attend a **Coptic Mass** at the Hanging Church (Friday 8–11am and Sunday 9–11am) and hear the sound of the pharaohs, as the Copts claim to be their direct descendants. The instruments, music and language you hear are similar to those in ancient Egypt. On 1 June, a festival commemorates the Holy Family's stay in the area.

Hidden gems To the right of the entrance of the Hanging Church is a beautiful 10th-century **icon of the Virgin and Child** with obvious Egyptian facial features.
■ Walk along the alleys behind the 11th-century St Barbara's church to discover a hidden Christian cemetery.

❸ Sharia al Muizz li Din Allah

This is the main thoroughfare of the original Fatimid city of al Qahira (Cairo), and is lined with some of the city's most glorious mosques and palaces. As it was customary to build shops outside mosques, it's also home to some of Cairo's less touristy bazaars.

The 11th-century **Fatimid walls** and the **gate called Bab al Futuh** mark the northern end of Sharia al Muizz. Built before the Crusades by Armenians (using stones from pharaonic structures), they were reinforced by Saladin (➤ 25) a century later. To appreciate the architectural and military genius, take

A minaret overlooks the ablution fountain of al Hakim mosque

a torch and walk the ramparts to **Bab al Nasr**, and back for marvellous views over the Northern Cemetery and Cairo.

Adjacent is the mosque of **al Hakim** (➤ 24), with a marble courtyard and huge minarets that are among the oldest in the city. You may guess from the smell that this part of the street is also home to the onion and garlic market.

Farther to the right, the **mosque and** *sabil-kuttab* **of Sulayman Agha al Silahdar** is built in a mixture of Turkish and Cairene styles, and has a slim pencil minaret. Opposite is **Darb al Asfar**, a narrow side street with several renovated merchant houses, a sign of the government's plans for the entire old city. The finest mansion is Beit al Suhaymi, two 17th- and 18th-century houses knocked together. Its rooms are decorated with inlaid marble and mashrabia woodwork, and a fabulous shaded courtyard is filled with birdsong. Back along Sharia al Muizz to the left is the elegant mosque of **al Aqmar** ("the moonlit"), a rare surviving Fatimid monument. On the next left corner is the prominent **sabil-kuttab of Abd al Rahman Katkhuda**, which has a fountain downstairs and Quranic school upstairs, with a beautiful carved ceiling. Here, Sharia Muizz opens out to **Bayn al Qasrayn** ("Between the

Two Palaces"), after the long-gone Fatimid palaces at the core of the original city. This area is undergoing extensive renovation. Only two of the original five storeys of the 14th-century palace of **Qasr Amir Bashtak** have survived (on the left of the street), but this is one of Cairo's most impressive secular medieval buildings.

Opposite is the 185m (610-foot) facade of the epitome of Mameluke architecture. This complex includes the cruciform *madrasa-khanqah* of Sultan Barquq (1384), the *madrasa-mausoleum* of al Nasir (1304) with a marble Gothic doorway, and the *madrasa-mausoleum and maristan* of Sultan Qalawun, al Nasir's father. The *maristan* functioned as a medical centre until the 19th century.

Opposite Qalawun's complex, **Sultan Ayyub's** *madrasa-mausoleum* was built in 1242 as Cairo's first Quranic school. Lined with coppersmith shops, the street turns into the Gold Bazaar, where a small alley to the left leads into **Khan al Khalili** (➤ 71). Past the busy shopping street of al Muski is the imposing *madrasa* of **Sultan Barsbay** (1425), and at its southern end an alley leads into the **Perfume and Spice Market**. Across Sharia al Azhar is the impressive **Ghuriya complex** of Mameluke Sultan al Ghuri, with its mausoleum on the left and *madrasa* on the right.

Beyond the city's last *tarboush* (fez) shop, the street ends at **Bab Zuwayla**, the beautifully restored southern city gate, former place of execution. Beside the gate is the **mosque of Sultan al Muayyad** (1415) with a splendid raised facade and twin minarets on top of the gate.

Enjoy the peacefulness of the delightful shady courtyard of Beit al Suhaymi

TAKING A BREAK

For a sumptuous café with drinks, snacks and water pipes head for the **Naguib Mahfouz Café** (►76) or the authentic café-terrace of **al Fishawi** (►75), both in Khan al Khalili.

➕ 197 E4

🕐 Most monuments daily 9–5; mosques may close during prayer times; less-visited monuments such as the ramparts and Qasr Bashtak may appear closed, but a custodian is usually on duty near by 💰 Moderate; the mosques are free but the custodian will invariably ask for a tip, so bring plenty of change

SHARIA AL MUIZZ LI DIN ALLAH: INSIDE INFO

Top tips Explore the street in the morning or late afternoon when it's cooler.
- Dress modestly, covering arms and legs, as this is a socially traditional part of town. Women should take a scarf to cover their heads when needed and everyone should remove their shoes before entering a mosque.
- Climb up one of the minarets for a view over the historic centre and then rest in one of the mosque courtyards, which are often oases of calm.
- Visit on Sunday: most shops are closed so one can admire the architecture.

Hidden gems Stroll around in the area behind al Azhar Mosque to discover several great shops and fine mansions.

4 Saqqara and Memphis

Saqqara was one of the largest burial grounds in Egypt and in use for more than 3,000 years. Most of it remains unexcavated, but among the wonders on show is the impressive Step Pyramid of Zoser. The tomb was built by the innovative architect Imhotep for King Zoser in the 27th century BC. But instead of the king's traditional mudbrick *mastaba* grave, Imhotep built in stone and stacked several *mastabas* on top of each other to create the first pyramid and the first large stone building.

Originally the Step Pyramid complex was enclosed in a limestone wall, which had fake doors to confuse intruders

With its original shiny limestone casing, Zoser's pyramid stood 62m (203 feet) high and 118m (387 feet) by 140m (460 feet) around its base. A 28m (92-foot) deep shaft leads into the burial chamber. Part of the original limestone enclosure wall has been rebuilt near the entrance in the southeastern corner. Enter the complex via a pillared corridor, and on the right is the Heb Sed Court, where the king's vitality was symbolically renewed at a festival held every seven years. The Houses of the South and the North are thought to represent older shrines

of Upper and Lower Egypt, and the Serdab has a copy of Zoser's statue (the original is in the Egyptian Museum in Cairo, ▶ 50–53). Across the Great Court is the shaft of the South Tomb that probably contained the king's internal organs.

Other Tombs

To the south rises the less impressive **pyramid of Unas**, built 350 years after Zoser's with its interior walls covered with the Pyramid Texts, the earliest-known examples of decorative writing in a tomb. To the southeast of Unas's pyramid are the recently opened **B Tombs** (separate charge, moderate) and the Persian Tombs.

Northeast of Zoser's complex you can see the magnificent 6th-Dynasty *mastabas* of the viziers Mereruka, Ankh-Ma-Hor and Kagemni, containing the finest reliefs of the Old Kingdom. The double *mastaba* of Akhti-Hotep and Ptah-Hotep shows the different stages of tomb decoration and also has some superb reliefs. The walls of the *mastaba* of the royal hairdresser Ti are covered with wonderful scenes of daily life in ancient Egypt. But the strangest place in Saqqara is the **Serapeum**, where mummified sacred bulls were buried like pharaohs in underground, rock-hewn galleries.

Memphis

Just a short way from Saqqara lie the remains of Memphis, the world's first imperial city, founded in about 3100 BC by King Menes (▶ 22). Old Kingdom pharaohs and nobility were buried in its necropolis at Saqqara.

As the first capital of a united Egypt, Memphis was symbolically built at the place where the delta met the

Part of the original portal leading to the Saqqara complex

The approach to the Step Pyramid is through a pillared corridor

southern valley. Even after the 5th century BC, when Thebes had long taken over as the capital of Egypt, it was a splendid city, a thriving commercial centre and an important cult centre dedicated to the God Ptah. It's hard to imagine such splendour today, as the mudbrick palaces have dissolved and the stones of its temples, including the grand temple of Ptah, were plundered centuries ago for other buildings.

The sleepy village of Mit Rahina has a few minor statues. Its tiny museum has a fine limestone colossus of Ramses II as a young man, and a beautiful alabaster sphinx in the garden.

TAKING A BREAK

Saqqara has a small **café** selling cold drinks and tea, but Egyptian families like to picnic in the shade of the ruined 6th-century Monastery of Jeremiah, near the car-park. If the weather's not too hot you could also **picnic in North Saqqara**, with Imhotep's masterpiece as a backdrop.

Saqqara
➕ 199 E3 ✉ 21km (13 miles) south of Giza pyramids; 32km (20 miles) from Cairo ◎ May–Sep daily 8–5, Oct–Apr 8–4 🚌 Bus from Downtown to Pyramids Road (Sharia al Haram); from the Marioutiya Canal (1km/ 0.5 mile before the pyramids) get a microbus to Saqqara 🎟 Step Pyramid moderate; separate charge for other tombs

Memphis
➕ 199 E3 ✉ Mit Rahina, 3km (2 miles) from Saqqara ◎ May–Sep daily 8–5, Oct–Apr 8–4 🍴 Cafeteria across the road (£) 🚌 No public transport 🎟 Inexpensive

SAQQARA AND MEMPHIS: INSIDE INFO

Top tips The most spectacular approach to the Step Pyramid is on horseback across the desert. You can rent a horse from the stables in Saqqara (➤ 78).
■ It gets hot in Saqqara, so make sure you take enough liquids.

Ones to miss The Persian and B Tombs have some fine reliefs, but can be skipped if time is short.

5 Giza Pyramids and Sphinx

The Pyramids of Giza (al Ahram in Arabic), sole survivors of the seven wonders of the ancient world, embody the mystery and magic of antiquity. Along with the Sphinx, they have attracted more speculation and explanation than any other monument. Despite their enduring fascination, countless questions remain that may never be answered.

Many people dream of seeing these pyramids once in their lives but, strangely enough, the first sight can be disappointing. Perhaps because they are so familiar, the pyramids seem smaller than you might expect and the mystique often disappears in the face of relentless hassle from touts and camel drivers at the entrance. But if you take time to walk around them, preferably early in the morning, it's still possible to sense their overwhelming grandeur and to evoke the 45 centuries of history they represent.

The pyramids and the Sphinx remain mysterious

The **Great Pyramid of Khufu** (second king of the 4th Dynasty, 2589–2566 BC) is the oldest and largest of the three main pyramids. Built out of 2.3 million blocks weighing an average of 2.5 tonnes each (but sometimes up to 15 tonnes), with its original casing it reached a height of 146.6m (481 feet) but is now 10m (33 feet) lower than that.

Since it was first reopened in the 9th century, three chambers have been found inside the pyramid, all empty except for Khufu's sarcophagus. But some archaeologists believe there's a fourth chamber, containing the king's treasure. From the entrance a claustrophobic corridor descends steeply into an unfinished chamber. Alternatively, an ascending corridor leads left into the Queen's Chamber or right into the spectacular 47m (154-foot) long Great Gallery and, beyond it, the King's Chamber with the sarcophagus. East of the pyramid are the remains of the king's funerary temple and causeway, and the three smaller Queens' Pyramids.

A mortuary temple stands at the entrance to the vast Great Pyramid of Khufu

The King's Guardian

Khufu's son **Khafre** (fourth king of the 4th Dynasty, 2558–2532 BC) built the second pyramid, which is 136.4m (448 feet) high,

but the higher ground makes it appear taller than his father's. This pyramid has two chambers, one of which houses the king's sarcophagus. To the east are the remains of Khafre's Funerary Temple and of the causeway leading to his Valley Temple, guarded by the legendary **Sphinx**, carved out of the hillside.

Known as *Abu 'l Hol* ("the Father of Terror") in Arabic, this massive statue remains a mystery: the face is clearly Khafre's, but the lionesque body has been suggested to be as much as 2,600 years older. The Sphinx is in a poor condition – the old story goes that its nose fell off after apparently being used as a target by Mameluke and Napoleonic soldiers, while its beard is in the British Museum in London. The soft limestone has

The pyramids at Giza and the Sphinx are the most instantly recognisable monuments in the world

not stood the test of time but recent restorations have added thousands of hand-cut limestone blocks to support the legs and haunches.

Khafre's son **Menkaure** (2532–2504 BC) built the third pyramid, which is only 70m (230 feet) high but surrounded by the smaller pyramids of the royal family.

TAKING A BREAK

There are a few fast-food restaurants in Nazlat al Samaan, but for a more sumptuous lunch with a view of the pyramids, head for the poolside restaurant of the **Mena House Oberoi hotel** (➤ 73), or relax in the garden of **Andrea's** (➤ 74).

🔟 199 E4 ⊠ Giza, 18km (11 miles) southwest of Cairo ☎ 02-383 8823
(tourist office); www.guardians.net/hawass ⏰ Daily 7:30–4, Great Pyramid
7:30–4 🍴 Cafeteria (£) 🚌 CTA buses 355 and 357 from beside the Egyptian
Museum to Oberoi hotel at the foot of the pyramids. Microbus to al Ahram from
Abd al Moneim Riyad bus station 🎟 Pyramid plateau and Sphinx moderate;
extra charges for Khufu's pyramid (expensive), and two other pyramids
(inexpensive); Solar Boat Museum moderate

Camel and
horse drivers
around the
pyramids can
be annoying

GIZA PYRAMIDS AND SPHINX: INSIDE INFO

Top tips Visit the pyramids in the **early morning or late afternoon** to avoid the
crowds. Follow the road past the pyramids to reach a plateau for a panoramic
view of all three, but souvenir stalls and touts may disturb your enjoyment.
- **Tickets** to enter the Great Pyramid of Khufu are limited to 300 a day:
  150 go on sale at 7:30am, and 150 at 1pm, and often they sell fast,
  particularly in winter on Wednesdays and Thursdays.
- Avoid taking a **horse or camel** from the Pyramid plateau, as you will most
  likely be overcharged. Instead try one of the stables beyond the Sphinx
  (► 78) and watch the sun go down behind the pyramids.
- A **son et lumière** show is held several times daily at a theatre beside the
  Sphinx. For infomation tel: 02-2386 3469 or check online at
  www.soundandlight.com.eg

Hidden gem The **Solar Boat Museum** (Jun–Sep daily 9–5, Oct–May 9–4;
moderate) behind the Great Pyramid contains a superb 43m (140-foot) boat that
was intended to carry the king through the underworld. The vessel was found in
1,200 pieces which restorers spent a total of 10 years putting back together.
Another well-preserved boat was found near by, but it remains unexcavated.

At Your Leisure

6 Downtown (Wust al Balad)

Midan Tahrir (Liberation Square) is the centre of modern Cairo. Landmarks to look for include the Egyptian Museum (➤ 50–53); the Nile Hilton (built over the remains of the British barracks after the 1952 revolution); the Mugamma, a Soviet-inspired "temple" of bureaucracy; Umar Makram Mosque and the American University.

Khedive Ismail developed the downtown area in the 1860s as part of a modernisation drive connected with the opening of the Suez Canal. The scheme was heavily influenced by Hausmann's plans for Paris boulevards. The main streets of Talaat Harb and Sharia Kasr al Nil are lined with elegant buildings that now house offices, shops and banks. The famous but dilapidated Groppi Café graces Midan Talaat Harb, while the picturesque food market of Tawfiqiya sits at the north end of Sharia Talaat Harb, a road lined with shoe shops. With its seedy nightclubs and backstreet bars, 26th-of-July Street leads to the once-grand Ezbekiya Gardens.

✚ 196 C4

7 Mr and Mrs Mahmoud Khalil Museum

This splendid museum houses Egypt's finest collection of Western art. The works of French Impressionist and Post-Impressionist artists, including Rodin, Monet, Gauguin, Renoir, Van Gogh and Delacroix, belonged to the prewar minister Mahmoud Khalil and his French wife, who bequeathed them to the State on condition that they were exhibited in their elegant former residence.

✚ 196 B3 ✉ 1 Sharia Kafour, near the Cairo Sheraton, Giza ☎ 02-2338 9720; www.mkm. gov.eg 🕐 Tue–Sun 10–6 (holidays 10–3) 🚇 Doqqi 💷 Inexpensive (passport required)

8 Gayer-Anderson House (Beit al Kritliya)

The Beit al Kritliya gives a fascinating insight into the life of stylish and wealthy medieval Cairenes. Englishman Major Gayer-Anderson, a doctor to the royal family from 1935 to 1942, joined two houses together and lovingly restored and furnished them with Oriental *objets d'art* and

Men's reception room at the Beit al Kritliya

paintings picked up on his travels. The ornate reception room on the ground floor featured in the James Bond movie *The Spy Who Loved Me* (1977). The museum is even more splendid after its restoration. The entrance is via Ibn Tulun mosque.

🚩 197 D2 ⊠ Midan Ahmed Ibn Tulun ☎ 02-2364 7822 ⏱ Daily 9–5 🚌 Bus 174 and minibus 54 from Midan Tahrir 🎟 Moderate

9 Ibn Tulun Mosque

A masterpiece of classical Islamic architecture, and the largest and oldest intact mosque in Cairo, Ibn Tulun's mosque impresses with its vast scale and elegant simplicity, despite the controversial restoration. It was built in AD 879 by the Abbasid sultan Ahmed Ibn Tulun, who was clearly influenced by the mosques in his native Iraq. The spiral minaret was probably based on the mosque in Samarra (Iraq), although legend has it that Ibn Tulun was in fact inspired by a rolled-up piece of paper. The vast paved courtyard has a peaceful quality and is surrounded by elegant arcades. A 2km (1-mile) long sycamore frieze below the ceiling is inscribed with about one-fifth of the Quran.

🚩 197 D3 ⊠ Sharia Saliba, Midan Ahmed Ibn Tulun ⏱ Summer daily 8–6 🚌 Bus 174 and minibus 54 from Midan Tahrir 🎟 Free, but tip the custodian

Top: Muhammad Ali's mosque is a Cairo landmark
Below: Fine plasterwork at the Mosque of Ibn Tulun

10 Citadel (al Qalaa)

The largest fortification in the Middle East and still dominating Cairo's skyline, al Qalaa stands on a spur of the al Muqattam hills. It was the royal residence for more than 700 years. The citadel was built in 1176 by Salah ad Din (Saladin, ► 25) as part of his programme of fortifications against the Crusaders. The impressive walls still remain, but the original buildings were torn down first by Sultan al Nasir, whose striped mosque with faïence minaret is the only reminder of that period. In the 19th century Muhammad Ali (► 26) tore down more to build his mosque and palaces.

The Muhammad Ali Mosque, built between 1824 and 1848 and modelled on Istanbul's Sultanahmet Mosque, is more striking from a distance than close up. The interior is disappointing, but the views from the terrace are impressive. The clock in the courtyard was a gift from King Louis Philippe of France (1773–1850), given in return for the obelisk that now stands in Paris.

The Gawhara Palace houses a small museum of Muhammad Ali's family belongings. Of the other museums, only the Carriage Museum and the bizarre National Police Museum are interesting.

🚩 197 E3 ⊠ Midan al Qalaa (entrance in Sharia Salah Salem) ☎ 02-2512 1735 ⏱ Summer daily 8–6; winter 8–5; museums 8:30–4:30 🍽 Cafeteria (£) 🚌 Bus 174 from Midan Ramses and minibus 54 from Midan Tahrir 🎟 Moderate

11 Sultan Hasan Mosque-*Madrasa*

One of the finest Islamic monuments in Egypt, this was built between 1356 and 1363 on an unprecedented grand scale, as it included shops, schools and apartments. The first mosque to have a cruciform plan, it has four *iwans* (vaulted spaces around a courtyard), and within each corner is a *madrasa* (Quranic school) dedicated to the four main legal rites of Sunni Islam.

The entrance to this splendid building is through a dark corridor leading into the dazzling courtyard, with its sense of overwhelming peacefulness and monumental simplicity. The light is most beautiful in the morning. Huge portals on either side of the *mihrab* (niche indicating the direction of Mecca) lead into a sombre mausoleum. There's some confusion as to whether anyone is buried here – some sources say the Sultan's sons are interred inside, while others say that the grave is empty.

🔲 197 E3 ✉ Midan Salah ad Din ⏰ Summer daily 8–6; winter 8–5 🚌 Bus 174 and minibus 54 from Midan Tahrir 💲 Free

FIVE BEST VIEWPOINTS

- **Top of Cairo Tower on Gezira Island:** terrace, cafeteria and revolving restaurant
- **Citadel terrace** before sunset
- **The Revolving Restaurant** on the 41st floor of the Grand Hyatt Cairo and Lounge Bar have glorious 360° views over Cairo and the Nile
- Top of the minaret of **al Muayyad Mosque** (▶ 57), Bab Zuwayla
- **Al Azhar Park** (▶ 71), magnificent views over Fatimid Cairo and beyond

12 Islamic Art Museum

A visit to this rich collection is essential for a clearer understanding of the Islamic monuments in Cairo, as most of the objects were salvaged from local mosques, *madrasas* and palaces. The collection contains some exquisite masterpieces including an elegant Mameluke fountain and mosque lights, gorgeous *mashrabeya*

Spectacular view from the citadel over the mosque of Sultan Hasan

FIVE PLACES FOR CHILDREN
- **Cairo Zoo**, Midan al-Gamaa, Giza (daily 9–4, tel: 02-3570 8895, inexpensive)
- **Dream Park**, Oasis Road, 6th of October City, 20km/12.5 miles south of Cairo (tel: 02-3855 3191, www.dreamparkegypt.com, Sat–Thu 4pm–midnight, Fri noon–9pm, expensive) more than 30 rides for children.
- **Dr Ragab's Pharaonic Village** St Jacob's Island, 2km/1 mile south of Giza Bridge on the Corniche, Giza (tel: 02-3571 8675; www.pharaonicvillage.com; summer daily 9–9; winter 9–6). A kitsch but fun two-hour boat tour taking in scenes of ancient Egypt, all performed by costumed Egyptians.
- **Horse- or camel-riding** at the pyramids (▶ 78).
- **Fagnoon Art School**, Saqqara Road, Sabil Om Hashim (tel: 02-3815 1014; daily 10–7). Children can let their creativity loose in Mohammed Allam's wonderful art centre.

woodwork, some unusual woodwork from the Tulunid period, superb illuminated manuscripts and some fine Egyptian glass. Unfortunately, the museum has been closed for restoration for several years, and no one knows when it will reopen.

✚ 197 E4 ✉ Sharia Bur Said, Bab al Khalq
🕐 Closed for restoration

🔟 Al Azhar Mosque

Al Azhar ("the most blooming" or "the radiant"), was built in AD 971 as the first mosque in Fatimid Cairo. It is often claimed to be the oldest university in the world, and is also Egypt's supreme theological authority, presided over by the influential Sheikh of al Azhar. The entrance to this splendid mosque is the ornate 15th-century Barber's Gate, where students traditionally had their heads shaved. The *sahn* (courtyard), part of the original Fatimid design, is overlooked by three minarets and flanked on the right by a Mameluke *madrasa* with rooms for the students. The university itself, which offers religious studies to students from all over the Muslim world, is now housed in modern buildings behind the mosque.

Colourful handicrafts for sale in Khan al Khalili bazaar

197 F4 ⊠ Sharia al Azhar ⏰ Daily 9–5. Closed during prayer times, particularly Fri noon 🎫 Free, but tips are requested

14 Khan al Khalili

The Khan, a confusing maze of alleys and bazaars that are mostly organised by trade, has been the bustling commercial soul of Cairo's old city since the Middle Ages. The main street, al Badestan, is now mostly devoted to souvenirs, but for more interesting buys stroll into the smaller alleys to find out where the locals shop. A good place for lunch or a snack is the Naguib Mahfouz Café-Restaurant (➤ 76) on al Badestan. The gold market around Sharia al Muizz li Din Allah (➤ 56–58) is big and busy, as the amount of gold given by a groom to his bride is still an important part of the marriage contract.

The spice and perfume bazaar in an alley to the side of the Barsbay mosque, on Sharia al Muizz li Din Allah (just follow your nose), still has an authentic medieval atmosphere. Near the mosque of al Husayn is al Fishawi (➤ 75), a café that claims to have been serving continuously since it opened in 1773 – perhaps something of an exaggeration but still worth a visit.

197 E4 ⊠ Between Midan al Husayn and Sharia al Muski ⏰ Mon–Sat 9–6 🍴 Al Fishawi and Naguib Mahfouz café and restaurant (£–££) 🎫 Free

AL AZHAR PARK

The Aga Khan Trust for Culture created **al Azhar Park** (Sharia Salah Salem, tel: 02-2510 7378, www.alazharpark.com, daily 9am–midnight, inexpensive), a much-needed green zone, **behind al Azhar Mosque**, from an ancient rubbish tip. The result is stunning – over 1.5km (1 mile) of 12th-century Ayyubid city walls were uncovered and restored, the neighbourhood of Darb al Ahmar is being restored and revitalised, and 30ha (74 acres) of **beautifully landscaped gardens**, in Islamic tradition with more than 50 different water features, have been created. Just how needed this green space was in one of the world's most densely populated areas is clear from the numbers of families who come for **a stroll or a picnic**. The grounds include a theatre, a children's playground, fruit orchards, a lake, a gallery and a wonderful tearoom-restaurant, Citadel View (➤ 75), all with 360 degree views over the city.

Where to... Stay

Prices
The prices are for a double room per night.
£ under 400LE   ££ 400–900LE   £££ over 900LE

As Egypt's main city, Cairo has a huge range of accommodation, from the sleazy fleapits near Ataba market to sumptuous palaces with spectacular views of the Nile or the pyramids. Whatever your priorities might be, in summer try to get a room with air-conditioning, as it can get incredibly hot and sticky even at night. Try to book ahead in high season (winter) or you'll be lucky to find a bed anywhere.

Cairo Marriott £££

The 19th-century ruler Khedive Ismail built this superb palace on the Nile to house the French empress, Eugenie, and other foreign guests attending the opening of the Suez Canal in 1869. The palace and garden now form the central part of the hotel, and the bedrooms are in two modern towers. Many of the well-equipped, recently renovated rooms have splendid views over the Nile and the city, but they lack the grandeur of the palace. The khedival garden with its swimming pool is an oasis of calm in busy Cairo, while you can drink cocktails in Empress Eugenie's impressive bedroom. There's also a casino for those seeking extra excitement.

🚹 196 C4 ⊠ 16 Sharia Saray al Gezira, Zamalek ☎ 02-2728 3000; www.marriott.com

Carlton Hotel £

Good for nostalgic souls, this old-fashioned downtown hotel near Cinema Rivoli has a range of rooms in various states of renovation and size, but all with plenty of character. All rooms are clean with private bathrooms, and the hotel boasts a great rooftop cafeteria where cool beers are served with a view, a coffee house and a restaurant.

🚹 196 C4 ⊠ 21 Sharia 26th of July, Downtown ☎ 02-2575 5022; www.carltonhotelcairo.com

alcoholic drinks in the evening. Book well ahead as it fills up with people who regularly visit Cairo.

🚹 196 B5 ⊠ 21 Sharia Ismail Mohamed, Zamalek ☎ 02-2735 2311; www.hotellongchamps.com

Luna £

In this excellent budget option you will find spacious and immaculate rooms, with fresh, crisp bedlinen provided on a daily basis, and air-conditioning. Some rooms have a private bathroom, other share an immaculate communal bathroom, and guests can use the kitchen or salon to hang out.

🚹 197 D4 ⊠ 5th floor, 21 Sharia Talaat Harb, Downtown ☎ 02-2396 1020; www.hotellunacairo.com

Mayfair £

A quiet and good-value budget option, well located on a leafy street at the heart of the island of Zamalek. In a renovated grand art-deco building, the rooms have wooden floors, high

Longchamps ££

This is a long-established, mid-range option located in the quiet residential area of Zamalek, close to many restaurants and bars. The spacious rooms are immaculate, and come with spotless bathrooms, and sometimes a balcony. A good breakfast is served, as well as

ceilings, balconies and immaculate bathrooms, although the single room are on the small side. The large terrace is a pleasant place to read or take afternoon tea. The hotel is close to restaurants and shops.
🚹 196 B5 ☒ 2nd floor Sharia Aziz Osman, Zamalek ☎ 02-2735 7315

Mena House Oberoi £££

Here, you can be one of the lucky few with a view of the pyramids from their room. The beautifully decorated, Oriental-Moorish rooms in the 19th-century wing of this former *khedival* hunting lodge sit beside the Great Pyramid. Standard rooms in the modern garden annexe are spacious and, although they lack the immediacy of the palace rooms, you might still get a glimpse of the ancient wonders. Even the swimming pool has a view. You can eat breakfast on the garden terrace, and the garden restaurant is perfect for lunch or afternoon tea, while the Moghul Room is the best Indian restaurant in town.
🚹 196, off A1 ☒ Sharia al Ahram, near the pyramids of Giza ☎ 02-3377 3222; www.menahouseoberoi.com

Nile Plaza Four Seasons £££

One of two Four Seasons hotels in town, this is the most luxurious of Cairo's five-star hotels. The stylish rooms are spacious, with large marble bathrooms and sweeping views over the Nile or the old city and citadel. The level of service here is unmatched and the hotel boasts two swimming pools, a spa and five excellent restaurants – a real treat!
🚹 196 B3 ☒ 1089 Corniche al-Nil, Garden City ☎ 02-2791 7000; www.fourseasons.com

Osiris £

In this excellent family-run budget hotel in a quiet corner of downtown Cairo the rooms are lovely and have a homey feel to them. A delicious breakfast is served on the terrace with great views over Cairo.
🚹 197 D3 ☒ 49 Sharia Nubar, 12th floor, Downtown ☎ 02-2794 5728; http://hotelosiris.free.fr

Pension Roma £

Madame Cressaty's diligence has maintained this 1940s hotel as one of the best inexpensive options downtown. Behind the Moorish facade, the clean rooms have polished wooden floors, high ceilings and comfortable old furniture. Book ahead as the hotel is extremely popular with backpackers and students.
🚹 197 D4 ☒ 4th Floor, 169 Sharia Muhammad Farid ☎ 02-2391 1088

President ££

Modern and unassuming from the outside, but cosy, quiet and friendly on the inside, the President offers comfortable rooms in the leafy residential area of Zamalek, with its many shops and restaurants. The hotel boasts a well-equipped business centre, an excellent bakery, a rooftop restaurant, and a top-floor bar which can get quite lively in the evenings.
🚹 196, off B5 ☒ 22 Sharia Taha Hussein, Zamalek ☎ 02-2735 0718

Talisman ££

Cairo's one and only boutique hotel is full of atmosphere, and wonderfully located in a quiet alley off a busy shopping street. The hotel, in a large downtown flat, has colourful and luxuriously decorated rooms with Egyptian and Syrian furniture, great bathrooms with Egyptian toiletries. Communal spaces are equally sumptuous.
🚹 197 D4 ☒ 5th floor, 39 Sharia Talaat Harb ☎ 02-2393 9431; www.talisman-hotel.com

Villa Belle Époque £££

This is an exciting new boutique hotel opening in early 2009. Located in a lovely 1920s villa in the quiet residential area of Maadi, well connected by metro to the centre of Cairo, the hotel features 13 spacious and luxurious bedrooms, and a garden with a small pool in the shade of fruit trees.
🚹 Off map 197 F1 ☒ Belle Epoque Travel, 17 Sharia Tunis, New Maadi ☎ 02-2516 9649/53/60; www.dahabiya.com

Where to...
Eat and Drink

Prices
Expect to pay per person for a meal, excluding drinks and tips.
£ under 100LE   ££ 100–150LE   £££ over 150LE

Cairo's wide variety of restaurants reflects the city's cosmopolitan character. National dishes such as *fuul*, *koshari* and kebabs are inexpensive and widely available from food vendors and eateries on many street corners, but most of these places don't serve alcohol. Restaurants serving ethnic or international cuisine are often part of a hotel. Note that wealthy Cairenes like to dress up for dinner.

Abu al Sid ££-£££
This very popular and trendy Egyptian restaurant serves very well-prepared classics such as stuffed pigeon and *meloukhiya* (a soup of a spinach-like vegetable with chicken, served with bread, onion and condiments), as well as *mezze* and *sheeshas* (water pipes). The atmosphere is great, and the place is decorated with wonderfully kitsch Louis Farouk-style furniture and features work by local artists. Reservations are essential.
🕀 196 B5 ⬜ 157 Sharia 26 July, Zamalek ☎ 02-2735 9640 ⏰ Daily noon–2am

Abu Tarek £
Proclaimed the best of all Cairo's *koshari* places, Abu Tarek serves the national carbohydrate treasure of lentils, macaroni, rice and fried onions with a spicy tomato sauce. The restaurant is always expanding due to its popularity.
🕀 196 C4 ⬜ 40 Sharia Champollion, Downtown ⏰ Daily 8am–midnight

Americana Fish Market ££
An excellent fish restaurant situated on the upper deck of a permanently moored boat on the Nile, the Americana is arguably the best in town. You choose from a large catch of the day with a wide selection of Mediterranean and Red Sea fish and seafood. Your choice is weighed, cooked to order, and served with hot freshly made bread and delicious Middle eastern salads. Reservations are essential.
🕀 196 B2 ⬜ Americana boat, 26 Sharia an Nil, Giza ☎ 02-2570 9693 ⏰ Daily noon–2am

Andrea £-££
The real pleasure here is to be had outdoors, sitting at tables covered in red-and-white checked cloths, in a garden of bougainvillea and shady trees. Start with a selection of *mezze* and fresh salads that are presented on a large tray, and scooped up with delicious pitta bread (made by women working at the entrance). Main courses are limited to grilled meat and poultry, with the roast chicken coming particularly recommended. Andrea's is perfect after a visit to the pyramids, though it does sometimes suffer from an influx of tour groups.
🕀 199 E4 ⬜ 59–60 Marioutiya Canal, near the Giza pyramids ☎ 02-3383 1133 ⏰ Daily 10am–1am

Aqua £££
This is an expensive but excellent fusion restaurant with some of the best sushi in town. Pacific Rim cuisine is complemented by views over the Nile. Book ahead and dress for the occasion.
🕀 196 C3 ⬜ Four Seasons Nile Plaza, 1089 Corniche an Nil, Garden City ☎ 02-2791 6076 ⏰ Daily 7pm–1am

L'Asiatique £££

This award-winning Asian restaurant, voted third best in Africa and the best in Egypt by World's 50 Best Restaurants (UK), is deservedly popular with Cairo's glitterati and well-heeled crowds. The service is swift, the decor elegant and the menu features a delicious selection of well-prepared Asian dishes. Reservations are essential.

🚉 **196 C4** ⊠ **Le Pasha 1901 Boat, Sharia Saray al Gezirah, Zamalek** ☎ **02-2735 6730** 🕐 **Daily 7pm–2am, also lunch Fri 2–5**

La Bodega ££-£££

This very hip lounge bar serves Asian fusion food in a stylish contemporary Asian décor. The more down-to-earth bistro on the same floor serves an inventive and delicious selection of popular Mediterranean dishes, ranging from a good couscous to fresh pasta and paella.

🚉 **196 B5** ⊠ **157 Sharia 26 July, Zamalek** ☎ **02-2735 6761** 🕐 **Daily noon–2, 7pm–4am**

Cedars £££

In this swish Lebanese restaurant with a large terrace they serve *mezze* and good Lebanese dishes as well as *sheshas* (water pipes). It attracts a younger crowd who arrive later in the evening. Book ahead to be sure of a table.

🚉 **196 A5** ⊠ **42 Sharia Geziret el-Arab, Muhandesseen** ☎ **02-3345 0088** 🕐 **Daily noon–1am**

Citadel View ££

Overlooking the beautiful al Azhar Park (▶ 71) and the city of Cairo, this is a perfect place to lunch on the terrace, take tea in one of the upstairs traditional salons, with cushions and low tables, or have a more intimate dinner. At lunch time there is a good-value buffet offering a wide choice of Egyptian *mezze* and main courses. This establishment is recommended, but book ahead on Fridays.

🚉 **197 F3** ⊠ **Al Azhar Park, Sharia Saleh Salem** ☎ **02-2510 9151** 🕐 **Daily lunch and dinner**

Egyptian Pancake House £

Places to eat in and around Khan al Khalili bazaar are limited, but this one has become reliable. Egyptian pancakes (*fiteer* in Arabic) are a cross between a pizza and a crêpe. *Fiteer* can come sweet with nuts and honey, or savoury with cheese, tomatoes and chilli. Inside the restaurant is calmer and cooler, but outside you have the opportunity to sit still and watch the endless fascination provided by Islamic Cairo.

🚉 **197 E4** ⊠ **Between Sharia al Azhar and Midan al Husayn, Khan al Khalili** 🕐 **Daily from morning until the last customer leaves late evening**

Felfela £-££

If you know nothing about Egyptian food but are keen to find out and experiment with a variety of flavours and textures, then this is as good a place to start as any. The clientele is predominantly foreign, but locals come here as well for the traditional dishes, if not the wacky décor of stuffed animals and Egyptian artefacts. Try a selection of salads and *mezze* to start, followed by a kebab or grilled pigeon. Felfela has now become a chain, but this is the original and best.

🚉 **196 C4** ⊠ **15 Sharia Hoda Shaarawi, Downtown** ☎ **02-2392 2833** 🕐 **Daily 8am–midnight**

Al Fishawi £

The claim that they have never closed al Fishawi since 1773 may be a slight exaggeration, but this is the oldest teahouse in Cairo. It's also one of the few cafés where you'll find Egyptian women and families sitting with their men. It's a great place to relax, sip mint tea or smoke a sweet water pipe and watch the world go by. During the day it's a good place to stop for a break while visiting the sights of the old city, and at night it gets extremely lively with locals. As it's close to the mosque of al Husayn no alcohol is served.

🚉 **197 E4** ⊠ **Khan al Khalili, just off Midan al Husayn** 🕐 **Daily 24 hours**

Galleria Food Court ££

One of the many good restaurants in the Grand Hyatt Cairo hotel on the Nile, the Galleria Food Court has several corners offering different food choices, including the Cappucci Café, Bites & Fries deli, Mama Mia pasta and pizza, Salam Middle Eastern Café and the Sugar, which are great for a coffee break, a quick snack or a good lunch. A big window looks onto the Nile.

🛈 196 C2 🗷 Grand Hyatt Cairo, Corniche an Nil, Roda Island, Garden City 🕿 02-2365 1234; www.cairo.grand.hyatt.com 🕒 Daily 11am–1am

Greek Club £

For nostalgic souls this is the perfect place to be. The old club, with its faded neoclassical interior and noisy outdoor terrace, is the perfect place to stop and enjoy a cold and cheap beer with some mezze. This is a Cairo institution.

🛈 197 D4 🗷 3 Sharia Mahmoud Bassioni, above Groppi, Downtown 🕿 02-2575 0822 🕒 Daily 7am–2am

La Mezzaluna ££

A popular Italian restaurant in a little alley close to the 26th-of-July main street, La Mezzaluna serves pastas and copious salads but no alcohol. A favourite with young Cairenes and Cairo ex-pats.

🛈 Off map 196 B5 🗷 Sharia Aziz Osman, Zamalek 🕿 02-2735 2655 🕒 Daily 7am–11pm

Marriott Garden ££

Cairo doesn't have many secluded outdoor spaces where you can have a drink or a meal in relative peace, but the Marriott Garden, all that remains of the original 1869 design, is a perfect place to restore your spirits and energy after sightseeing. Beyond the tourists, it's also a great place to watch wealthy Cairenes or young gulf Arabs relaxing. It serves drinks and ice-creams as well as sandwiches, pizzas and grilled Egyptian specialities.

🛈 196 C4 🗷 Cairo Marriott Hotel, Sharia Saray al Gezira, Zamalek 🕿 02-2735 8888 🕒 Daily 9am–1am

Naguib Mahfouz Coffee Shop £ & Khan al Khalili Restaurant ££

This popular combination of coffee shop and restaurant is the only "quality" place to eat in the bazaar area and, just as important, has the only decent lavatories. The coffee shop serves traditional Egyptian hot drinks (including delicious mint tea), fresh juices, sheeshas (water pipes) and sweets in an attractive Oriental décor. The more expensive restaurant serves mezze and a wide selection of authentic Egyptian or Middle Eastern main courses. Although the clientele is comprised almost exclusively of tourists, it's still a cosy and quiet place – a haven of tranquillity situated off a very busy street.

🛈 197 E4 🗷 5 Sikket al Badestan, an alley in Khan al Khalili 🕿 02-2590 3788 🕒 Daily 10am–2am

Sabaya ££–£££

In this delightful Lebanese restaurant the best of authentic Lebanese cuisine is served, with an amazing selection of mezze and salads. The friendly waiters often recommend the delicious specialities of the house, like kibbeh nayyeh (raw pounded lamb) or hummus (chickpea paste) served with fried lamb and pine nuts.

🛈 196 C3 🗷 Semiramis InterContinental, Corniche al Nil, Garden City 🕿 02-2795 7171 🕒 Daily 7:30pm–1am

Sequoia ££

Sequoia has everything going for it, and it is hugely popular with wealthy Cairenes. Situated on the tip of Gezira Island, this outdoor restaurant (there are heaters during the winter months) has all-round views of the Nile. The excellent Egyptian food is reasonably priced for such a hip venue and they offer what must be the largest selection of flavours for the sheesha. In addition, there is an extensive cocktail list to choose from. The Sequoia is the place in Cairo to see and be seen.

🛈 196 B5 🗷 End of Sharia Abou al Feda, Zamalek 🕿 02-2576 8086 🕒 Daily lunch and dinner

Where to... Shop

Cairo often seems like one big bazaar, so there should be no shortage of shopping opportunities, from exotic spices to cotton clothing and silver Bedouin jewellery.

Books and Music

The most extensive range of books on Egypt and the Middle East, many published by the American University in Cairo (AUC Press), is available at the AUC campus, Sharia Mohammed Mahmoud, Downtown). **Lehnert and Landrock** (44 Sharia Sherif, Downtown) also has a good book selection as well as old photographs and postcards of Egypt. In Zamalek there is **Diwan** (159 Sharia 26th July) with a great selection of books, Arabic videos/DVDs and music. The best places to buy music are **Mirage Megastore** (71 Sharia Gami'at al Duwal al Arabiya, Mohandiseen) or **Vibe** (1A Sharia Sayed al Bakry), behind the Diwan bookshop.

For valuable antiquarian Oriental books, maps and prints check out l'Orientale (Shop 757 in the basement of the Nile Hilton Shopping Mall, Midan Tahrir, Downtown).

Craft Shops

Khan al Khalili (▶ 71) sells a selection of souvenirs, but the better crafts are in more specialised shops. Dr Ragab, who reinstated the making of papyrus, sells top-quality papyri with matching prices at **Dr Ragab's Papyrus Institute** (Corniche al Nil, near Cairo Sheraton, Giza). **Khan Misr Touloun** (opposite Ibn Tulun Mosque; tel: 02-2365 2227) and

Azhar Mosque, sells contemporary Egyptian crafts. Near by is **Abd al Zaher** (31 Sharia Mohammed Abduh; tel: 02-2511 8041; www. abdelzaherbinding.com), a traditional bookbinder who makes leather bound notebooks and albums, engraved with your name in gold leaf.

Clothes and Jewellery

Arcadia (Corniche al Nil, Bulaq) is Cairo's top-quality shopping mall, but the mall at the **First Residence** (35 Sharia al Giza, Giza) provides some competition. For belly dance outfits go to **Haberdashery**, reached via a dark stairway signposted "Everything a Belly Dancer Needs", on Sharia Gawhar al Qayed near al Fishawi Café in Khan al Khalili.

Dina Maghawry (16 Sharia Sayed al Bakry, Zamalek; tel: 02-2737 8210; www.dinamaghawry.com) makes funky jewellery with amazing Oriental designs as does **Azza Fahmy** (Al Ain Gallery, 73 Sharia al Husayn, Dokki; tel: 02-3749 3940; www.azzafahmy.com).

Fair Trade Egypt (27 Sharia Yahia Ibrahim, 1st floor, apt 8, Zamalek; tel: 02-2736 5123) both promote high-quality Egyptian crafts at fixed prices. **Oum el Dounia** (1st floor, Sharia Talaat Harb, Downtown; tel: 02-2393 8273) is a colourful shop filled with the best crafts in Egypt, at fixed and reasonable prices. **Makan** (4 Sharia Ismail Mohamed, Zamalek; tel: 02-2738 2632) is another great shop where old furniture blends in with contemporary designs by local artists. **Nagada** (13 Sharia Refa'a Dokki, tel: 02-3748 6663; www.nagada. net) sells superb hand-woven cotton and pottery made in Fayoum Oasis. Crafts from Siwa oasis are on sale in the elegant **Nomad Gallery** (14 Saray al Gezira, 1st floor, Zamalek; tel: 02-2736 1917), or at the Cairo Marriott shopping arcade. Shops in **al Khiyamiya** (Tentmakers' Bazaar), outside Bab Zuwayla, sell traditional appliqué work for tents, cushion covers or wallhangings.

The **al Khatoun Gallery** (3 Sharia Mohammed Abduh), behind the al

Where to...
Be Entertained

Cairo is as alive at night as it is during the day. Check the daily *Egyptian Gazette*, the *al Ahram Weekly* and the monthly *Egypt Today*, or check the excellent website www.yallabina.com.

Ahwas (Coffee Houses)

Egyptian men like to spend the evening in their local *ahwa* or café, chatting over a water pipe and coffee – no alcohol is served (▶ 28–29). **Al Fishawi** (▶ 75) and the area near the mosque of al Husayn in the old city are particularly lively at night.

Music

Most classical concerts are performed at the **Cairo Opera House** on Gezira Island (tel: 02-2793 0144; www.cairoopera.org), where men must wear a jacket and tie. The **Al Sawy Cultural Centre** (Sharia 26th July, Zamalek, under the bridge to Aguza; tel: 02-2736 8881; www.culturewheel.com) is a very active cultural centre with nightly performances of experimental theatre, Arabic music or jazz. The **Cairo Jazz Club** (197 Sharia 26th July, Aguza; tel: 02-3345 9939; www.cairojazzclub.com) has daily live music. **After Eight** (6 Sharia Qasr an Nil; tel: 02-2574 0855; www.after8egypt.com) is a popular, funky, but small music venue downtown with live Egyptian bands and Egyptian DJs. In another downtown venue, **Makan** (1 Sharia Saad Zaghloul, Mounira; tel: 02-2792 0878; www.egyptmusic.org) you can hear traditional music. Every Wednesday at 9pm the Mazaher group performs a *zar*, a musical trance for exorcising demons.

Belly Dancing

The best dancers perform at clubs in expensive hotels, at 8pm for tourists and 1am for Egyptians. Shows at **Cairo Sheraton** (tel: 02-3336 9700) and **Semiramis InterContinental** (tel: 02-2795 7171) are popular.

Downtown nightclubs such as **Palmyra**, in the alley beside the Chemla store on Sharia 26th July, are sleazier – better dancers arrive only when enough money has been thrown on to the stage. Ask the price of things before you order.

Sufi Performances

The Mawlawiyya is an Egyptian Sufi sect known as **Whirling Dervishes.** The **Tannoura Egyptian Heritage Dance Troupe** gives whirling performances in the courtyard of the **Wikala of Al Ghoury** (just off Sharia al Azhar, Islamic Cairo) every Monday, Wednesday and Saturday evenings at 7pm in winter and at 8pm in summer (tel: 02-2512 1735).

Nightclubs

The big night out in Cairo is Thursday. Nightclubs in hotels will admit non-members or non-residents on quieter nights, or impose a hefty charge. The hippest places are **Latex** (Nile Hilton Hotel, Corniche al Nil, Downtown; tel: 02-2578 0444) and **Absolute** (Casino al Shaggara, opposite the World Trade Centre, Corniche an Nil, Bulaq; tel: 02-2579 6512). **Al Morocco** (Blue Nile boat, 9 Saray al Gezira, Zamalek; tel: 02-735 3114) is a bar that turns into a disco at night. **Exit** (Atlas Hotel, 2 Sharia Mohamed Rushdi, Downtown; tel: 02 391 8127) is down to earth.

Horse-riding

Rent horses from renowned stables. In the village near the Sphinx, Nazlet al Semaan, the best stables are near the **Sphinx Club** (tel: 02-3382 0435), **AA** (tel: 02-3385 0531) and **MG** (tel: 02-3385 3832). The **Saqqara Country Club Hotel** (Saqqara road to Abu al Nomros; tel: 02-384 6115) offers temporary membership.

Luxor

Getting Your Bearings

It was the capital of the New Kingdom for more than 500 years, and Luxor has some of the world's most extraordinary monuments, many of which have defied the passing of time. The city is currently undergoing a much-needed but not uncontroversial facelift.

Luxor is a bustling town, with the Temple of Luxor at its centre surrounded by a crowded *souk* and hotels. By day the Corniche is busy with locals coming off the ferry, tourists getting off their boats, and buses touring the sights. But at night, when people come to catch the breeze along the Nile after a hot day, it's calm.

There were settlements here from an early age, but the town (then known as Waset and later as Thebes) became important only when the princes of Thebes established the New Kingdom (1550–1069 BC). Successive pharaohs vied to build ever-greater additions to the state temple of Amun in Karnak and its sister temple in Luxor. As secular buildings were made of mudbrick, little else remains of the fabled city that Homer described as "hundred-gated".

Luxor Temple and its god Amun were popular even after the Romans camped in the sacred precinct

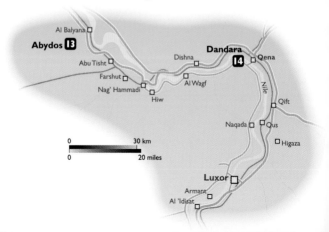

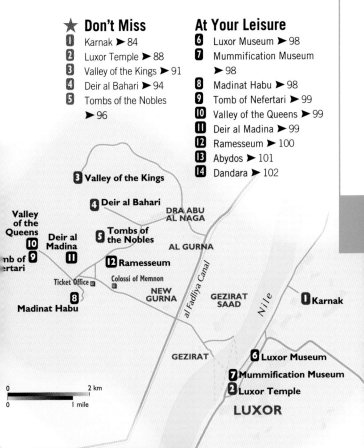

★ **Don't Miss**
1. Karnak ➤ 84
2. Luxor Temple ➤ 88
3. Valley of the Kings ➤ 91
4. Deir al Bahari ➤ 94
5. Tombs of the Nobles ➤ 96

At Your Leisure
6. Luxor Museum ➤ 98
7. Mummification Museum ➤ 98
8. Madinat Habu ➤ 98
9. Tomb of Nefertari ➤ 99
10. Valley of the Queens ➤ 99
11. Deir al Madina ➤ 99
12. Ramesseum ➤ 100
13. Abydos ➤ 101
14. Dandara ➤ 102

3 **Valley of the Kings**

4 **Deir al Bahari**

DRA ABU AL NAGA

Valley of the Queens
10

Deir al Madina
9
11

5 **Tombs of the Nobles**

AL GURNA

12 **Ramesseum**

Ticket Office

Colossi of Memnon

NEW GURNA

al Fadliya Canal

GEZIRAT SAAD

Nile

1 **Karnak**

8 **Madinat Habu**

GEZIRAT

6 **Luxor Museum**

7 **Mummification Museum**

2 **Luxor Temple**

LUXOR

0 ——— 2 km
0 ——— 1 mile

The mosque of Luxor's patron saint Abu al Haggag sits atop Luxor Temple

The dead were buried on the west bank of the Nile, and the kings hid extraordinary treasures in a secluded valley in the Theban mountains, although their security measures failed to foil the tomb robbers. The queens and nobles had less secretive burial grounds, facing the pharaohs' mortuary temples. Ferries sail between the two banks, leaving just opposite Luxor temple, or a bridge crosses the river, 6km (3.75 miles) farther south.

In 1997 Luxor suffered Egypt's worst act of terrorism, when 58 tourists were shot at Deir al Bahari. Since then it has been peaceful, but security remains tight and visitors leaving town by road do so as part of an armed convoy.

In Three Days

If you're not quite sure where to begin your travels, this itinerary recommends a practical and enjoyable three days in Luxor, taking in some of the best places to see using the Getting Your Bearings map on the previous page. For more information see the main entries.

Day One

Morning
Start early, before it gets hot, by taking a *calèche* (horse-drawn carriage) to ❶ **Karnak Temple** (right, ►84–87), where you can easily spend a morning. Have lunch in the pleasant Egyptian restaurant Sofra (►104).

Afternoon
After lunch stroll over to ❷ **Luxor Temple** (►88–90) for a leisurely walk around the ruins. It's then a short walk to the **Old Winter Palace** (►103) for a touch of grandeur and tea on the terrace. That will take you to early evening, and time for shopping in the *souk*.

Day Two

Morning
Make another early start, especially in the summer. Take a taxi to the ticket booth on the West Bank, where you must buy tickets for some of the West Bank sites you want to visit. Back in the cab, head first for the exposed ❸ **Valley of the Kings** (►91–93), which gets very hot by noon. Ask the driver to wait for you, as there's little other transport back. The Nour al Gurna (►105) is good for a simple lunch.

Afternoon
Walk next door for a visit to the ⓬ **Ramesseum** (►100–101). There's no problem getting a cab here, but for some local flavour flag down a passing pick-up truck *(kabut)*, most of which go to the ferry terminal *(al mina)*. Once across the river, walk to the small, but beautifully arranged ❻ **Luxor Museum** (►98) for a short visit. Afterwards, rent a *felucca* and, wind permitting, sail into the sunset. After dinner, visit the ❷ **Luxor Temple** (►88–90), which is perhaps even more striking when floodlit.

Day Three

Morning

Rent a bicycle (▶ 182–183) or take a taxi (first agree a price that includes all your chosen sights) and then take the ferry to the West Bank, stopping again at the ticket booth as tickets are valid only for the day they're purchased. Carry on to the temple of **4 Deir al Bahari** (below, ▶ 94–95), passing the two **Memnon Colossi** (▶ 183). From Deir al Bahari retrace your steps to the **5 Tombs of the Nobles** (▶ 96–97), with their realistic depictions of daily life. Have a late lunch in the garden of Restaurant Muhammad (▶ 105), near the ticket office.

Afternoon

After lunch, walk or cycle to the **8 Temple of Madinat Habu** (▶ 98–99), which is at its best in the softer afternoon light. Take time to walk around the temple precinct and watch the sunset from one of the cafés opposite, or head back to the stables near the ferry (▶ 106) for a countryside ride.

Evening

Dress up for dinner and eat in the elegant dining room of the Old Winter Palace (▶ 103). It is advisable to book ahead. Take a leisurely stroll through the mature gardens after dinner.

Karnak

The ancient Egyptians called Karnak "Ipet-Isut" ("The Most Perfect of Places"), and for 1,500 years this was the most important place of worship in the country, dedicated to their great god Amun. Much more than just a temple, it was also an important intellectual centre, a spectacular complex of temples, chapels, pylons, obelisks and sanctuaries, covering more than 400ha (990 acres) – enough space for 10 cathedrals. Every pharaoh of note built, destroyed, enlarged, embellished or restored part of the complex to express his devotion to Amun. In the process, Karnak became one of the largest and most magnificent temple complexes in the ancient world.

Take a *calèche*, taxi or even a small motorboat along the Corniche to get to Karnak which, with all its splendour and history, can be a confusing place to visit. The complex consists of several temple compounds and many additions by different kings. But, as Egyptologist T G H James put it, "Karnak is an archaeological department store containing something for everyone". One rule to remember is that the monuments mostly get older the deeper inside you go.

The Temple of Amun and the Great Hypostyle Hall in Karnak never fail to impress the visitor with their overwhelming grandeur

THE TRIAD OF THEBES

The temples of Luxor and Karnak are both dedicated to the Theban triad of the gods Amun, Mut and Khonsu. Amun, the most important of these, later became a state deity as the Supreme Creator Amun-Ra, the fusion of Amun with the sun-god Ra. Mut, the Mistress of Heaven, was his wife or consort and Khonsu, also known as "the traveller" or the moon-god, was their son.

The most accessible part of Karnak is the **Precinct of Amun**, which seems like an endless succession of massive pylons (temple gateways), monumental statues and grand hypostyle halls. The precinct is approached from the **Processional Way** of ram-headed sphinxes (Amun was often represented as a human wearing ram horns), which connected with the temple of Luxor (► 88–90). This leads to the **First Pylon** which, at

43m (141 feet) high and 130m (426 feet) wide is the largest in Egypt, even though it was never finished. In the forecourt you'll find **Seti II's shrine**, which housed the sacred boats of the triad and, in the south corner, the superb **Temple of Ramses III** (20th Dynasty), also thought to be a way station for the sacred boats. The walls of this small temple, which follows the perfect plan of the classical temple, are decorated with scenes of the annual Opet festival. In front of the **Second Pylon** rises the granite colossus of the ubiquitous Ramses II with one of his many daughters beside him.

Behind the Second Pylon lies the most spectacular sight of all, the 13th-century BC **Great Hypostyle Hall** – an amazing "forest" of more than 140 tall papyrus pillars covering 5,500sq m (59,200sq feet), built by Seti I and his son Ramses II. Beyond the Hypostyle Hall lies a rather larger and more confusing section of the temple, built during the 18th Dynasty (1550–1295 BC). In the courtyards beyond the Third and Fourth Pylons are the finely carved **obelisks** of Tuthmosis II and, farther on, of the female pharaoh, Queen Hatshepsut

Every day, water birds were led through a stone tunnel from the fowl yard to the Sacred Lake

(1473–58 BC, ▶ 94). The tip of her second fallen obelisk lies on the way to the Sacred Lake.

Past the Sixth Pylon stand two elegant pillars carved with lotus and papyrus flowers, symbolic of Upper and Lower Egypt, and the granite **Sanctuary of Amun**, built by Philip Arrhidaeus, the half-brother of Alexander the Great. This is where Amun's effigy was kept and where, as the images on the walls show, daily offerings were made in his honour. Beyond lies a large **Central Court** and the **Jubilee Temple of Tuthmosis**, where the king's vitality and authority was symbolically renewed during his jubilee. It's interesting that this huge temple complex was only entered by the powerful priesthood; lay Egyptians were excluded and used intermediary deities, whose shrines they built against the temple's enclosure wall. One such series of chapels, known as the **Chapels of the Hearing Ear**, lies at the back of the Jubilee Temple.

Between the Third and Fourth Pylons the temple spreads southwards along the side of the **Sacred Lake**. In 1903, in the Cachette Court in front of the lake, some 17,000 bronze and 800 stone statues were uncovered. The finest of them are now in the Egyptian Museum in Cairo (▶ 50–53).

The **Open Air Museum** houses a few reconstructions of earlier buildings, two fine *barque* shrines and an elegant 12th-Dynasty white chapel with fine carvings.

TAKING A BREAK

The **café near the Sacred Lake** is a relaxing place to have a drink under the trees. For a later lunch leave the site and head for **Dawar al Umda** on the Corniche (▶ 104), or the coffee shop of the quiet Luxor Hilton Hotel near by.

➕ 202 C4   ✉ 2.5km (1.5 miles) north of Luxor   🕐 Daily 6–5:30 (6am–6pm in summer)   🍴 Café by the Sacred Lake (£)   💲 Complex moderate; museum inexpensive

KARNAK: INSIDE INFO

Top tips The temple **can get very crowded** with tour groups from 10:30am to 3pm, but earlier or later, when the light is at its best, you could have the place more or less to yourself.

■ A splendid 90-minute *son et lumière* show is held three or four times, in different languages, each evening. The first part of the show is a walk through the floodlit temple, the other part is viewed from a theatre beyond the Sacred Lake. Buy your ticket at the site. For information check the ticket booth (tel: 02 3386 3469; www.soundandlight.com.eg).

Hidden gems The **bas-reliefs** on the northern side of the Hypostyle Hall, representing Seti I's victories and battles, are exquisite. Look for the columned vestibule, known as the Botanical Garden, beyond the Middle Kingdom Court, with beautiful reliefs of local flora and fauna.

Ones to miss The badly ruined **Precincts of Mut** to the south and of **Mont** to the north are rarely visited, as are the courts beyond the 7th Pylon.

② Luxor Temple

This magnificent structure, known in ancient times as the "Harem of the South", is connected to the Temple of Karnak (► 84–87) by a 3km (2-mile) processional Avenue of Sphinxes. Like Karnak, Luxor's temple was dedicated to the Theban triad of Amun, Mut and Khonsu, whose statues stood here during the Opet festival.

Even though Luxor Temple was expanded several times throughout the ages, it's much more compact and coherent than Karnak, perhaps because its core was built by just one pharaoh, Amenhotep III (1390–1352 BC). The walls are decorated with some of the finest (and often best-preserved) carvings in Egypt, protected because much of the temple was buried until 1885. Before excavations, only the heads of the Ramses II (1279–1213 BC, ► 23) colossi and the tips of the obelisks stuck out above the pile of debris on which Luxor village was built. The village was removed bit by bit as the excavations started, but when it came to destroying the tomb and mosque of Luxor's patron saint, Abu al Haggag, the people refused.

A Latin inscription on this pylon is evidence of Roman occupation

ABU AL HAGGAG

The patron sheikh of Luxor, Abu al Haggag, was born in Baghdad around AD 1150, moved to Mecca and later made his way to Luxor where he founded a Sufi school. Every year during the saint's *moulid* (festival), huge floats move slowly through the streets and a few *feluccas* are dragged around his mosque by local people. These represent the boats that were pulled around the temple during the ancient Opet festival.

The First Pylon and obelisk are dramatically illuminated at night

As a result, the pretty mosque now perches awkwardly on top of the excavated temple.

The **Avenue of Sphinxes** leads to the monumental **First Pylon** built by Ramses II, which was once fronted by two obelisks and six colossi of the man himself. One obelisk and two of the statues were taken to France in the 19th century, but the remaining ones are still very impressive. The pylon is decorated, as so many other Egyptian temples, with Ramses II's favourite story, the Battle of Qadesh. Beyond the pylon, the large Court of **Ramses II** is surrounded by two rows of papyrus-bud columns, interspersed with more statues of the king.

THE OPET FESTIVAL
During the splendid annual Opet (fertility festival) priests would bring the statues of the gods Amun, Mut and Khonsu in a procession of holy barges up the Nile from Karnak to Luxor, where they would spend a symbolic honeymoon. This festival, held during the second month of the Nile flood, was intended to ensure a good harvest for the season

To the left of the court, the **Mosque of Abu al Haggag** hangs over the temple, while to the right is the *barque* shrine that was used for the three statues that came from Karnak during the annual Opet festival (➤ panel, left). Also of interest on this side are reliefs of the temple itself and of a funerary procession led by Ramses II's sons. Beyond the Second Pylon the impressive **Processional Colonnade** of Amenhotep III, with huge papyrus columns, was the model for the Great Hypostyle Hall at Karnak. The carvings on the walls were added by Tutankhamun and give a picture of the Opet celebrations: one wall shows the outward journey, the other the return of the procession.

At the end of the colonnade is perhaps the temple's most impressive part, the **Great Sun Court**, also built by Amenhotep III, its fine decorations developed over the millennium between the reigns of Amenhotep and Alexander the Great. Unfortunately this court has suffered badly from the rising water level and a major restoration project is underway. A large cache of statues unearthed here in 1989 can now be seen in Luxor Museum (➤ 98).

Behind a columned portico, used as a chapel by Roman soldiers, lies the temple's **inner sanctuary**, with Alexander the Great's Sanctuary of Amun's Barge and Amenhotep III's Birth Room, which has images of the king's divine conception and birth, and his nurturing by goddesses. The bedrock on which this part of the temple was built was believed to be the site where Amun was born.

TAKING A BREAK

Enjoy Nile views down by the water and a cool beer at the pleasant **Metropolitan Café** (➤ 104).

🕂 202 C4 ✉ Corniche, East Bank 🕓 Summer daily 6am–10pm; winter 6am–9pm 💷 Moderate

LUXOR TEMPLE: INSIDE INFO

Top tips It's best to explore Luxor Temple early in the day, and return at night when **floodlights** add to the mysterious atmosphere and accentuate the fine carvings.
■ Ask the tourist office when the *moulid* happens, as it's quite spectacular.

Hidden gem Study the reliefs on the walls carefully to understand the **rituals of the Opet festival**.

❸ Valley of the Kings

Ever since Howard Carter discovered Tutankhamun's tomb in 1922, filled to the brim with untold wonders (➤ 52), the Valley of the Kings (Wadi al Muluk) has excited, intrigued and fuelled the imagination of the world. For more than 500 years this barren and secluded valley, also known as "The Place of Truth", was the last abode of the mighty New Kingdom pharaohs. Their elaborate tombs were carved into the mountain, their mummies covered with gold and jewels, and surrounded with treasure and everything else they would need in their afterlife.

The barren hills hide richly decorated tomb interiors

These tombs were intended to be secure places where the mummies could rest eternally, ensuring the deceased pharaohs a happy afterlife. But the prize was too great – treasure hunters and tomb raiders were not easily deterred and most tombs had been raided before much time had passed. But even without the mummies and their treasure, the massive scale of some of these tombs and the magnificence of their wall paintings allows you to imagine the original splendour, particularly if you can get away from the crowds.

Into the Underworld
As the pyramids had proved relatively easy to break into, pharaohs of the New Kingdom chose to be buried with less ostentation. The architecture of the tomb in some way

reflected the journey the dead pharaoh was making, so rock-hewn tombs with long corridors leading down into antechambers and finally into the burial chamber represented the underworld. Artists and workers from Deir al Madina (▶ 99–100) decorated the tomb walls with mysterious and complicated inscriptions and images from the Book of the Dead, to help guide the pharaoh to the underworld.

It's All Relative

Tutankhamun's tomb may be famous for the treasure it contained, but as the king died young and insignificant, his tomb is small and the decorations hastily executed. Just try to imagine the amount of gold and wealth that would have been buried with more powerful pharaohs such as Ramses II or Tuthmosis III. Tuthmosis (1479–1425 BC) was one of the first to be buried in the valley; his is a very secretive space, high up in the cliffs past a ravine. That the Tomb of Ramses IV was already a tourist attraction in antiquity is obvious from the centuries of graffiti near the entrance.

THE ROYAL MUMMIES
In 1876 the greatest cache of mummies was discovered near the Temple of Hatshepsut. The mummies of 40 pharaohs, queens and nobles including Amenhotep I, Tuthmosis III, Seti I and Ramses II, were found in a huge burial pit (tomb No. 320). It's believed that New Kingdom priests, realising the mummies' allure to robbers, moved them to this secret communal tomb. Some of the mummies are now on display in the Mummy Room of the Egyptian Museum in Cairo (▶ 50–53).

THE THEBAN MAPPING PROJECT

The Theban Mapping Project (TMP) has been working since 1978 at a comprehensive map of Thebes, one of the world's most important archaeological sites, in order to protect and preserve the area. During the last decade TMP has focused its attention on the Valley of the Kings. In 1995 they rediscovered and started excavating KV5, so far the largest tomb in the valley, with more than 128 rooms. This tomb probably belonged to the 50 sons of Ramses II. In 2006 another tomb was discovered, KV63, with several intact coffins (www.thebanmappingproject.com).

The Tomb of Ramses III is one of the longest and grandest in the valley, his sarcophagus is in the Louvre in Paris. Horemheb's tomb is interesting as it was left in different stages of decoration. As to be expected the Tomb of Ramses II was the largest, but it suffered serious damage from floods. The most beautiful tomb belongs to his father Seti I (1294–1279 BC), with carvings even finer than those in the pharaoh's temple at Abydos (▶ 101–102), but it is closed to the public for the foreseeable future.

TAKING A BREAK

At the time of writing the café at the entrance to the Valley of the Kings was closed. Stalls sell cold drinks and ice-creams.

The secluded tomb of Tuthmosis III
Right: The entrance to the tomb of Ramses VI

🔲 202 B4 ✉ West Bank, beyond al Gurna 🕐 Summer daily 6am–7pm; winter 7–5 🍴 Cafeteria (£). Closed at present 💰 Expensive

---

VALLEY OF THE KINGS: INSIDE INFO

Top tips Tickets are sold per **three tombs,** with a separate ticket for the tombs of Ay and Tutankhamun, from the ticket office at the entrance to the Valley of the Kings. Also here is the **Visitor Centre** where you can see a film about the discovery of the tomb of Tutankhamun. A *tuftuf* train (inexpensive) takes visitors to the site, but you can also walk.

■ Tomb openings are **rotated to protect paintings** from human damage.

■ To **avoid the crowds** head for the tombs farther away from the entrance.

■ Early Tuesday morning is **market day** on the West Bank. The market is held at the start of the road to the Valley of the Kings, in an open space behind the modern cemetery and across from the temple of Seti I.

Ones to miss Tutankhamun's tomb is **small and often disappointing** because the treasure is in the Egyptian Museum in Cairo (▶ 50–53).

❹ Deir al Bahari

The magnificent Mortuary Temple of Hatshepsut is set dramatically against the cliff face of the Theban hills. The imposing terraces look surprisingly stark and modern, but you have to imagine them in Hatshepsut's days, when they were filled with exotic perfumed trees, and fountains to cool the air. Hatshepsut called her temple Djeser Djeseru ("the Sacred of Sacreds"). It was a ruin when excavated in 1891, but it's been carefully restored over many years.

In ancient times the temple was connected to the Nile by a wide avenue of sphinxes. The Lower Terrace (closed for restoration at the time of writing) would have been lined with sweet-smelling myrrh trees and refreshing fountains. The pylons have disappeared and the colonnades were defaced by Tuthmosis III, but you can still see the stumps of a few 3,500-year-old trees. A massive ramp connects the terraces and the fabulous reliefs on the portico of the Second Terrace. On the north side is the Birth Colonnade, with scenes confirming the queen's divine parentage and her right to rule. To the south is the Punt Colonnade, depicting the expedition to Punt (probably in present-day Somalia) sent by Queen Hatshepsut to bring back myrrh trees, ebony, ivory and spices.

Beyond lies the Chapel of Hathor, with a hidden representation of the queen's favourite, and architect of the temple, Senenmut. The Third Terrace, architecturally the finest part of the temple, has a pink granite portico leading into the rock-cut Sanctuary of Amun.

TAKING A BREAK

Several vendors sell cold drinks, but for a rest head for one of the **cafés near the Ramesseum**.

➕ 202 B4 ✉ Al Gurna, West Bank ⏰ Summer daily 6am–7pm; winter 7–5 💷 Moderate

THE FEMALE PHARAOH
Tuthmosis I's daughter, Queen Hatshepsut, was one of Egypt's rare female rulers and her life was full of intrigue. Her husband Tuthmosis II died before she produced a son, so she usurped Tuthmosis III, son of another wife, and became the absolute ruler of Egypt from 1473 to 1458 BC. She is often represented as a man. After her death Tuthmosis III tried to obliterate her name from history, defacing her images and cartouches.

The setting of Hatshepsut's mortuary temple against the pink Theban hills is spectacular

DEIR AL BAHARI: INSIDE INFO

Top tips Tickets for this temple are available from the ticket office at the entrance to the site.
- Visit early in the day to avoid the worst of the heat and bring lots of water.
- Two paths lead up the mountain near Deir al Bahari. Climb to the top for some fabulous views, or walk across the hill to the Valley of the Kings (▶ 91–93).

5 Tombs of the Nobles

The nobles – local rulers, ministers and governors under the pharaohs – enjoyed a good life and were keen for pleasures to continue after their death. As a result, their tombs are not decorated with cryptic texts from the Book of the Dead, but with realistic and vividly coloured depictions of their lives. The work is inferior to that of the royal tombs, but it provides a wonderful insight into ancient Egyptian society and the daily life of wealthy Egyptians and their servants.

Whereas the pharaohs' tombs were hidden in the Theban hills, the nobles built theirs ostentatiously on the frontline, facing the mortuary temples of their masters. There are many tombs in this necropolis, but only seven are open to the public. The farthest two are the tombs of **Rekhmire** and **Sennofer**. The first has scenes of the vizier Rekhmire receiving tributes from foreign lands and overseeing the agricultural revenue, while the second is known as the "tomb of the vines" for its ceiling of beautifully painted vines. The decorative style of the nearby tomb of **Ramose** reflects that he was a vizier immediately before and after the Amarna revolution (➤ 22). The superb carvings along the entrance wall are all in the classical style, showing Ramose making offerings, but on the opposite side they also reveal the more naturalistic Amarna style. Immediately south, the tomb of **Khaemhat**, a royal scribe, contains fishing, family and funerary scenes and has exceptionally well-preserved colours.

Farther north lies another beautiful group of tombs. **The Tomb of Nakht** has fascinating scenes of a banquet with dancers and a blind harpist, with a cat eating fish under his chair, while that of **Menna**, an inspector of estates, depicts scenes of rural life and of Menna and his wife performing ceremonies for the gods.

**Opposite:
Part of a wall painting in the tomb of Sirenput II
Below:
Entrance to the tomb of Rekhmire**

TAKING A BREAK

Two **cafés near the Ramesseum** sell cold drinks or tea. **The Nour al Gurna hotel** restaurant (➤ 103), near by, is good for lunch.

➕ 202 B4 ✉ Old Gurna ⏰ Daily 7–5, but smaller tombs often close around 3pm 🍴 Cafés (£)
💶 Tickets per group of tombs inexpensive (from the kiosk near the crossroads opposite the Nour al Gurna Hotel)

TOMBS OF THE NOBLES: INSIDE INFO

Top tips A visit involves walking and climbing stairs, so avoid midday heat.

- Tombs are divided into four groups, each requiring a separate ticket. It takes an hour to visit all the tombs, but most visitors limit themselves to the best of each group, or just one group.
- Guards will light up tombs the traditional ancient way, using a mirror to reflect sunlight, in return for *baksheesh*. Be sure to refuse their services on arrival if you don't want them.
- Most of the villages here were moved to New Gurna several kilometres further north, and the houses were pulled down in 2007 to protect these tombs.

Ones to miss The tombs of Khonsu, Userhet and Benia are the least impressive.

Hidden gem Many visitors skip Sennofer's tomb as it requires a good climb, but it's delightful and colourful, reflecting Sennofer's eternal love for his beautiful wife.

At Your Leisure

6 Luxor Museum

This small museum of antiquities is an absolute gem. The choice selection of statues and objects found in local tombs and temples is well labelled in English and perfectly displayed against a dark background to bring out the best features. Among the many highlights are a strikingly beautiful statue of an eternally young King Tuthmosis III, an extraordinary statue of Amenhotep III held by the crocodile god Sobek, and furniture from Tutankhamun's tomb. The important cache of statues, among them Ramses II and Tutankhamun, found a few years ago under Luxor Temple, is also on display here in the hall to the left of the entrance. An interesting new wing is dedicated to the glory of Thebes during the New Kingdom period. The highlight is the two royal mummies of Ahmose I and Ramses I.

🚩 202 C4 ✉ Corniche al Nil, Luxor
☎ 095-238 0269 ⏰ Summer daily 9–1, 5–10; winter 9–9 💰 Moderate, camera permit extra

Fine relief of King Tuthmosis III wearing the long royal beard and the "atef" crown

7 Mummification Museum

This interesting little museum highlights the beliefs and the historical development of mummification, and also explains the different stages of the lengthy process. Exhibits include mummification instruments and even some fine animal mummies.

🚩 202 C4 ✉ Corniche al Nil, East Bank, near the ferry terminal ☎ 095-238 1501
⏰ Summer daily 9–1, 5–10; winter 9–1, 4–9 💰 Moderate

8 Madinat Habu

The grand mortuary temple of Ramses III (1184–1153 BC), modelled on the Ramesseum (▶ 100–101) of his ancestor Ramses II, was the last great classical pharaonic temple to be built in Egypt. Ramses III, however, was more fortunate than his namesake because this temple has survived the millennia remarkably well, but the Hypostyle Hall and Sanctuaries were severely damaged during an earthquake in the 1st century BC. The entrance to the temple complex is a lofty Syrian-style gatehouse with an upper

Above: All around Madinat Habu are reminders of the Coptic settlement of Djeme
Below: Entrance to the temple of Deir al Madina

room decorated with musicians and dancers, where Ramses III apparently entertained guests. To the right are several older chapels and what remains of the Sacred Lake, where local women still come in search of a cure for infertility. The towering First Pylon, like the Second Pylon, is decorated with scenes of battles fought by Ramses II and leads to the First Court, which features well-preserved carvings of Ramses himself making offerings to the gods.

Mudbrick remains of the Coptic town of Djeme, which covered the entire enclosure until the 19th century, can be seen above the perimeter wall.

202 B4 Kom Lola, near the ticket office Daily 7–5 Café-restaurants opposite the entrance (£) Moderate

9 Tomb of Nefertari

The New Kingdom pharaoh Ramses II created one of the most beautiful tombs in Egypt as a shrine to the beauty of Nefertari, his wife of some 34 years. The corridors and walls in its three chambers are decorated with brightly coloured images, most famously of the stunning queen in a transparent white dress with a two-feathered golden head-dress. The ceiling is painted with bright golden stars. The tomb was reopened in 1995 after extensive restoration, but the closed again in 2003 until further notice.

202 B4 Valley of the Queens, West Bank (see below) Closed until further notice Expensive

10 Valley of the Queens

This is a slight misnomer as the 80 tombs belong not only to queens, but also to princes and princesses. But only four, including the tomb of Nefertari, are open to the public. The tomb of Amun-Her-Khopshef, son of Ramses III, shows beautiful scenes of the father introducing his son to the gods. Also in the tomb is the mummy of a five-month-old foetus, believed to be lost when the mother heard of the death of her nine-year-old son Amunwas. Another son of Ramses III, Prince Khaemweset, is also buried here, surrounded by similar scenes of Ramses leading him through the underworld.

202 B4 West Bank Daily 7–5 No public transport Inexpensive; separate charge for Tomb of Nefertari

11 Deir al Madina

This village sheds a rare light on the lives of less exalted Egyptians. The artists, masons and labourers who worked on the tombs in the Valley of the Kings (► 91–93) lived here

"I met a traveller from an antique land
Who said: Two vast and trunkless legs of stone
Stand in the desert...Near them on the sand,
Half sunk, a shattered visage lies...

... Nothing beside remains. Round the decay
Of that colossal wreck, boundless and bare
The lone and level sands stretch far away."
From "Ozymandias", Shelley

with their families, segregated from the rest of the population to keep the location of the royal tombs secret. Many inhabitants were literate and a large amount of papyri records the strict organisation of their lives, as well as their complaints about hardship and working conditions. Despite this, they worked 8-hour days, staying in the Valley of the Kings for 10-day shifts, so there was plenty of spare time to work on their own tombs.

Near the entrance to the village are the tombs of artists Sennedjem and Ankherkha, with colourful inter-pretations (often parodies) of designs they worked on in the royal tombs. The tomb of Peshedu has a painting of the dead artist praying under the tree of regeneration, while Iphy's tomb is decorated with scenes of everyday life.

A temple dedicated to the goddesses Maat and Hathor stands at the northern end of the village.

✚ 202 B4 ✉ West Bank, opposite the ticket office 🕐 Daily 7–5 💷 Inexpensive; separate ticket for Peshedu's tomb (inexpensive)

🔟 Ramesseum

Ever since the English poet Percy Bysshe Shelley (1792–1822) eternal-ised the broken statue of Ramses II in his poem "Ozymandias" (▶ panel, left) as a symbol of the vanity of transient human glory, visitors have

Parts of Ramses II's colossus are scattered all over the Ramesseum

come to the Ramesseum looking for its colossal fragments. Ramses II, who built some awe-inspiring monuments elsewhere in Egypt, intended this mortuary temple to be his eternal monument, but unfortunately chose a site that was annually flooded. It would almost certainly have been as grand as his fabulous temple at Abu Simbel (➤ 118–120), but it's ironic that only this one, intended to be the most important, fell to pieces.

The colossal statue, once the largest in the world at 18m (60 feet) high and weighing more than 900 tonnes, destroyed the Second Pylon and the Second Court as it fell. You can still see its remains and marvel at the proportions. In addition to the statue itself, at the far end of the court is a smaller

The wall carvings at Seti I's temple in Abydos are among the finest from the New Kingdom

colossus with a more intact face. The walls of the First and Second Pylons are decorated with scenes of Ramses' famous victories, as are the walls of the Great Hypostyle Hall, where 29 of its original 48 columns still stand. Beyond lie two smaller hypostyle halls, one with an astronomical ceiling which boasts the oldest-known 12-month calendar. The vaulted mudbrick rooms surrounding the temple were used as workshops, servants' quarters and storage houses.

🚼 202 B4 ✉ Al Gurna, West Bank, Luxor
🕐 Daily 7–5 🚍 No public transport, so cycle or take a taxi 🎟 Inexpensive]

🔟 Abydos

Abydos is situated about 130km (80 miles) north of Luxor. For nearly 2,000 years Abydos was Egypt's prime burial ground, as it marked the entrance to the underworld and is where Osiris's head was buried (➤ 12–13). Ancient Egyptians aspired to make a pilgrimage once in their lives and, if they weren't to be buried here, endeavoured to have

BEST FOR CHILDREN
■ *Felucca* ride on the Nile (➤ 106)
■ Horse-riding (➤ 106)
■ Mummification Museum (➤ 98)
■ Tombs of the Nobles (➤ 96–97)
■ Al Aboudi bookshop (➤ 105): a huge selection of children's books on Egypt

their mummies brought here before being taken for burial elsewhere in Egypt.

The 14th-century BC Temple of Seti I is one of Egypt's finest monuments, with exquisite decoration, but the facade was finished less carefully by Seti's son, Ramses II, who also built a smaller temple here.

➕ 202 B5 ✉ Al Araba al Madfuna, 10km (6 miles) southwest of al Balyana ⏰ Daily 7–6 🍴 Café opposite 🚂 Train or bus from Luxor to al Balyana, then in convoy to the site 💷 Inexpensive

🔟 Dandara

The well-preserved Temple of Hathor was built here in the classic Egyptian style by the Ptolemies and the Romans, between 125 BC and AD 60. Hathor, wife of Horus, was the goddess of pleasure, beauty and love, often associated with the Greek goddess Aphrodite.

During the annual New Year festival, Hathor's statue was taken to the roof to be exposed to the sun-god, before being reunited

Wall reliefs at the Temple of Hathor

with Horus at his temple in Edfu (▶ 121). Scenes of this festival decorate the walls of the temple.

➕ 202 B5 ✉ 4km (2.5 miles) across the Nile from Qena, 64km (40 miles) north of Luxor ⏰ Daily 7–6 🍴 Café (£) 🚂 Train or bus to Qena, horse-carriage to the site (check first for travel restrictions) 💷 Inexpensive

LUXOR FROM THE AIR

You'll get the most spectacular view of Luxor's monuments and villages from a hot-air balloon. Each flight of about one hour is slightly different depending on the wind, but the experience is unforgettable. Three companies offer flights in the early morning: **Hod Hod Soleiman** (tel: 095-237 0116), **Magic Horizon** (tel: 012-226 1697; www.magic-horizon.com) and **Sky Cruises of Egypt** (tel: 095-237 6515).

Where to...
Stay

Prices

The prices are for a double room per night.
£ under 400LE   **££** 400–900LE   **£££** over 900LE

EAST BANK

New Emilio Hotel ££

All the rooms in this excellent hotel are equipped with their own private bathroom, air-conditioning, minibar, TV and there is a hotel video channel. There's also a small rooftop pool with comfortable chairs for guests to relax while sunbathing. The staff are particularly helpful and friendly. Book in advance in high season, as the New Emilio can fill up with tour groups.

✚ 202 C4 ⊠ Sharia Yussef Hassan
☎ 095-237 3570

Old Winter Palace £££

The Old Winter Palace is a colonial building overlooking the Nile and the Theban Hills beyond, while the interior mixes colonial paraphernalia with new fabrics and *objets d'art* inspired by the old glory days. The large and comfortable rooms have high ceilings and are elegantly decorated, and there's a marvellous, large swimming pool in well-tended gardens filled with songbirds. The hotel has an excellent central location in East Bank Luxor.

✚ 202 B4 ⊠ Sharia Corniche an Nil
☎ 095-238 0422

WEST BANK

Al Moudira £££

This palatial desert retreat is like no other hotel in Egypt. The wonderful Egyptian architect Olivier Sednaoui excelled himself in this formidable building, with its vast luxurious rooms, beautifully decorated with locally made furniture and finds from antique markets. Set on the edge of the desert and the farmed land, the fabulous swimming pool is surrounded by the perfumed garden that overlooks the Thebes mountains. This hotel is a real delight for its guests!

✚ 202 B4 ⊠ Daba'iyya, 15km
(9 miles) south of ticket office on the West Bank ☎ 012-325 1307/392 8332

Beit Sabee £–££

Mudbrick painted in bright blues, with beds and furniture made out of palm wood, and 1950s-style fabrics, this funky hotel is a rural Egyptian house made hip. There are only eight rooms. If you prefer

lots of peace and quiet, this is the perfect hideaway in Luxor. Dinners are available upon request.

✚ 202 B4 ⊠ Kom Lolah, West Bank
☎ 010-632 4926; www.nourelnil.com

Nour al Gourna £

In this delightful small hotel, the simple, stylish rooms overlook sugarcane fields or a pretty palm grove. All rooms have fans and mosquito nets, local furniture and a stereo sound system.

✚ 202 B4 ⊠ Opposite the ticket office,
Gurna, West Bank ☎ 095-231 1430/
010-129 5812

Sheherezade £

This new hotel, near the ferry landing on the West Bank, is built in a traditional style with comfortable and tastefully decorated rooms. There is a very friendly welcome from the owner who also organises tours in the region.

✚ 202 B4 ⊠ Al Gezira, West Bank
(500m/545 yards from the ferry) ☎ 010-611
5939; www.hotelsheherazade.com

Where to...
Eat and Drink

Prices
Expect to pay per person for a meal, excluding drinks and tips.

£ under 100LE   ££ 100–150LE   £££ over 150LE

Most hotels on the East Bank have adequate restaurants serving international cuisine. Most restaurants on the West Bank are basic, offering simple but fresh Egyptian stews, grilled chicken and kebabs.

EAST BANK

1886 £££
The only gourmet experience in town, the 1886 has a French chef preparing delightful French and Egyptian-inspired dishes. The period dining room is elegant and guests are expected to dress for dinner.

202 C4 ⊠ **Old Winter Palace, Corniche an Nil** ☎ **095-238 0422** ⊙ **Daily dinner**

Dawar al Umda ££
A good Egyptian restaurant set in the pleasant hotel gardens, offering an excellent selection of *mezze* and classical Egyptian fare such as kebabs, *kofta* and vegetable stews. On winter evenings there is often a belly dancer or folkloric show.

202 C4 ⊠ **Mercure Inn, Sharia al Karnak** ☎ **095-237 3321** ⊙ **Daily lunch and dinner**

La Mamma ££
In the middle of the hotel garden and beside a pond with ducks and pelicans, La Mamma is one of the most reliable restaurants in town, and is especially popular with children. Fresh pastas, thin-crust pizzas and Italian meat dishes make a change from Egyptian fare.

202 C4 ⊠ **Sheraton Hotel, Sharia Khalid Ibn Walid** ☎ **095-237 4544** ⊙ **Daily lunch and dinner**

Metropolitan Café £–££
This pleasant café down by the water, overlooks the Nile and the *felucca* captains going about their business. Food, Egyptian and international, is served. This is a perfect place for a cold beer while watching the sunset.

202 C4 ⊠ **Lower level, Corniche an Nil, opposite the Old Winter Palace, East Bank** ☎ **No phone** ⊙ **Daily 10am–11pm**

Oasis Café £
A great café-restaurant in a 1920s building in the heart of Luxor, with simple but cosy décor. The food ranges from snacks and pastas to pastries and grilled meats.

202 C4 ⊠ **Sharia Dr Labib Habashi** ☎ **012-336 7121** ⊙ **Daily 10–10**

Snobs ££
Popular and lively, this western-style restaurant serves steaks, salads and Mediterranean dishes prepared by their enthusiastic chef. No alcohol is served but you are welcome to bring your own and drink it on the premises.

202 B4 ⊠ **Just past the Sonesta Hotel, off Sharia Khaled Ibn al Walid** ☎ **095-236 0356** ⊙ **Daily 10am–midnight**

Sofra £
A fabulous Egyptian restaurant in a 19th-century house with small garden and rooftop terrace, Sofra serves well-prepared traditional Egyptian dishes and *mezze* in a lovely atmospheric décor. Service is very friendly. There is no alcohol on the menu, but delicious fresh juices are served.

202 C4 ⊠ **90 Sharia Mohamed Farid, off Sharia al Manshiya** ☎ **095-235 9752; www.sofra.co.eg** ⊙ **Daily 11am–midnight**

WEST BANK

Al Moudira £££

The poolside restaurant or the Oriental fantasy indoor restaurant offer the most romantic dining in town. The food, a mixture of the best of Western and Lebanese cuisine, is delicious, and the whole experience is worth travelling the few miles from Luxor. Book ahead.

╬ 202 B4 ⊠ Daba'iyya, 15km (9 miles) south of the ticket office on the West Bank ☎ 012-325 1307/392 8332 ◉ Daily 8am–11pm

Nile Valley £

Delightful Egyptian food is served on the rooftop terrace of the Nile Valley Hotel, which offers views of the Nile. Alcohol is available.

╬ 202 B4 ⊠ Nile Valley Hotel, Al Gezira, right near the ferry landing ☎ 095-231 1477 ◉ Daily 8am–11pm

Nour al Gurna £–££

This simple restaurant, in a shady garden, serves local dishes like *meloukhiya* (a soup of a spinach-like vegetable with chicken, served with bread, onion and condiments) and stuffed pigeon. No alcohol is served.

╬ 202 B4 ⊠ Opposite the ticket office, Gurna ☎ 095-231 1430 ◉ Daily 10–10

Restaurant Muhammad £

Simple, Egyptian dishes in a cool house with a shaded terrace. The menu is small, but if you pass by in the morning, he may be able to serve a delicious *meloukhiya*, stuffed pigeon or grilled duck for lunch.

╬ 202 B4 ⊠ Next to the Pharaoh's Hotel, near the ticket office, West Bank ☎ 095-231 1014 ◉ Daily noon–10 or later

Tutankhamun £

Simple but delightful local specialities are cooked by Amm Mahmoud. His chicken with rosemary and duck a l'orange are legendary, but his *tagens*, stews cooked in local earthware, are good too. There is a rooftop terrace.

╬ 202 B4 ⊠ On the waterfront near the ferry landing, Al Gezira ☎ 095-231 0918/010-566 8614 ◉ Daily noon–10pm

Where to... Shop

Luxor Town, particularly around the temple, is one big tourist bazaar with hundreds of vendors selling cheap souvenirs, from small statues and colourful skullcaps to carpets and painted papyri. It's hard to avoid these, as vendors know every trick to lure innocent-looking tourists. Few have fixed prices, so the rule here, as elsewhere in Egypt, is to bargain hard, and you might well find some evocative souvenirs. The little statues of ancient Egyptian gods are a good choice, as are scarves (watch out for synthetic ones) and hand-woven cotton tablecloths from Akhmim. Another great buy is traditional clay cooking pots, sold at two stalls beside the police station. If cooking is your thing, look out for cheap spices like cumin, chilli and black pepper. The bazaar is open in the morning until 1pm, and again from 5 to 9pm or later.

Alabaster

Alabaster is quarried 80km (50 miles) north of the Valley of the Kings and in workshops on the West Bank you can see how the stone is treated and polished. Several large shops sell kitsch statuettes and sphinx lamps, as well as beautiful unpolished alabaster vases or bowls in simple shapes.

Bookshops

Luxor has some excellent bookshops stocking a wide selection of titles on Egypt, Arab culture and the Middle East, in several European languages. Al Aboudi (tel: 095-237 3390) in the tourist bazaar, next to the Winter

Palace has an excellent children's section and several well-priced books on Egypt. It sells postcards too. Also next to the Winter Palace is **AA Gaddis** (tel: 095-238 7042), with books on modern and ancient Egypt, postcards, Egyptian papyrus stationery and quality souvenirs.

Quality Crafts

Fine fabrics have been hand-woven in Akhmim for centuries, and the best selection from there is available at the **Winter Akhmim Gallery** (tel: 095-238 0422) in the arcade of the Old Winter Palace Hotel. **Fair Trade Centre Luxor Outlet** (tel: 012-356 3445; www.egyptfairtrade.org) on Sharia al Karnak is an excellent shop with a selection of fairtrade crafts from projects throughout Egypt. **Habiba** (Sharia Sidi Mahmoud, off Sharia as-Souq; tel: 010-124 2026; www.habibagallery.com) is run by an Australian woman promoting Egyptian crafts that provide women with income. She has cotton towels, leather bags and jewellery.

Where to...
Be Entertained

Luxor has so many monuments to visit that the only entertainment most tourists want at the end of the day is a dive in the pool, a cool drink, a good dinner and a soft bed. And that's just as well because there isn't really much else to do. But if you do still have the energy, you'll find listings of special events and exhibitions in the monthly magazine *Egypt Today***, usually available from bookshops in Luxor.**

Feluccas and Boats

Here, as elsewhere on the Nile, taking a trip in a *felucca* is a great way to wind down, once you've negotiated the price. The most popular destination is Banana Island, 4km (2.5 miles) upriver, where souvenir vendors await

unwary tourists (so you might want to avoid it).

Instead, take a boat for a few hours and just sail up the Nile, enjoying the beauty of the river and the landscape. It's particularly lovely around sunset. If there's no wind, you will be rowed – or it's an opportunity, perhaps, to take a trip along the river in one of the small motorboats available.

Horse-riding

Another way to relax is to rent a horse or camel from one of the stables. Try the **Nobi Horse Stable** (tel: 010-504 8558) or **Pharaoh's Stables** (tel: 095-231 0015), both behind the Mobil filling station on the West Bank. An hour-long circuit will take you through some lush countryside and then back along the Nile.

Swimming

Nearly all hotels will open their pools to non-residents, either for an entrance fee or for a minimum charge for any drinks and snacks that are purchased.

Nightlife

Luxor has a few nightclubs in hotels, but don't expect the latest dance music or a laser show. The liveliest nightclubs are at the **Mercure Inn Hotel** and at the **Tutotel** on 1 Sharia Salah al Din, East Bank (tel: 095-237 7990). The **Dawar el Omda** (▲ 104) restaurant has a popular folkloric show with belly dancers and snake charmers on a Thursday when the Oriental buffet is served.

Sightseeing by Night

An excellent **Sound and Light Show** happens daily, in different languages, at Karnak Temple (▲ 84–87). Luxor Temple (▲ 88–90), dramatically floodlit at night and open until 10pm, makes for an unusual evening stroll.

Upper Egypt
and Nubia

Getting Your Bearings

During the 19th century, as more and more archaeological discoveries were made, it became fashionable to spend the winter in Upper Egypt. Wealthy Europeans would rent a private *dahabeyya* (sailing houseboat) and set off on the river from Cairo, stopping to explore ruins and monuments.

Today, the best and most relaxing way to visit the sights along the Nile is by *dahabeyya* (➤ 122, panel). These old-fashioned sailing boats have four to ten cabins and often take a week to go from Esna to Aswan, taking in sights the big cruise boats can't stop at. Luxury cruise ships run three- to five-day cruises between Luxor and Aswan that stop at the temples, but leave plenty of time to idle around on deck. The more adventurous can get even closer to the river on a three-or four-day *felucca*

Right: There seem to be temples and necropolises everywhere in Aswan

ride, sleeping under the stars. Several cruisers also offer a four-day trip on Lake Nasser, taking in rescued Nubian monuments, or fishing for the huge Nile perch.

Visitors can travel only in a private vehicle from Luxor to Aswan in an armed police convoy, which leaves twice a day from both places; only the morning convoy stops briefly at Kom Ombo and Edfu Temples. Security concerns have also made travel by road from Aswan to Abu Simbel possible only in buses organised by tour operators and in a police convoy.

South of Luxor the landscape changes and the desert closes in on the Nile. The people change too, as many Nubian families who lost their land when the area was flooded after the Aswan Dam was built moved north to Aswan and beyond.

By the time you reach Aswan you know you've left the Mediterranean and the Middle East behind and entered an exotic, more African environment. Aswan, with fewer important monuments than Luxor, is the perfect place to slow down and relax, enjoying views on the river and the islands.

Sailing by *felucca* between Luxor and Aswan is an idyllic way to experience the temples

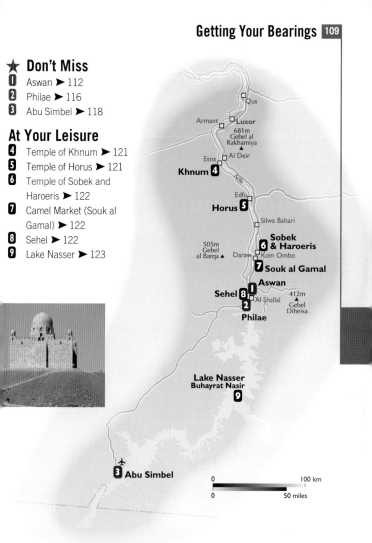

★ Don't Miss

At Your Leisure

Qus
Armant   Luxor
681m
Gebel al
Rakhamiya ▲
Esna   Al Deir
Khnum 4
Nile
Edfu
Horus 5
Silwa Bahari
Sobek
& Haroeris
6
505m
Gebel
al Barqa ▲   Daraw Kom Ombo
7 **Souk al Gamal**
Aswan
Sehel 8 1
412m
▲
Al Shallal   Gebel
2   Diheisa
Philae

Lake Nasser
Buhayrat Nasir
9

✈
3 **Abu Simbel**

0 ——————— 100 km
0 ——————— 50 miles

Some nomads
still roam the
desert south
of Aswan, but
most have
been pushed
farther south

In Three Days

If you're not quite sure where to begin your travels, this itinerary
recommends a practical and enjoyable three days in Upper
Egypt and Nubia, taking in some of the best places to see using
the Getting Your Bearings map on the previous page. For more
information see the main entries.

Day One

Morning
Start early and hire a private taxi for a half day. Leave **❶ Aswan**
(➤ 112–115) along the road past the **Fatimid Cemetery** (➤ 112) and
the **Unfinished Obelisk** on the outskirts of the town. Continue via the Old
Aswan Dam to the dock in Shallal to buy a ticket to the site and take a
boat to **❷ Philae island** (➤ 116–117). Spend about 90 minutes here, then
drive on for a look at the **Aswan High Dam** (➤ 115) and return to Aswan via
the Old Dam. Have a late lunch at the Panorama restaurant (➤ 125).

Afternoon
From the terminal opposite the Egypt Air office, take a ferry out to
Elephantine Island on the Nile to visit the **Aswan Antiquities Museum** and its
peaceful garden for an hour or so (➤ 114). Stroll to the north of the island
through the palm groves and Nubian villages. Back at the ferry landing,
you can take a *felucca* (above) around the islands. Have the *felucca* wait
while you walk through the botanical garden on **Kitchener Island** (➤ 115)
and then sail around the islands, past the **Aga Khan's Mausoleum** on the
West Bank (➤ 114).

Evening
Finish the day with dinner at the **Nubia Beach Restaurant** (➤ 126).

Day Two

Morning
Take a taxi for a round trip south to
9 Kalabsha Temple on Lake Nasser (right,
➤ 123). Depending on the height of the
lake you may have to take a boat from
the harbour. Boatmen usually allow for
an hour's visit, which is enough. Return
to Aswan for lunch in one of the places
along the Corniche (➤ 125–126).

Afternoon
Stock up on water and good sun
protection and take a *felucca* on a
two-hour round trip to **8 Sehel Island**
(➤ 122–123). After returning to Aswan,
walk over to the **Nubia Museum** (➤ 114) for a late afternoon visit. Stroll
back to the Old Cataract Hotel for an early evening drink on the terrace and
dinner at the beautifully restored Moorish restaurant (➤ 126).

Day Three

Morning
Take a morning bus or minibus to **3 Abu Simbel** (below, ➤ 118–119) and
head for the Eskaleh Hotel (➤ 124) for lunch (book ahead).

Afternoon
Stroll over to the temple, enjoying more tranquillity in the afternoon as
most of the day trippers who came by plane will have left on their return
journey. Watch the sun go down and stay on for the *son et lumière* show.

Evening
Walk back to the Eskaleh Hotel and have dinner. If you are lucky the owner
will play Nubian music with his friends, otherwise enjoy the peace and
quiet of the lake.

◻ Aswan

Aswan's setting on the Nile is dramatic and idyllic. Here the
river is squeezed between the Eastern Desert and the Sahara.
Its cool, sparkling blue waters contrast starkly with the hot,
golden desert sands, the pink granite boulders and the lush
green islands in its stream. But the views over Aswan and the
Nile are the real spectacle, particularly in the late afternoon.

The town of Aswan has been a frontier since ancient times,
as Egypt's southernmost city and the gateway to Nubia and
Africa. It has a sweet, exotic smell and its tall, dark Nubian
population has more in common with the Sudanese than with
other Egyptians. The climate is fabulous in winter – warm
and dry – and the atmosphere is totally laid back. Aswan has
fewer spectacular sights than Luxor or Cairo, so there's more
time to hang out in the riverside cafés watching the sun set
and the *feluccas* sail by, and to stroll in its quirky *souk*.

Modern Aswan

Aswan is a relaxed and easy town to explore, and its attractive
Corniche is lined with pleasant waterfront café-terraces.
Sharia al Souk, the main market street, still retains an
exotic air even though it's become increasingly touristy. At
the southern end of the Corniche are the Ferial Gardens, a
tranquil place to sit and watch the sunset if you can't get on
the terrace of the Old Cataract Hotel (➤ 126).

Behind the hotel grounds is the **Nubia Museum**, a tribute
to the culture and art of the Nubian people whose lands were
flooded when the dams were constructed to create Lake Nasser.
The museum's impressive collection, well displayed and labelled
in English, traces the history of Nubia from prehistoric times.

About 1.5km (1 mile) south of Aswan is the vast **Fatimid
Cemetery**, with domed mudbrick tombs from the 9th century,
and the gigantic **Unfinished Obelisk** that was abandoned after a

A *felucca* trip
is a relaxing
way to pass
the time

***Feluccas* sail peacefully around the small islands on the Nile at Aswan**

flaw was discovered. It's thought that it was intended to stand in Tuthmosis III's temple at Karnak (➤ 84–87).

Upriver from the First Cataract (➤ 122) is the Old Dam built in 1902, and farther on the High Dam, completed in 1971.

Ancient Aswan

In ancient times the main town and temple area were on Elephantine Island, mid-river opposite modern Aswan, mainly on its southern tip which was known as Yebu (meaning "ivory" and "elephant"). The fortress of Yebu, protected by the turbulent waters of the Nile, was a perfect base for Egyptian expeditions into Nubia,

NILOMETERS

These instruments were used to record the annual flooding of the Nile, until it was controlled by the Aswan Dam. It was vital to know the accurate level of the Nile waters, as it formed the basis of tax calculations: The higher the waters rose, the bigger the harvest and therefore the higher the taxes.

ASWAN DAMS: VITAL STATISTICS
- The Old Dam was the world's largest when built (1898–1902) and was raised twice.
- It's 50m (165 feet) high, 2km (1 mile) long, 30m (100 feet) wide at the base.
- The High Dam is 111m (365 feet) high, 3.8km (2.5 miles) long and 980m (1,072 yards) wide at the base.
- Lake Nasser, the world's largest reservoir, covers 6,000sq km (2,300sq miles).
- It's forbidden to take photos of the Aswan Dam.

Sudan and Ethiopia and an important cult place dedicated to Khnum – the god who controlled the Nile's level – his wife Satis and their daughter Anukis. During the Islamic period Yebu became an important trading post for the caravans of camels and elephants laden with ivory, gold, spices and slaves. Excavations of the extensive ruins of ancient Yebu are still underway, but so far you can see a small early Old Kingdom step pyramid, a gateway on which Alexander II is shown worshipping Khnum, and the 30th-Dynasty Temple of Khnum. Farther north there's a Nilometer with Greek, Roman, pharaonic and Arabic numerals.

Both the Nilometer and the ruins of Yebu now form part of the **Aswan Antiquities Museum**, which is housed in the villa of Sir William Willcocks, the British engineer who designed the Old Aswan Dam. The villa itself contains an interesting but rather musty collection of artefacts found on Elephantine including a beautiful gilded statue of Khnum. However, the more recent annexe has a fascinating and well-labelled display illustrating life on the island in ancient times. Stroll through the Nubian villages Siou and Koti on Elephantine, set amid lush, scented gardens and stop for a drink at the Nubia café between them.

The West Bank

The most visible landmark opposite Aswan on the Nile's west bank is the **Aga Khan's Mausoleum** (now closed to the public) where Aga Khan III, and his wife the Begum, are buried. Farther north, the **Tombs of the Princes of Elephantine Island,** cut into the rock, are floodlit at night and command excellent views.

Watch the sun set from the terrace of the colonial Old Cataract Hotel

TAKING A BREAK

Café terraces along the Nile, particularly the **Panorama** (➤ 125), serve fresh juices and good, simple Egyptian food. Alternatively, the terrace of the **Old Cataract Hotel** (➤ 126) is the traditional place for an English tea and to watch the sunset, but non-residents pay a minimum charge.

🚩 202 C3

✉ 215km (135 miles) south of Luxor ☎ 097-231 2811 (tourist office in Midan al Mahatta)

Aswan Museum/Nilometer/Ruins of Yebu
✉ Southern tip of Elephantine Island ⏰ Summer daily 8:30–6; winter 8–5
🚢 Ferry from opposite the Egypt Air office 💰 Inexpensive

Fatimid Cemetery/Unfinished Obelisk
✉ 1.5km (1 mile) south of Aswan ⏰ Obelisk summer daily 8–6; winter 7–4
💰 Moderate, tip at the cemetery

Nubia Museum
✉ Sharia Abtal al Tahrir, between the Old Cataract and Basma hotels
☎ 097-231 9111 ⏰ Daily 9–1, 5–9 🚶 Walk or private taxi 💰 Moderate

The colourful souk in Aswan is still busy at night-time

Botanical Garden
✉ Kitchener's Island
⏰ Summer daily 8–6,
winter 8–5 🍴 Cafeteria
(£) 🚢 Ferry from west
side of Elephantine Island
or rented boat or *felucca*
💰 Moderate

Tombs of the Nobles
✉ West Bank, Aswan
⏰ Summer daily 8–5; winter
8–4 🚢 Ferry from northern
end of Corniche, then hike
uphill 💰 Inexpensive

High Dam Pavilion
✉ A few kilometres south of
Aswan ⏰ Daily 7–5 💰 Tip
for the guardian to open it
💰 Inexpensive

ASWAN: INSIDE INFO

Top tips Take at least one *felucca* ride around the islands as there's nothing more relaxing, particularly around sunset when local children go out on their home-made boats and sing Nubian songs.
- Visit the sweet-smelling **Botanical Garden** on Kitchener Island, where General Kitchener planted shrubs imported from all over the world.

Hidden gems There's a good if tiring 30-minute walk across the desert from the tombs of Elephantine's nobles to the beautiful ruins of 7th-century **St Simeon Monastery** (open daily 8–5; admission moderate). A guardian will open the basilica and show you the place where St Simeon's beard was tied to the ceiling to stop him falling asleep during his prayers.

One to miss You can skip the simple tombs of the princes of Elephantine if you've been to the West Bank in Luxor.

2 Philae

The splendid Temple of Isis, set on an island in the blue waters of Lake Nasser, is one of Egypt's most romantic sights. For more than 800 years, until AD 550, this temple to Isis and Osiris was one of the most important Egyptian cult centres.

Ptolemaic and Roman rulers, keen to identify themselves with this powerful ancient Egyptian cult, all added their mark, making for an interesting blend of styles. The worship of Isis as the Mother of the Gods eventually spread all over the Roman Empire, and early Coptic art clearly associates the Virgin Mary and baby Jesus with Isis suckling her infant son Horus.

Originally the Temple of Isis was built on the island of Philae (the "Island from the Time of Re") facing Bigah Island, which was believed to be one of the burial sites of Osiris. But Bigah was accessible only to priests, so all the religious festivities took place on Philae. With the building of the first Aswan Dam the temple was submerged for half the year. In the 1970s, when the High Dam threatened to submerge it completely, UNESCO and the Egyptian Antiquities Organisation painstakingly moved the entire complex to nearby Agilkia Island, which had been landscaped to resemble Philae.

Temple Highlights

Boats land near the oldest structure on the island, the Vestibule of **Nectanebo I**, beyond which lies a large court flanked by two elegant colonnades and the impressive **First Pylon** of the Temple of Isis. The small door to the left leads into a 3rd-century BC **Birth House**, whose outside back

The lofty Kiosk of Trajan supported by 14 columns is locally known as the "Pharaoh's Bed"

Golden sandstone columns are decorated with intricately carved capitals

wall shows some lovely scenes of Isis nursing Horus in the marshes. The main gate, with two granite lions, leads to the **Second Pylon**, opening up to a **Hypostyle Hall**. The inner temple lost most of its decoration when it was converted into a church around AD 553, but the Sanctuary still contains Isis's sacred *barque*.

Near by, the **Temple of Hathor**, the cow goddess of music (among other things), has a wonderful relief of the gods playing musical instruments. And an elegant monument here is the **Kiosk of Trajan** (used as a gateway to the temple in Roman times), from where there are superb views across the lake.

TAKING A BREAK
There are a few simple cafés at the dock, and on the island there is a cafeteria with a terrace, selling cold drinks, tea, snacks and ice-cream.

➕ 202 C3
✉ Agilkia Island, between the Old Dam and the High Dam, 9km (6 miles) south of Aswan 🕐 Summer daily 7–5; winter and during Ramadan 7–4 🍴 Cafeteria (££) 🚕 Taxi to Shallal dock for a boat to the island 🎟 Moderate

---

PHILAE: INSIDE INFO

Top tips Check the official price list for boats at the docks before hiring one. The price allows for a one-hour visit, but pay the captain extra if you want to spend more time.
■ The sound and light show at the Temple of Isis is often considered the best in Egypt (➤ 128).

Hidden gem The Osiris Room on the upper floor, where Osirian mysteries were enacted, has interesting reliefs illustrating the story of Isis and Osiris. It's usually closed, but the guards may open the doors for some *baksheesh*.

③ Abu Simbel

The 13th-century BC rock-hewn Temple of Ramses II at Abu
Simbel is the most impressive monument in Nubia, expressing
the imperial ambition of the New Kingdom period. The four
21m-high (70-foot) seated figures of Ramses II that guard the
temple's facade are among the largest sculptures in Egypt, and
seem designed to warn the Nubians of Egypt's mighty power.

No modern Europeans had seen the temple at Abu Simbel
until the Swiss explorer Jean Louis Burckhardt sailed past it in
1813. But by then the massive statues were buried up to their
necks in sand and it took 20 days of digging in 1817 to clear
the entrance, then under some 15m (50 feet) of sand. In the
1960s a different operation was underway, as the international
community united to raise this wonderful temple high above
the rising waters of Lake Nasser. The temple and the hillside
into which it was cut were sawn into 1,050 blocks weighing
up to 30 tonnes each, and painstakingly reassembled on
higher ground beyond the reach of the lake. Before the salvage
operation few people visited Abu Simbel, but today it's a
major tourist attraction.

A Labour of Love

It took Ramses II about 30 years to build his "Temple of
Ramses, Beloved of Amun". He dedicated it to Ra-Herakte,
Amun-Ra and Ptah, but most of all to the deified image of
himself. Next door he built a smaller temple for his favourite
wife Nefertari, where she is identified with the cow goddess

**Colossi of
Ramses II
front the main
temple at
Abu Simbel**

Hathor. The original temple was perfectly oriented so that the sun's rays would illuminate the statues deep in the sanctuary on Ramses II's birthday and on the day of his coronation. The relocated temple catches the rays a day later, and at dawn on 22 February and 22 October the sun's rays reach into the inner sanctuary of the Sun Temple and illuminate the remains of the four deities there.

The temple's facade is dominated by magnificent colossi of Ramses II, staring eternity in the face. The statues' heads and torsos are finely sculpted (but one lost its upper half during an earthquake in 27 BC), while the feet and legs seem rather crude. Members of the royal family, including Nefertari, Ramses' mother Muttuya and several of his children, stand at his feet.

Following the classic temple design, the interior reveals a series of increasingly smaller

The massive doors to the temple are opened by an *ankh* key, the symbol of life

chambers with a floor that rises noticeably. The massive rock-hewn Hypostyle Hall contains eight 10m-high (33-foot) statues of the king as Osiris. The walls are decorated with scenes from his military campaigns, including the Battle of Qadesh which was fought against the Hittites, Libyans and Nubians. On the back wall he offers his captives to the gods. A smaller hall leads to a vestibule and the Sanctuary, with four statues of Ptah, Amun-Ra, the pharaoh-god Ramses II and Ra-Herakte.

Queen Nefertari's Temple

To the north is the smaller temple of Nefertari, dedicated to Hathor. As with Ramses' temple, the rock was smoothed and angled to resemble a pylon, with six 10m (33-foot) colossi (four of Ramses and two of Nefertari) flanking the facade. Although smaller, this temple follows a similar plan, containing a hypostyle hall with carved Hathor images, a vestibule and small sanctuary.

TAKING A BREAK

There's only a small **café** on the site, with cold drinks and very little to eat, so bring a picnic to enjoy in the shade of the trees near the lake.

The scale of the inner rooms of the Great Temple is progressively smaller as you approach the sanctuary

---

✚ 202 A1

✉ 280km (175 miles) south of Aswan, 40km (25 miles) from the Sudanese border ⏰ Summer 6–6, winter 6–5 🍴 Café (£) 🚌 Bus from Aswan in armed convoy ✈ Egypt Air flights from Cairo and Aswan. Flights from Aswan are sold as packages, including return trip and transfer to and from the site. This leaves you only about one to one and a half hours to enjoy the site, which can be quite short, particularly if the outward flight is delayed 💷 Expensive including tour by a local guide

---

ABU SIMBEL: INSIDE INFO

Top tips Stay on board ship (if you're cruising) or at an Abu Simbel hotel and have the temple almost to yourself in the early morning or later afternoon. Sit on the left of the plane from Cairo or Aswan for a good view of the temple.

■ There are several *son et lumière* shows daily starting at 6pm in winter and 8pm in summer (tel: 02-3386 3469; www.soundandlight.com.eg).

Hidden gem Usually an ancient Egyptian queen was represented as a tiny figure coming up to her husband's knees only. Perhaps as proof of Nefertari's status, her own temple here in Abu Simbel is fronted by two statues of her husband Ramses II and four statues of herself at equal heights.

At Your Leisure

The Hypostyle Hall at Esna

4 Temple of Khnum (Esna)

The temple of Khnum at Esna is located 155km (96 miles) north of Aswan. The temple, rebuilt by Ptolemy VI (180–145 BC) on an older structure, was probably once as large as the one at Edfu (see below). Nowadays people come to see the temple's wonderful 1st-century AD Roman Hypostyle Hall – the only part that's been excavated. Here you get a true sense of what the hall was meant to represent. With 24 columns topped by various finely carved floral capitals, it really feels like a beautifully enclosed garden. The walls are decorated with carvings of various Roman emperors making offerings to Egyptian deities.

🚩 202 B4 ✉ Esna, 54km (34 miles) south of Luxor, 155km (96 miles) north of Aswan
🕐 Summer daily 6–5; winter 6–4 🚌 Bus or taxi from Luxor or Aswan 🚃 Trains from Luxor, Edfu or Aswan to Esna, then a *calèche* to the site 🎟 Inexpensive tickets from the riverside kiosk near the tourist bazaar

5 Temple of Horus (Edfu)

The Ptolemaic temple at Edfu (105km/65 miles north of Aswan), built from 257–237 BC, is the best

preserved and one of the finest in Egypt. Built in classic pharaonic style, it gives a clear idea of the appearance and purpose of an Egyptian temple, and explanations are inscribed on the walls. The site was chosen because the falcon-headed god Horus fought here with Seth (► 12) for power over the world. Visitors approach the temple from the back. It's best to start from the First Pylon, fronted by two falcons. Carvings on the inside walls record the annual Festival of the Beautiful Meeting, where the statue of Horus joined the statue of Hathor at her temple in Dandara (► 102). The annual festivals were celebrated in the Festival Hall, and recipes for incense and perfumes line the walls of a small side chamber. During the New Year festival, the statue of Horus was carried on to the roof to be revitalised by the sun. Outside the temple is the Birth House. Look at the carvings of Horus being suckled by his mother Isis.

🚩 202 C4 ✉ Edfu, 115km (71 miles) south of Luxor, 105km (65 miles) north of Aswan
🕐 Summer daily 7am–8pm; winter 7–7
🍴 Stalls selling drinks (£) 🚌 No public transport; cruise ships, *feluccas* or taxis
🎟 Moderate

Some carvings are remarkably well preserved at the temple at Kom Ombo

6 Temple of Sobek and Haroeris (Kom Ombo)

The remains of this Graeco-Roman temple at Kom Ombo, unusually dedicated to two deities, still look truly imposing, particularly from the river. The temple has two identical halves: the eastern part is devoted to the crocodile god Sobek, and the western to Haroeris, or Horus the Elder, the "Good Doctor", who attracted thousands of pilgrims hoping to find a cure for their illnesses. Its spectacular location on a bend of the river was responsible for the pylon and the forecourt eventually disappearing into the water, but much of the inner temple remains. The Chapel of Hathor near the entrance housed mummified crocodiles, while live ones swam in the well. A double entrance leads into the inner Hypostyle Hall, with elegant floral columns and two ceremonial paths leading into the symmetrical sanctuaries. Behind are seven chapels whose outer

---

DAHABEYYAS

A luxurious way to see the Nile is on a *dahabeyya* (➤ 108), a sailing boat with cabins. Nour an Nil has the best, four different *dahabeyyas* with 8 to 10 cabins (tel: 010-657 8322/ 010-570 5341; www.nourelnil. com). They offer 6- or 7-day cruises, mooring at small islands on the way.

---

walls reveal a fascinating display of sophisticated instruments that were used to perform brain surgery.

✚ 202 C3 ✉ Kom Ombo, 45km (28 miles) north of Aswan ◷ Summer daily 6–5; winter 6–4 🍽 Cafeteria just outside the temple (£) 🚌 Bus or taxi from Aswan in convoy 🎟 Inexpensive

7 Camel Market (Souk al Gamal)

Egypt's largest camel market is a fascinating place, especially early in the morning when Sudanese traders go noisily about their business. Herdsmen walk the camels across the desert along the Forty Days Road from Sudan, to somewhere north of Abu Simbel where the animals are driven to Daraw and sometimes to Birqash (35km/22 miles northwest of Cairo).

✚ 202 C3 ✉ Outskirts of Daraw, 5km (3 miles) south of Kom Ombo – ask or just follow the crowds ◷ Sun 6:30–2 in winter (also Tue mornings, best before 10:30) 🍽 Cafés (£) 🚌 Service taxi from Aswan, private taxi taking in Kom Ombo in convoy

8 Sehel

This small island commands superb views over what was the white water of the First Cataract, where the Nile is channelled through dramatic outcrops of granite. Ancient Egyptians believed this to be the source of the Nile, from where the river flowed south into Nubia and north into Egypt. The Nile gods Hapy and Khnum were thought to live in a cave under the rapids from where they controlled the annual flood. Locals made offerings on Sehel for a good harvest and travellers prayed here for a safe return, as the area remained a danger for anyone travelling south until the Aswan dams were built.

These days the waters are less stormy and the *felucca* ride is the main attraction. However, two hills made up of granite boulders reveal more than 250 roughly carved ancient Egyptian inscriptions that record expeditions upstream. The Famine Stele, on top of one of the hills, relates how King Zoser

CRUISES ON LAKE NASSER

Several luxurious cruise boats make three-, four- or seven-day tours from Aswan to Abu Simbel, stopping at the other Nubian temples. Happily, numbers have been limited. Choose between the stylish *Eugenie* (www.eugenie.com.eg) and *Qasr Ibrim* (www.kasribrim.com.eg) boats, run by Belle Epoque Travel (tel: 02-516 9653), or *Prince Abbas* (tel: 097-231 4660) or *Nubian Sea* (tel: 012-322 2065).

(► 22) ended a seven-year famine by building a temple on Sehel Island.

On the other side of Sehel the Nubian villages, with their lovely gardens, are also worth exploring.

➕ 202 C3 ✉ 4km (2.5 miles) upriver from Aswan 🍴 Some villagers offer tea for *baksheesh* (£) 🚤 Accessible only by *felucca* or motorboat from Aswan (► 128)

🟑 Lake Nasser

The building of the Aswan dams buried the Nubian Nile and created this, the world's largest reservoir, stretching more than 500km (310 miles) south of Aswan. The Nubian communities who lived along the Nile for thousands of years lost their homes, land and much of their rich culture to the dams and lake, but many of the ancient monuments were relocated to drier ground, with help from the international community. These include the little-visited Temple of Mandulis at Kalabsha. This healing temple, dedicated to the Nubian fertility god Marul (Mandulis in Greek), was mostly rebuilt during the Ptolemaic-Roman period, which is obvious from the blend of styles on the fine wall carvings. Next door is the photogenic Ptolemaic Kiosk of Kertassi and the small rock-hewn temple of Beit al Wali. This was built in honour of Ramses II, who is shown on the colourful reliefs in a

A cruise on Lake Nasser offers a more peaceful and more relaxing alternative to the traditional Nile cruise

battle with the rebellious Nubians. The interesting but more remote temple groups of Wadi al Sebua, Dakka and Amada and the fortress site of Qasr Ibrim can only be visited on a luxury cruise, although new roads are being built.

Fishing trips are increasingly popular on the blue waters of the lake, which is home to a few crocodiles, the elusive tiger fish and the Nile perch – one of the largest freshwater fish (► 128).

Kalabsha Temple/Beit al Wali
➕ 202 C2 ✉ Next to the High Dam ⏰ Daily 8–4 🚗 Private taxi, also rented boat from the harbour 🎟 Inexpensive

Wadi al Sebua/ Amada/Qasr Ibrim
➕ 202 C2 ⏰ Daily 6–6 🚤 Currently accessible by cruise boat only 🎟 Inexpensive

SOMETHING FOR THE CHILDREN

There are no attractions specifically for children but they might enjoy:

■ A *felucca* ride around the islands in Aswan

■ The camel market in Daraw (► 122)

■ Baby crocodiles in the *souk* (► 127)

Where to... Stay

Prices

The prices are for a double room per night.

£ under 400LE   ££ 400–900LE   £££ over 900LE

ASWAN

Elephantine Island Mövenpick £££

Apart from its ugly tower, which dominates Aswan's skyline, the Mövenpick is a comfortable hotel set in lush gardens on quiet Elephantine Island. The spacious rooms have good views of the Nile.

🕀 202 C3 ☒ Northern tip of Elephantine Island ☎ 097-230 3455; www.moevenpick-hotels.com

Keylani Hotel £

This friendly, centrally located hotel with Internet café, has been popular with visitors for years. The rooms are spotless and comfortable, all with shower, air-conditioning or fan.

🕀 202 C3 ☒ 25 Sharia Keylani, off main Sharia al Suq ☎ 097-231 7332; www.keylanihotel.com

Nile Hotel £

A good-value hotel in a new building, this place has 30 well-equipped rooms with very clean bathrooms, satellite TV and a balcony with Nile view. The hotel has a restaurant, library with books about Egypt and Internet access. The staff are very welcoming.

🕀 202 C3 ☒ Corniche an Nil ☎ 097-231 4222; www.nilehotel-aswan.com

Nuba Nile £

This is another good budget option. It is situated near the train station, and offers simple, clean rooms, some with the benefit of a private bathroom and air-conditioning. There is a popular café just next door for meals.

🕀 202 C3 ☒ Just off Midan al Mahatta ☎ 097-231 3267

Old Cataract Hotel £££

Immortalised in the film of Agatha Christie's *Death on the Nile*, this is one of Egypt's most famous hotels. The splendid Moorish building is set in lush gardens and most rooms command stunning views. Some rooms are still impressive, as are the public areas of the hotel. For real indulgence, stay in one of the amazing suites with terraces over the river.

🕀 202 C3 ☒ Sharia Abtal al Tahrir ☎ 097-231 6000

Sara Hotel ££

Well out of the centre, but quiet and with views over the first cataract on the Nile and the Western Desert on the other side, this mid-range hotel offers great value for money. The rooms have little local flavour, but they are spacious and clean and some have big balconies. There is a swimming pool.

🕀 202 C3 ☒ On a cliff, 1km (0.5 mile) south of Nubian Museum ☎ 097-232 7234; www.sarahotel-aswan.com

ABU SIMBEL

Eskaleh £–££

This delightful guesthouse is run by the charming Nubian musician and guide Fikri Kachif. There are just five simple rooms decorated with Nubian furniture, all with a terrace on the lake, a library with books on Nubia and a restaurant serving produce from the organic garden. The atmosphere is totally relaxing.

🕀 202 A1 ☒ On the waterfront Abu Simbel ☎ 012-368 0521

Where to...
Eat and Drink

Prices
Expect to pay per person for a meal, excluding drinks and tips.
£ under 100LE   **££** 100–150LE   **£££** over 150LE

Don't expect grand cuisine in Aswan. It seems that most tourists visiting Aswan eat on board their cruise ships. Restaurants on the Corniche serve good but basic food, such as *kofta* and vegetable stews. Eateries in the *souk* specialise in cheap snacks such as *kebab*, *taamiya* or *fuul* sandwiches, and *koshari*. The food in international restaurants in the hotels can be a touch bland.

1902 Restaurant £££
The date refers to the opening of the Old Aswan Dam but the decor is less historical and more pure Oriental-Moorish fantasy, where you can dine in style under a huge dome. The four-course set menu prepared by a French chef is overpriced and not always very inspired, but with a good Oriental show and white-glove service, it makes for a memorable night out.

⊞ 202 C3 ⊠ Old Cataract Hotel, Sharia Abtal al Tahrir ☎ 097-231 6000 ⓖ Daily 7pm–midnight, but can be closed to non-residents when the hotel is full

Aswan Moon £
The entrance through a mock castle gate may be alarming, but it gets a lot better after that. The restaurant has a floating extension, and there's also an attractive terrace for watching the sunset over the Nile while smoking a water pipe. By day it's the perfect place for fresh juice, breakfast or a light lunch in the shade. But at night it gets lively and the Nubian music is turned up. The food is simple Egyptian fare, but everything is well prepared (often in earthenware pots). No alcohol is served.

⊞ 202 C3 ⊠ Corniche al Nil ☎ 097-232 6108 ⓖ Daily 8am–11pm (or until the last customer leaves)

Aswan Panorama £
The food is similar to that of the Aswan Moon, but the restaurant is a lot quieter. This is a good place for breakfast or to while away a lazy afternoon, sitting in the shade of some greenery and looking over Elephantine, with a cold drink and a delicious *roz bi laban* (milky rice pudding with a few drops of rose water). No alcohol is served.

⊞ 202 C3 ⊠ Corniche al Nil, opposite the duty free shop ☎ 097-231 6169 ⓖ Daily 8am–11pm (or until the last customer leaves)

Biti Pizza £
Bright and shiny, this eatery serves a really good Egyptian pizza (*fateer*), sweet or savoury, as well as Italian-style pizzas.

⊞ 202 C3 ⊠ Near the train station, Midan al Mahatta ☎ No phone ⓖ Daily all day

Chef Khalil £–££
A popular fish restaurant, unassuming but good, this place serves fresh fish from Lake Nasser and the Red Sea. Choose your fish, and after it is weighed, choose how you like it cooked. All fish dishes are served with good french fries and salads.

⊞ 202 C3 ⊠ Sharia al Suq ☎ 097-231 0142 ⓖ Daily lunch and dinner

Emy £
A popular place on a double-decker boat on the Nile, one of the few

to still sell alcohol – perfect for a sundowner. This is also a good place to find the *felucca* captains who gather here at night, if you want to organise a *felucca* trip down the river. The menu features most backpackers' favourites from pancakes to spaghetti bolognese, as well as a few tasty Egyptian stews, but the fresh fruit juices are excellent and refreshing.

✚ 202 C3 ⊠ Next to Aswan Moon, Corniche al Nil ⏱ Daily 9am–midnight

Al Masry Restaurant £

Go local in this simple family restaurant that's famed for serving the best grilled *koftas* and kebabs in the town. The décor is loud Islamic kitsch, with brightly coloured vinyl tablecloths, plastic flowers and Swiss mountain views on the walls. But the service is friendly and the delicious kebabs come with fresh bread, *tahina* and a good salad. The front room is for men only, but women and mixed couples are welcome to eat in the family room at the back of the restaurant, which is very popular with locals. However, there is no alcohol.

✚ 202 C3 ⊠ Sharia al Matar, off Sharia al Souk ☎ 097-230 2576 ⏱ Daily noon–11pm (or until the last customer leaves)

Al Madina £

The Madina is a popular backpackers' dive serving good-value set meals of fish, *kofta* or kebab with salad, *tahina* and rice. No alcohol is served.

✚ 202 C3 ⊠ Sharia al Souk, near the Cleopatra Hotel ⏱ Daily all day

Nubia Restaurant ££

Try this for a Nubian night out. There's a three-course set menu followed by a folklore show of regional music and dance. The food is tasty – grilled meats and stews as usual – but this time prepared and cooked the Nubian way, which usually means with more spices. Be warned that it mostly seems to cater for tour groups. No alcohol is served.

✚ 202 C3 ⊠ Essa Island, south of Elephantine: free shuttle boat from opposite the Egypt Air office ☎ 097-230 2465 ⏱ Daily 7–11:30pm

Nubian Beach £

Set on its own with just a huge beautiful sand dune as its neighbour, this Nubian café-restaurant is the perfect place to linger away the afternoon, either for lunch, an afternoon drink or a dinner under the stars. The good-value food, simple Egyptian/Nubian dishes prepared with fresh local produce, is really good. You have to get there by boat, but call ahead for instructions.

✚ 202 C3 ⊠ West Bank, past the Aga Khan Mausoleum ☎ 012-773 7885/012-169 9145 ⏱ Daily 11–11

Nubian House Café £

This delightful café-restaurant is set in a traditional Nubian house overlooking the Nile. If you don't want to pay the premium for the Old Cataract Terrace, this is a perfectly relaxed place to hang out in the afternoon and watch the sunset, while drinking tea and smoking a water pipe. Listen to Nubian music or order some food from the small menu.

✚ 202 C3 ⊠ Corniche, 700m (750 yards) south of Nubia Museum ☎ 097-236 6226

Old Cataract Terrace ££

Set in a legendary location, this splendid terrace, shaded by traditional Egyptian tent material, is a perfect place to watch the sunset. The view over the Nile, the peaceful garden and the boulders on the tip of Elephantine Island are spectacular, and the afternoon tea (Earl Grey, cakes and sandwiches) is a real treat. It's also a lovely place to while away a lazy evening but beware of the minimum charge imposed for non-residents from 4pm to dusk.

✚ 202 C3 ⊠ Old Cataract Hotel, Sharia Abtal al Tahrir ☎ 097-231 6000 ⏱ Daily 8am–11pm

Where to...
Shop

There's only one place to shop in this area and that's in the **Aswan souk** (market), smaller but certainly far more exotic than most Egyptian markets. The best time to shop is late afternoon, after the heat of the day. The souk is relaxed, and the colours, spices and amulets confirm that you are definitely in Africa.

Aswan is famous for *karkadeh*, dried hibiscus flowers which are soaked in boiling water to make a delicious blood-red tea, drunk hot or cold. You can also find good-quality **henna** powder, used by local women to paint their hands and feet, and *fuul sudani*, excellent roast peanuts, at good prices. If buying **spices**, stick to those used locally such as cumin, black pepper and chilli, as other spices are often fake. The **Nubian baskets** make good wall decorations,

and look for the handmade Nubian **skullcaps** worn by local men. Everywhere in the *souk* you can find brightly coloured, woven **scarves** that travel well but, contrary to what you'll be told, they may not be silk.

In the *souk* you will find intriguing Nubian and Sudanese charms and sculpture, but the best selection of **African beads** and **crafts** is available from **Hanafy Bazaar** (41 Corniche al Nil; tel: 097-231 4083/230 6630), which specialises in genuine Nubian and Beshari products.

For something very different visit **Atelier du Palmier** (16 rue al Berba, Ksar al Hagar; tel: 012-316 9547; atelierdupalmier@hotmail.com) where local artesan Amer Awadalla creates unique furniture from palm fronds. His workshop is open by appointment only.

Where to...
Be Entertained

Aswan is a quiet and pleasant provincial town. Most tourists are more occupied with sightseeing during the day, or lying by the hotel pool. The best entertainment is probably to stroll along the Corniche and watch the parade of locals who come to do exactly the same thing, often dressed in their Sunday best. The Nile offers a shifting view at all times of the day, but is particularly spectacular at sunset or later at night when several sites are floodlit. The best place to go for a drink is one of the terraces beside the Nile.

Swimming

Aswan is often hot, and temperatures are even pleasantly warm in winter,

so a dip in a pool is usually welcome. It's not advisable to swim in the Nile in Aswan because of the risk of bilharzia (a chronic waterborne disease caused by parasitic flatworms), except for places where the current is quite strong. *Feluccas* and motor boats make the trip to a beach on the West Bank opposite Seluga Island, south of Aswan, where it is delightful to swim.

Foreigners are not allowed in the public pool on the Corniche, so you'll have to resort to hotel pools. For a fee, non-residents can use the small rooftop pool at the **Cleopatra Hotel**, or the large but more expensive pools of the **Basma** and **Isis Island** hotels. At quiet times you might also be allowed into the **Mövenpick** hotel's pool on Elephantine Island.

Felucca Trips

One of the best ways to enjoy Aswan and the islands on the Nile is to take a *felucca*, particularly just before sunset, when the light works its magic. Boats are moored all along the Corniche and you can just turn up and leave at once, after agreeing on a price. The usual trip sails up and past the islands of Elephantine and Kitchener and past the Mausoleum of the Aga Khan, but another slightly longer, and even more beautiful, trip goes to Sehel Island (▶ 122).

The most romantic way to get to Luxor from Aswan is to sail by *felucca* or *dahabeyya*. It's more practical than travelling by road, because you don't have to travel in an armed convoy. The journey takes four to seven days, and you'll visit the temples of Kom Ombo, Edfu and Esna on the way, eating and sleeping on the boat.

The tourist office in Aswan lists official prices for all the different excursions and can help you arrange trips with reliable boat captains. Always take enough water and protect yourself from the sun. You'll also need to buy provisions from the food market around the railway station and Sharia al Suq.

Fishing

Fishing is popular on Lake Nasser (▶ 123), as it contains some of the largest freshwater fish in the world, including the Nile perch (which can weigh up to 200kg/40 pounds).
Lake Nasser Adventure (tel: 012-240 5897; www.lakenasseradventure. com) is run by a Frenchman and a Nubian, both passionate about fishing and the area. They organise fishing safaris and trips into the rarely visited south of the Eastern desert.
The **African Angler**, run by former Kenyan safari guide Tim Bailey, offers a range of outings, including week-long fishing safaris. Contact them in Aswan (tel: 097-230 9748; www.africanangler.co.uk).

Sound and Light Show

There are two or three performances of the spectacular *son et lumière* at the temple of Philae per day, when a 60-minute tour leads through the dramatically floodlit temple to the accompaniment of a rather melodramatic soundtrack.

The tourist office has a timetable of shows in several foreign languages, or you can check online at www.soundandlight.com.eg. You can buy tickets at the Shallal dock and also get a ferry across to the site (tel: 02-3386 3469; www. soundandlight.com.eg).

Music and Dance

Most live Nubian music is performed at Nubian weddings. As the singers and band are a major part of the wedding expenses, the bridegroom often invites plenty of friends and relatives to the wedding, charging them about 20LE or more a head. Foreign guests are thought to bring good luck to the couple, so you may well be invited to join in the week-long celebrations. A similar offering of money will be more than welcome.

But beware of occasional touts who invite foreigners to weddings in their village, get them drunk or stoned and then rob or cheat them.

The **Nubian Folk Troupe** performs at the austere-looking building of the **Palace of Culture** (tel: 097-231 3390) on the Corniche daily from 9:30 to 11pm from October until March, and all through Ramadan. The show, which is popular with locals, includes story-telling, Nubian stick dancing and traditional wedding and harvest songs. A nightly show featuring live Nubian music is also held at the Nubia House Restaurant (▶ 126).

The nightclubs held at the **New Cataract Hotel** (Sharia Abtal al Tahrir, tel: 097-231 6002) and the **Elephantine Island Mövenpick Hotel** (Elephantine Island, tel: 097-231 4666) put on a floor show especially designed for international tourists comprising Western and Nubian music, while the **Isis Hotel** (Corniche, tel: 097-232 4744) offers a nightly disco (except Mondays) which plays a selection of popular Western music.

Mediterranean Coast and Oases

Getting Your Bearings

Although most foreigners left at the time of the Revolution in 1952, Alexandria retains something of its cosmopolitan flair. The city has been undergoing something of a cultural revival since the opening of the new Bibliotheca Alexandrina. The mix of the underlying ancient history and the vibe of a modern Arab Mediterranean city makes for a unique and pretty exciting place to spend a few days.

Because it's been inhabited continuously since antiquity, most historic monuments have disappeared beneath the sea or the modern city, so the National Museum of Alexandria is the best place to start a visit. Other layers will be revealed as you walk the downtown streets, which follow the ancient pattern.

The rest of the coast seems to have rejected its links to the Mediterranean and become 100 per cent Egyptian. What was a pristine sandy coastline has been developed into a string of mediocre resorts aimed at Egyptian holiday-makers. The Western Desert oases, some of which were important agricultural centres in Roman times, have their own idiosyncratic character because of their long isolation. Roads in the Western Desert are relatively recent. Before them, the oases – separated from each other by hundreds of kilometres of desert and cut off from the Nile Valley – were accessible only by camel caravans. Life in the oases is slow and traditions die hard. Siwa in particular has retained its very distinct character. A road was laid in the early 20th century, but it's only in the last few years that travellers no longer require a special permit to get there. But with the advent of television, the growth of desert tourism and the Egyptian government's plan to relocate people from the crowded Nile valley to the oases, change is at an alarming rate.

Colourful fishing boats in Alexandria's Eastern Harbour

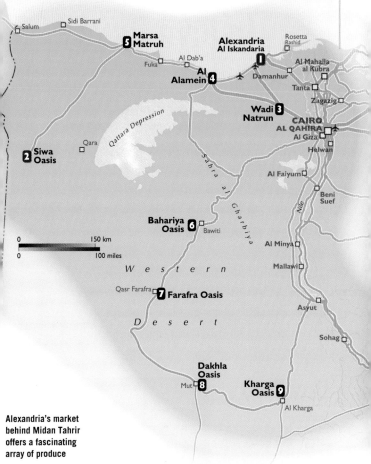

Salum · Sidi Barrani

Marsa Matruh 5

Fuka · Al Dab'a

Al Alamein 4

Alexandria Al Iskandaria 1

Rosetta Rashid

Al Mahalla al Kubra

Damanhur

Tanta

Zagazig

Wadi Natrun 3

CAIRO AL QAHIRA

Al Giza

Helwan

Qara · Qattara Depression

Siwa Oasis 2

Al Faiyum

Beni Suef

Sahra al Gharbiya

0 — 150 km
0 — 100 miles

Bahariya Oasis 6
Bawiti

Al Minya

Mallawi

W e s t e r n

Qasr Farafra **Farafra Oasis** 7

D e s e r t

Asyut

Sohag

Dakhla Oasis 8
Mut

Kharga Oasis 9
Al Kharga

Alexandria's market
behind Midan Tahrir
offers a fascinating
array of produce

★ Don't Miss

1 Alexandria ➤ 134
2 Siwa Oasis ➤ 138

At Your Leisure

3 Wadi Natrun Monasteries
➤ 141
4 Al Alamein ➤ 141
5 Marsa Matruh ➤ 142
6 Bahariya Oasis ➤ 142
7 Farafra Oasis ➤ 143
8 Dakhla Oasis ➤ 143
9 Kharga Oasis ➤ 144

In Five Days

If you're not quite sure where to begin your travels, this itinerary
recommends a practical and enjoyable day in Alexandria and a
four-day tour to the oasis of Siwa, taking in some of the best places
to see using the Getting Your Bearings map on the previous page.
For more information see the main entries.

Day One

Morning
Your first stop in **1 Alexandria** (➤ 134–137) must be the **National Museum
of Alexandria** (➤ 135) as only here and at the **Roman Odeon** (➤ 135), in
the city centre, can you really get a feel of what the city once was. Take a
taxi or walk along the Corniche to the **Bibliotheca Alexandrina** (➤ 136) for a
visit and have a light lunch at the Hilton Café on the site.

Afternoon
Hire a taxi for two hours to visit the **Serapeum and Pompey's Pillar** (➤ 135)
and the nearby catacombs of **Kom al Shuqafa** (➤ 134). Back in downtown
Alexandria, stroll through the streets admiring the grand facades of
19th-century buildings or sniffing out antiques in the **Attarin junk shops**
(➤ 149). Have a drink in the Sofitel Alexandria Cecil Hotel lounge
(➤ 145) and walk along the Corniche to one of the fish restaurants. The
dome of Abu al Abbas Mosque is pictured below.

Day Two

Morning
Leave by car or taxi
to **5 Marsa Matruh**
(➤ 142), a journey of
about three hours, and
stop for a simple lunch
and then a swim in the
brilliantly clear sea at
the small resort of Sidi
Abd al Rahman.

Afternoon
Continue to Marsa
Matruh and visit the
little town on foot, or
explore some of the
nearby beaches of
Cleopatra or Agiba
before returning to Marsa
Matruh for dinner at the
Beausite Restaurant on
the beach.

Day Three

Morning
Drive to **2** **Siwa** (above, ➤ 138–140), a journey of about four hours through the desert, and arrive in time for lunch at the Kenooz restaurant (➤ 149), set in a palm grove.

Afternoon
A half-hour walk through splendid palm groves leads to **Aghurmi** where Alexander the Great consulted the Oracle (➤ 138). Continue to Cleopatra's Bath, where you can stop for a drink at the cafeteria. A further 10 minutes through the palms is Gebel Dakrur, with wonderful views over Siwa. Return by foot along the first dirt road for about half an hour, and back in town climb up to Shali (the old town) for some more superb views.

Day Four

Morning
Visit on foot the Traditional Siwan House (➤ 138), then take the Matruh road out of town and continue walking for about 30 minutes to the tombs of **Gebel al Mawta** (➤ 138). Have lunch back in town.

Afternoon
Take an organised tour into the desert around Siwa for a chance to see the sand dunes and swim in the saltwater lakes and hot-water pools.

Day Five

Take a bus or taxi back to Alexandria (about seven hours), stopping *en route* for lunch and a swim in Marsa Matruh.

0 Alexandria

Modern Alexandria may be a little worn, but its name still conjures up dazzling images. Alexander the Great founded the city in AD 331; Cleopatra had her passionate love affair with Mark Antony here; the Alexandrian Library was the intellectual centre of the ancient world; while the lighthouse, the Pharos, was one of the seven wonders of the world.

The city's wealth and glory slowly vanished after the Arab conquest of AD 641, but in the 19th century Alexandria regained some of its wealth and grandeur, growing rich from trading in cotton and adopting the cosmopolitan air evoked in Lawrence Durrell's series of novels, the *Alexandria Quartet*.

But in spite of all its history and legends, modern Alexandria reveals very little of its past. Fragments of Cleopatra's Palace and the Pharos have been found in the Mediterranean, but for centuries rulers and archaeologists have searched in vain for Alexander the Great's tomb.

Watch Your Step

You may not see so much of it, but Alexandria's past is always beneath your feet, and every construction site reveals new sections of the hidden city, yielding the remains of buildings, statues and pottery. Elsewhere, holes suddenly appear in the city's roads, leading to the discovery of underground treasures. Egypt's largest Roman burial site, the eerie catacombs of **Kom al Shuqafa**, were discovered when a donkey fell through a hole in the ground. These 2nd-century AD catacombs are decorated in a uniquely Alexandrian blend of Egyptian, Greek and Roman motifs, even including some bearded serpents, images of Medusas and the Egyptian gods Anubis and Sobek dressed as Roman legionnaires.

City Highlights

**Below left:
A brooch in
the Royal
Jewellery
Museum
Below: The
Corniche
curves around
the Bay of
Alexandria**

At first, modern Alexandria, a sprawling and overpopulated town, may seem disappointing, but time spent discovering its hidden splendours is well rewarded. The fascinating **National Museum of Alexandria** clearly illustrates the city's history from antiquity until the modern period, through well-displayed artefacts. The museum is laid out chronologically over three floors: the basement is devoted to the pharaonic period, the ground floor to the Graeco-Roman period, which includes a sphinx and other sculptures found in the Eastern Harbour, and the top floor covers Coptic, Muslim and modern Alexandria. The old Graeco-Roman Museum has

one of most comprehensive collections of Graeco-Roman art in the world, so typical for Alexandria, with more than 40,000 objects, but it is closed for restoration at the time of writing. The recently renovated **Royal Jewellery Museum** has a stunning collection of the jewellery that belonged to the former royal family, and is housed in a great villa in the suburbs.

Kom al Dikka ("Pile of Rubble"), a short walk away from the National Museum, has an elegant 2nd-century AD Roman Odeon with a marble seating area and the remains of a mosaic floor. A Graeco-Roman street nearby passes late-Roman ruins. The Roman Villa of the Birds has been uncovered, with large floor mosaics (charge: inexpensive).

In the Karmouz neighbourhood is Pompey's Pillar, a 27m (88-foot) pink granite column, from around AD 295. Crusaders attributed it to Pompey, but the pillar probably supported a statue of Emperor Diocletian (AD 284–305). Two granite sphinxes and statues are the only other remains of the fabled Serapeum on Rhakotis, the settlement Alexander the Great developed into Alexandria. The Serapeum housed the magnificent temple of Serapis and the Second Alexandrian

Library, containing Cleopatra's private collection of 200,000 manuscripts. Until destroyed by Christians in AD 391, this was an important intellectual centre.

Downtown Alexandria

Alexander's city had two main streets – Canopic and Soma – which survive in the downtown streets of al Hurriya and Nabi Danyal. The area opposite the old-style Sofitel Alexandria Cecil Hotel (➤ 145) was the site of the Ptolemies' palaces and of the Caesareum, Cleopatra's monument to Mark Antony. Fragments of a royal palace, perhaps Cleopatra's, were discovered in the waters of the Eastern Harbour. The impressive modern building of the new **Bibliotheca Alexandrina** (Alexandrian Library) is intended to be an international centre of knowledge like its ancient ancestor, designed to hold 8 million books in many languages. The book collection is far from complete yet, but the complex includes a good manuscript collection, a small antiquities museum, a concert hall and a planetarium.

The **Nabi Danyal mosque** on Sharia Nabi Danyal houses the tombs of Danyal al Maridi and Lukman the Wise, and some believe Alexander's tomb is in the crypt. Nearby, the former home of Greek poet Constantine Cavafy (1863–1933) has become the **Cavafy Museum**, a place of pilgrimage for his many fans.

At the western end of the Corniche, 15th-century **Fort Qaytbey** and the Naval Museum covers the site of the 125m (410-foot) high Pharos, built in 279 BC by Sostratus for Ptolemy II, and destroyed by earthquakes in the 11th and 14th centuries. Underwater excavations have revealed fragments of the Pharos.

A sphinx guards the giant granite column of Pompey

TAKING A BREAK

Downtown Alexandria is a great place to stroll or hang out in one of the excellent pâtisseries or bars immortalised in Durrell's *Alexandria Quartet* and Cavafy's poems.

Alexandria Tourist Office
✛ 198 C5 ✉ Midan Saad Zagloul ☎ 03-485 1556 🕐 Daily 8:30–6

National Museum of Alexandria
✉ 110 Tariq al Hurriya ☎ 03-483 5519 🕐 Daily 9–4; public holidays 9–3
💲 Moderate

Kom al Dikka (Roman Odeon)
⊠ Behind Cinema Amir, Sharia Salman Yusuf ☎ 03-486 5106 🕘 Daily 9–5 🖐 Inexpensive

Pompey's Pillar
⊠ Sharia Amud al Sawari, Karmouz 🕘 Daily 9–4 🚃 Tram 16 from Ramla 🖐 Inexpensive

Bibliotheca Alexandrina
⊠ Corniche al Bahr ☎ 03-483 9999; www.bibalex.org 🕘 Sun–Thu 11–7, Fri–Sat 3–7 🖐 Moderate; separate charge for all museums

Kom al Shuqqafa Catacombs
⊠ Off Sharia Amud al Sawari, Karmouz ☎ 03-484 5800 🕘 Daily 9–5 🖐 Inexpensive

Cavafy Museum
⊠ 4 Sharia Sharm al Sheikh, off Sharia Sultan Hussein, Downtown ☎ 03-486 1598 🕘 Tue–Sun 10–4 🖐 Inexpensive

Royal Jewellery Museum
⊠ 27 Sharia Ahmed Yehia Pasha, Zizinia, Glymm ☎ 03-582 8348 🕘 Daily 9–4 🖐 Inexpensive 🚃 Tram 2 from Midan Ramla

Graeco-Roman Museum
⊠ Sharia Mathaf al Romani ☎ 03-486 5820/487 6434; www.grm.gov.eg 🕘 Currently closed for restoration

---

ALEXANDRIA: INSIDE INFO

Top tips Take time to explore the back streets downtown and in **Attarin** (➤ 149), to catch glimpses of history both in the monuments, the people and the junk shops.
■ Escape the urban sprawl in the **Muntazah Gardens** east of downtown, or in the elegant **Antionadis Gardens**.

Hidden gems Underwater archaeology has revealed that much of ancient Alexandria lies submerged near Fort Qaytbey and in the Eastern Harbour. There were vague plans for the world's first underwater museum but in the meantime a small company **Alexandria Dive** (tel: 03-483 2042; www.alexandria-dive.com) offers diving tours in both of these sites.

Ones to miss If time's short skip the **Naval Museum** in Qaytbey (closed for restoration) and the five faded tombs from 250 BC in the Anfushi Necropolis.

❷ Siwa Oasis

The oasis of Siwa is one of the most remote and idyllic places in Egypt, where lush palm groves and gardens appear like a mirage from the surrounding desert of rocks and sand. Here you'll find freshwater springs and natural hot pools, salt lakes and the dangerous sand dunes of the Great Sand Sea.

In late antiquity Siwa was famous for its Oracle of Amun, whose predictions were sought by people all over the ancient world. It was important enough for the Persian emperor Cambyses to send an army of 50,000 to conquer the oasis and destroy the Oracle. The troops were subsequently lost in the desert, thus enhancing the Oracle's reputation. In 331 BC the young Alexander the Great, having conquered Egypt, travelled eight days from Alexandria to consult the Oracle, hoping to confirm his divine birth.

Below: The Great Sand Sea at Siwa

Splendid Isolation

Until the late 19th century Siwa was virtually cut off from the Nile valley and the rest of the world and Siwans had a reputation for extreme hostility towards non-Muslims. They still have their own language, Siwi, and their own customs and rituals. Change came quickly in the 1980s with a new road from Marsa Matruh and the arrival of electricity and, therefore, television. This and the advent of tourism have made dramatic changes to the villages of Siwa, unfortunately not always for the best. Siwans now welcome foreigners, but they are proud of their traditions and keen to preserve them.

In and Around Siwa

Siwa town is still a sleepy and laid-back place, even though much of its old mudbrick architecture has been replaced by shabby breeze-block structures and hotels. The **Traditional Siwan House**, in a traditional mudbrick building, contains a beautiful collection of silver jewellery and costumes.

The new town is overshadowed by the ruins of **Shali**, the fortified hilltop town founded in 1203 and inhabited until 1926, when a heavy rainstorm caused serious damage and forced the inhabitants out. Shali's melting labyrinth of buildings and passages disintegrates more with every rainfall.

Just outside the town is **Gebel al Mawta** ("Mountain of the Dead"), a rock formation pitted with ancient Egyptian and Graeco-Roman tombs, only four of which are open to the public. To the south is **Aghurmi**, an older fortified settlement under which Siwans believe a large amount of treasure is buried. The 6th-century BC **Temple of the Oracle**, built over an older temple dedicated to Amun, is where Alexander the Great sought confirmation that he was Zeus or Amun's son, but he died before revealing what the Oracle told him.

A walk through the palm groves, past **Cleopatra's Bath**, leads to **Gebel Dakrur** where rheumatics are buried in the hot

Right: Siwans are keen to preserve their traditional way of life, despite the changes brought to the area by tourism

sands to help ease their condition. A few kilometres from Siwa is the edge of the **Great Sand Sea**, stretching more than 800km (500 miles) south and with dunes up to 150m (500 feet) high.

A popular corner shop in Siwa town

TAKING A BREAK

The best restaurants in Siwa are **Kenooz** (➤ 149) and **Abdu's** (➤ 148). These are also good places to meet desert guides or to find an organised tour into the desert.

➕ Off map 198 A5
Siwa Tourist Office
✉ At beginning of Tariq Mersa Matrouh, Siwa Town ☎ 046-460 1338
🕐 Sat–Thu 9–2 (also 5pm–8pm in winter)

Traditional Siwan House
✉ Siwa Town 🕐 Sun–Thu 10–noon 🎟 Inexpensive

SIWA OASIS: INSIDE INFO

Top tips The oasis is still very **traditional**, so dress modestly out of respect for local customs. Women in particular should keep their arms and legs covered and avoid wearing bikinis in the local baths. Also, avoid shows of affection in public.

■ Don't bring **alcohol** into the oasis.
■ The **best time to visit** is during spring and autumn when the climate is most pleasant. In winter the days are usually fine enough but the nights can get very chilly, while from May onwards it's just hot, hot, hot.
■ Around the full moon in October there's a big **Siyaha festival** on Gebel Dakrur that lasts for three days.
■ Friday is **market day** in the main square.

In more depth The Great Sand Sea, 800km (500 miles) of amazing sand dunes, starts just outside Siwa and it is a sight to behold. **Take a tour** with one of the desert guides who will slide down the dunes in his four-wheel drive or take you to one of the cool lakes or hot water springs. One of the best is Abdallah Baghi, who is passionate and very knowledgeable about Siwa and the desert (tel: 03-460 1111; email: shali55@hotmail.com).

At Your Leisure

3 Wadi Natrun Monasteries

Wadi Natrun played an important role in Egypt's Coptic Church, as for more than 1,500 years its popes have invariably been elected from these monasteries. The monastic tradition runs strong in the Coptic religion, and many educated Coptic men choose to retreat at some time during their life. One of Wadi Natrun's earliest monks was St Bishoi (AD 320–407), and more than 100 monks and hermits now live at his monastery. Deir al Suryani, originally inhabited by Syrian monks and formerly the home of the current Pope Shenouda III, has superb frescoes in its Church of the Virgin. Here also is St Bishoi's Cave where the saint's hair was tied to the ceiling to keep him standing. The church of the remote Deir al Baramus has a beautiful iconostasis, while Deir Abu Maqar (closed to the public) is the resting place of many Coptic popes.

🕂 199 D4 ✉ Valley off Cairo–Alexandria desert road ☎ Deir Anba Bishoi: 02-591 4448; Deir al Baramus: 02-592 2775; Deir al Suryani:

The Wadi Natrun monasteries are often a place of retreat for Coptic professionals
Below: A tank at al Alamein War Museum

02-592 9658 🕑 Daily 9–6 (Deir al Baramus Fri–Sun 9–5). Lent restrictions 🍴 Wadi Natrun Resthouse on desert road (£–££) 🚌 Cairo–Alexandria bus via desert road stop at Resthouse, then pick-ups to the monasteries 💵 Donations welcome

4 Al Alamein

This tiny coastal village was the site of the battle in 1942 that changed

GREAT NATURAL WONDERS IN THE OASES
- Surreal sculptures in the White Desert
- Acres of palm trees and gardens in Siwa
- Sand dunes near Mut in Dakhla
- Hot springs in all the oases

A farmer working in the fields near Bahariya Oasis

the course of World War II. Winston Churchill claimed "Before Alamein we never had a victory. After Alamein we never had a defeat". More than 70,000 soldiers were wounded and 11,000 killed in the battle between the German Afrika Korps under Field Marshal Rommel and Field Marshal Montgomery's British Eighth Army. The Commonwealth War Cemetery, overlooking the battlefield, is an eerie and moving place containing more than 7,000 graves. The smaller German and Italian cemeteries lie farther west. The War Museum houses a small collection of artillery, uniforms, maps and models related to the North Africa Campaign and the Battle of al Alamein.

🚹 198 B5 ✉ 106km (65 miles) west of Alexandria ☎ Museum 046-410 0031 🕐 Museum daily 9–4; Commonwealth War Cemetery daily 9–4 🍴 Alamein Resthouse (£) 🚌 Alexandria–Marsa Matruh buses stop near the War Museum, but there's no public transport to the cemeteries 💷 Museum inexpensive, cemeteries free

🟥 Marsa Matruh

Egypt's entire northern coast is being developed into an unattractive sprawl of resorts for Egyptian holiday-makers, and the once sleepy fishing village of Marsa Matruh has not escaped. During the summer its fantastic beaches are overcrowded with Egyptian families, fully dressed even in the water. And without sufficient services to cope with this influx, both beach and sea are polluted. Slightly cleaner is Rommel's Beach, where the World War II Field Marshal known as the Desert Fox reputedly took a dip. The nearby Rommel Museum has some of his

memorabilia, including his coat. The best beaches are farther out of town. Cleopatra's (or the Lovers') Beach has some interesting rock formations and, according to legend, Cleopatra's Bath is where the exotic queen took a dip with her lover Mark Antony. Agiba (Miracle) Beach seems to deserve its name for the beauty of its dazzling turquoise water.

🚹 Off map 198 A5 ✉ 290km (180 miles) west of Alexandria, 512km (318 miles) from Cairo ☎ Tourist office: 046-493 1841 🍴 Beausite Restaurant (££) 🚌 From Cairo, Alexandria and Siwa ✈ From Cairo 🚂 From Cairo

🟥 Bahariya Oasis

In ancient times Bahariya was a considerable agricultural centre, famous for its wines, but with the decline of the Roman Empire in the 4th century AD the rich fields and vineyards turned to desert. Today several villages make up the oasis, but the main town is al Bawiti, with more than 30,000 inhabitants. Over the last few years the town has seen a huge increase in tourism.

In 1996 a donkey dropped into a hole near the temple of Alexander the Great, and thus uncovered the "Valley of the Golden Mummies", a vast cemetery with probably more than 10,000 mummies. So far about 250 Graeco-Roman mummies have been excavated, and 10 of them are on show at the **museum**. The mummies are richly decorated but what is stunning are the realistically painted masks that cover the faces, like the famous Fayoum paintings.

The **Oasis Heritage Museum** has a display of local costumes, clay figures representing scenes of traditional oasis life and a small shop selling local crafts.

Towards the Roman well of Ain Bishnu are the mudbrick houses of Bawiti's old quarter. Hot water (30°C/86°F) flows into the palm-filled gardens. Farther along is the old settlement of al Qasr, which was built over the ancient capital. Notable are the ruins of the Temple of Bes (664–525 BC) and a Roman triumphal arch.

A trip into the desert, to the hot springs in the surrounding Black Desert, or the amazing rock formations in the White Desert, is a must.

➕ 198 B2 ✉ 330km (205 miles) southwest of Cairo ☎ Tourist office 02-3847 3035 🕐 Museum daily 8–2; sites 8–2, but no fixed hours 🍴 Popular Restaurant (£) 🚌 Buses daily from Cairo; from Farafra Sat, Mon and Thu 💷 Moderate: one charge for all sites

7 Farafra Oasis

Known as the "Land of the Cow" in ancient times, Farafra's cows look uncannily like those depicted in tomb paintings. Qasr Farafra is the only settlement in this beautiful oasis, and its only sight is Badr's Museum, a pretty mudbrick structure built by the eponymous local artist. Farafra's main attraction is its peace and quiet, especially in the palm groves and gardens, and its location near the spectacular White Desert, with its bizarre, eroded, white rock formations, shaped like moon craters or icebergs. Ain Besai, 15km (9 miles) from town, has ancient rock tombs and a cold freshwater spring.

➕ 198 A1 ✉ 180km (112 miles) south of al Bawiti, Bahariya 🕐 Museum (tel: 012-170 4710) 8:30–4, inexpensive 🍴 El Badawiyya Hotel restaurant (£–££) 🚌 Buses from Cairo, Bahariya and Dakhla daily except Wed

8 Dakhla Oasis

Excavations have shown that the lush oasis of Dakhla has been inhabited continuously since prehistoric times, when it was the site of a vast lake.

The mudbrick mosque in the medieval city of al Qasr at Dakhla Oasis

Mut, the ancient and modern capital, has an old citadel, hot sulphur pools and a small Ethnographic Museum with interesting scenes of oasis life. West of Mut are the colourful ancient Muwazaka Tombs, with their mummies intact, and the 1st-century AD Roman temple of Deir al Haggar.

Dakhla's medieval capital, al Qasr, is a charming place lined with mudbrick houses. The 12th-century mosque of Nasr al Din has an unusual mudbrick minaret. Next to the pottery factory you can see how mudbricks are still made in the ancient way.

The picturesque village of Balat, on the way to Kharga, also retains its medieval Islamic charm. Farther along the same road, just beyond Teneida, are strange rock formations bearing fascinating prehistoric rock paintings featuring antelopes, fish and giraffes.

🔲 Off map 198 A1 ✉ 310km (193 miles) southeast of Farafra ☎ Tourist office: 092-782 1685 ⓜ Museum Sat–Thu 8–2 🍴 Ahmad Hamdy (£) 🚌 Daily buses from Cairo, Asyut, Kharga, Farafra and Bahariya 🎫 Mostly free or inexpensive

Stunning rock formations rise from the White Desert

9 Kharga Oasis

Kharga Town, the capital of the New Valley, has retained little of its original character and charm, but there are still several individual attractions. The New Valley Museum houses a small collection of well-labelled archaeological finds from local excavations.

North of town is the ancient capital Hibis, its 6th-century BC temple built by the Persian emperor Darius I and dedicated to Amun. The nearby Roman Temple of Nadura commands fabulous views over the oasis, while the impressive Bagawat Necropolis has finely decorated mudbrick Christian tombs dating from the 3rd to the 7th centuries. The ruins of the monastery of Deir al Kashef overlook the crossroads of two major caravan routes.

🔲 Off map 200 A1 ✉ 195km (121 miles) east of Dakhla ☎ Tourist office 092-792 1206 ⓜ Museum daily 8–5; Bagawat Necropolis daily 8–5 🍴 Pioneers Hotel (£–££) 🚌 Daily from Cairo, other oases and Asyut, Minya and Beni Suef

Where to...
Stay

Prices
The prices are for a double room per night.
£ under 400LE   ££ 400–900LE
£££ over 900LE

Alexandria has some wonderful old-style and sumptuous new hotels, but accommodation elsewhere along the coast is usually basic. Some oasis hotels are set in luscious palm groves, but most are simple.

ALEXANDRIA

Egypt Hotel £
This great new hotel occupies an old Alexandrian house with comfortable rooms, and very clean bathrooms, mostly with sea views. A large and cosy lounge is full of period detail and antique furniture,

with all that history, the occasional old waiter to tell a story and magnificent sweeping views over the bay, it's still worth the stay. The mirrored tearoom and Monty's bar are a must, but you can give the restaurants a miss, with the selection of better restaurants near by.

➕ 198 C5   ⊠ 16 Midan Saad Zaghloul
☎ 03-487 7173; www.sofitel.com

SIWA

Adrère Amellal £££
This splendid ecolodge, on the edge of Siwa Lake, is built in mud and salt against the magical backdrop of the White Mountain. The rooms are simple, but comfortable and really stylish, decorated with local furniture and lit by oil lamps and lots of candles (there is electricity only in the kitchen and lobby). Drinks are served on the terrace with great views over the lake, and the wonderful chef creates some of the best food in Egypt, fresh

Le Metropole ££–£££
Not so long ago the Metropole was a cheap-and-cheerful alternative to the Cecil Hotel, but it is today a four-star establishment with all modern amenities. Overlooking the old harbour and the Mediterranean Sea, the beautiful art-deco building retains a colonial feel with large, cosy rooms decorated in a sumptuous style. The hotel is well situated in the heart of Alexandria, and has an art collection with paintings by both local and international artists, as well as a selection of antiques.

➕ 198 C5   ⊠ 52 Sharia Saad Zaghloul
☎ 03-486 1467; www.paradiseinnegypt.com

Four Seasons Alexandria £££
The new Four Seasons hotel has dramatically changed the hotel scene in Alex. With more than 100 spacious rooms overlooking the Mediterranean, it is by far the most luxurious hotel in town. There are nine superb restaurants to choose from, a huge European spa, a state-of-the-art fitness centre and a private cleaned-up beach.

➕ 198 C5   ⊠ San Stefano Mall, 2nd floor, 388 Tariq al Geish, Zizinya ☎ 03-581 8080;
www.fourseasons.com/Alexandria

Sofitel Alexandria Cecil Hotel £££
For a long time the grandest hotel in Alex and still an institution, the Cecil was immortalised by Lawrence Durrell in his *Alexandria Quartet* novels. It's no longer a celebrity hangout and the renovation was insensitive, but

➕ 198 C5   ⊠ 1 Digla, off Sharia Abdel Hamid Badawy ☎ 03-481 4483

from the hotel's own organic oasis' gardens. The swimming pool is fed by a natural spring set in a shady palm grove. Activities such as horse-riding, desert safaris and swimming in hot-water pools in the middle of the desert, are all included in the room rate. Rooms must be reserved in advance at the Cairo office, so that no money will be needed during a stay within the desert resort.

🚹 **Off map 198 A5** 🖂 **Near the White Mountain, Sidi al Jaafar, 18km (11 miles) from Siwa Town** 🕿 **02-736 7879/738 1321; www.adrereamella.net**

Shali Lodge £-££

In this beautiful mudbrick hotel, set in a lovely palm grove, there are only eight rooms surrounding a small pool. The large rooms are decorated with local furniture, and are pleasant and comfortable. The staff are friendly, and the restaurant Kenooz (▶ 149) is excellent value.

🚹 **Off map 198 A5** 🖂 **Sharia Subukha, Siwa** 🕿 **046-460 1299**

OASES

Aquasun Farafra £-££

Hisham Nessim runs a wonderful hotel in Farafra with 21 chalet-style rooms set in a garden. Every room has its own shady veranda made from palm fronds. The water in the swimming pool comes from the Bir Sitta well, the restaurant serves food from the organic garden, and Hisham organises interesting tours into the desert, including a search for the lost army of the Persian ruler Cambyses.

🚹 **198 A1** 🖂 **Bir Sitta, Farafra** 🕿 **012-780 7999; www.raid4x4egypt.com**

Desert Lodge ££

This delightful lodge is in traditional oasis style, overlooking the old town of al Qasr and the desert. Desert Lodge is the best accommodation in this oasis, and the nicest part of the oasis to be.

🚹 **Off map 200 A1** 🖂 **Al Qasr, 29km (18 miles) from Mut, Dakhla** 🕿 **092-772 7061; www.desertlodge.net**

Nature Camp £

At the foot of the Gebel Dist mountain is this pleasant eco-friendly camp, with candle-lit huts overlooking the desert, and adjacent to the spring of Bir Ghaba. The food is excellent and the owner Ashraf organises great tours into the desert.

🚹 **198 B2** 🖂 **Bir al Ghaba** 🕿 **012-337 5097**

Pioneers Hotel £££

One of the few more luxurious options in the oases, this modern rather uninspiring-looking, salmon-pink hotel provides a comfortable base for visitors travelling in the desert. There's a good swimming pool for a cooling dip. The bedrooms are surprisingly spacious and air-conditioned, and have many facilities, including satellite television if you're missing your favourite programmes from home.

🚹 **Off map 200 A1** 🖂 **Near the temple of Hibis, Kharga** 🕿 **092-792 7982; www.solymar-hotels.com**

Qasr el Bawity ££-£££

Set at the foot of the black Gebel al Ingleez mountain, and in the middle of a lush palm grove, is this friendly ecolodge built in traditional oasis style. There are 24 spacious rooms and 4 suites built in local stone, furnished with textiles from the oases and in the garden is a spring-fed pool and a hot spring.

🚹 **198 B2** 🖂 **At the foot of Gebel al Ingleez, 6km (4 miles) from al Bawiti, Bahariya** 🕿 **02-847 1880; www.qasrelbawity.com**

Taziry Ecolodge ££

This delightful ecolodge overlooks White Mountain (Adrere Amellal), and the lake. Run by an artist and engineer from Alexandria, this simple hotel is built from local materials. There is no electricity, and the pool is a natural spring. It's perfect for a few quiet days.

🚹 **Off map 198 A5** 🖂 **Gaary, 18km (11 miles) from Siwa Town** 🕿 **012-340 8492/012-642 1155; www.taziry.com**

Where to...
Eat and Drink

Prices
Expect to pay per person for a meal, excluding drinks and tips.
£ under 100LE   **££** 100–150LE   **£££** over 150LE

Alexandria may no longer have glamorous restaurants where the likes of the Aga Khan entertained international politicians and famous movie stars, but there are still some pleasant and fun places. Many specialise in fish and shellfish and the cuisine is generally more Greek-Mediterranean or Levantine than Egyptian. Some city bars have a typical port atmosphere with a mixed crowd of locals and visiting sailors. Food along the rest of the coast and in the oases is mostly standard Egyptian fare. In Kharga the only places to

eat are in the hotels, the best of which is probably the Pioneers Hotel (▶ 146), but even here the food is mediocre.

ALEXANDRIA

Cap d'Or £
This small but delightful art nouveau bar-restaurant is one of a kind. Cap d'Or is probably the type of bar you'd come across in a back street of Marseilles, serving cold beers and tasty, sizzling dishes of shrimps, casseroles and squid stew to the tunes of aged Euro-pop music. The patron races horses,

and his clients are mostly laid-back Egyptians and expat residents.
🔁 198 C5 ⊠ 4 Sharia Adib, off Sharia Saad Zaghloulm ☎ 03-483 5177 ⓖ Daily 10am–3am

Coffee Roastery £–££
In this lively and incredibly popular Western-style café-restaurant you can get a good coffee, fresh juices, sandwiches and salads as well as grilled meats. Large MTV screens and good music attract young Alexandrian students and families, and the place seems to hop all day. A great place to watch new Alexandria in the old part of town.
🔁 198 C5 ⊠ 48 Sharia Fuad, Downtown ☎ 03-483 4363 ⓖ Daily 7am–2am

Fish Market ££
Literally on the sea, this is the city's most upmarket fish restaurant with great views over the Med and a huge counter of the latest catch to choose from. Service is efficient and all fish and seafood comes with *mezze* and Oriental rice. Delicious

Oriental pastries can be bought from the bakery downstairs.
🔁 198 C5 ⊠ Beside the Kashafa Club, Corniche al Bahr ☎ 03-480 5119 ⓖ Daily noon–2am

Greek Club (Club Nautique Hellenique) £–££
As Mediterranean as it gets, the Greek Club has a flair of old Alexandria with a large terrace overlooking the sweeping bay of Alexandria. The food is OK, equally very Mediterranean with fish and fried calamari, but the best thing is to come for a sundowner, cold beer with *mezze*.
🔁 198 C5 ⊠ Sharia Qasr Qaytbay, Anfushi ☎ 03-480 2690 ⓖ Daily noon–11pm

Hoot Gondol Seafood £
Very popular with locals, this establishment is where they come to be sure of a delicious plate of the freshest grilled fish or fried calamari with *mezze*. The restaurant is located in a little alley near the Bibliotheca Alexandrina, but ask for

directions because everyone knows this place.

198 C5 ⊠ On the corner of Omar Lotfy and Mohammed Motwe ☎ 03-476 1779 ⊙ Daily 11–11

Qadoura ££

A popular fish restaurant, partly indoors, partly street terrace, this place is often considered to be the best in town, but no alcohol is served. Choose your fish or seafood from the counter and decide how you want it cooked. Specials include crab stew, clams with spaghetti and crayfish. The dishes come with mezze and salads.

198 C5 ⊠ Shari' Bayram et-Tunsi, Al Anfushi ☎ 03-480 0405 ⊙ Daily 9am–3am

Spitfire Bar £

This popular 1970s watering hole caters mainly for a few locals, ex-pats and visiting American marines. The walls are covered with pictures of warships, favourite customers and other memorabilia, the atmosphere is thick with smoke

and the music is pure rock and roll. For an unusual Egyptian souvenir, you can buy a Spitfire T-shirt over the counter.

198 C5 ⊠ 7 Sharia al Bursa al Qadima, off Sharia Saad Zaghloul ☎ 03-480 6503 ⊙ Daily noon–1am

THE OASES

Abdu's £

If you're on a tight budget, and even if you're not, this simple restaurant is the best in Siwa. It serves traditional Egyptian dishes and vegetable stews, as well as couscous and pizzas, and the yoghurt and pancakes are particularly recommended for breakfast. You might also pick up some useful tips about the oases here.

Off map 198 A5 ⊠ Siwa Town ☎ 046-460 1243 ⊙ Daily 8:30am–midnight

Ahmad Hamdy £

Another popular backpackers' meeting place, the Ahmad Hamdy serves not only the usual roast

chicken, kebabs and vegetable stews, but also delicious fresh lime juice and ice-cold beers.

Off map 200 A1 ⊠ Sharia al Saura, Mut, Dakhla Oasis ☎ 092-782 0767 ⊙ Daily 24 hours

Aquasun Farafra £

At this pleasant outdoor restaurant, freshly prepared Egyptian and Western dishes are served. Ingredients are mostly plucked straight from the restaurant's own organic garden.

198 A1 ⊠ Bir Sitta, Farafra ☎ 012-225 9660 ⊙ Daily 8am–10pm

Al Badawiyya Hotel Restaurant £–££

By far the best option in town, the Badawiyya has a shady courtyard and serves a selection of relatively expensive, but well-prepared standards, such as pasta dishes and chicken and rice, to weary desert travellers.

198 A1 ⊠ Farafra ☎ 092-751 0060/ 012-214 8343 ⊙ Daily 7am–11pm

Beausite Restaurant ££

The menu offers old-fashioned Graeco-Mediterranean food of the sort that once dominated Alexandrian cuisine. This beachside restaurant is spacious, a bit like a very large domestic dining room, and one member of the family of patrons is usually around to welcome newcomers, or to chat to the many returning regulars.

Off map 198 A5 ⊠ Sharia al Shati, Marsa Matruh ☎ 03-493 8555 ⊙ Daily breakfast, lunch and dinner

Dunes £

A very relaxed restaurant-bar, Dunes offers a large menu including vegetable stews, stuffed pigeon, pastas and couscous – some specialities need to be ordered in advance. Most of the day people hang out, drink tea and play backgammon, while puffing on a sheesha (water pipe).

Off map 198 A5 ⊠ Just off the central square, on Gebel Dakrour road, Siwa town ☎ 010-653 0372 ⊙ Daily all day

Kenooz £

Kenooz is set in a shady palm grove so you can eat in the shade of palm trees, and a palm tree grows up through the middle of the interior. The menu features authentic Egyptian and Siwan dishes and grills, as well as fruit juices and drinks. Go for tea and a water pipe on the delightful roof terrace as the food can be disappointing at times.

🚹 Off map 198 A5 ☒ Shali Lodge, Sharia Subukha, Siwa ☎ 046-460 1299 ⓒ Daily 8am–midnight

Popular Restaurant £ (also known as Bayyumi's)

This is the only restaurant outside the hotels in this oasis. Bayyumi, the owner, serves a basic selection of meat and vegetable stews, bread, omelettes, rice and soup. The restaurant is a meeting place for both locals and tourists and is the place to go for a cold beer.

🚹 198 B2 ☒ Main intersection of al Bawiti, Bahariya ⓒ Daily 5:30am–10pm

Tala Ranch £

Have dinner in a Bedouin tent, or stay in one of the ranch's six beautiful rooms. Sherif organises wonderful camel trips in the surrounding desert while his wife cooks up four-course meals in Egyptian-Bedouin style. The desert skies offer gorgeous star-watching after dinner. Call ahead as the owners are not always there.

🚹 Off map 198 A5 ☒ Gebel Dakrour ☎ 010-588 6003; www.talaranch-hotel.com ⓒ Dinner only on request

Tanta Wa Cafeteria & Restaurant £

A relaxed and "cool running" café-restaurant, this place is in a mudbrick structure overlooking Cleopatra's Bath. Here you will find salads, pastas, milkshakes and delicious fruit smoothies. If eating is too tiring you can relax in one of the hammocks.

🚹 Off map 198 A5 ☒ Next to Cleopatra's Bath ☎ 010-472 9539 ⓒ Daily 8am–11pm

Where to...
Shop

ALEXANDRIA

Alexandria has a small *souk* off Midan Tahrir selling cheap items. Alternatively, the **Attarin Market** has an amazing variety of antiques and junk shops, crammed into a maze of alleys. Dealers know the value of their stock, but there's still the occasional bargain. And if not, it's an atmospheric neighbourhood.

THE OASES

Most handicrafts sold in the Western oases are made of camel hair. **Ganoub Traditional Handicrafts** on Sharia Misr in Bawiti, has a selection of good crafts from the oasis, and the **al Badawiyya Hotel** in Farafra sells camel-hair hand-knitted socks and

sweaters made by the locally nicknamed "Dr Socks".

Siwa has a rich craft tradition, but most of the older pieces were sold to foreign collectors long ago, so most of what's on sale is new. Siwans traditionally wear large, heavy silver jewellery, including a wedding ring which covers half the hand. The oasis is also famous for its embroidery, with green, red, orange and black thread. The **Adrere Amellal** (➤ 145–146) has a shop with the best and priciest of Siwan crafts, but for something more authentic try **Siwa Original Handicrafts**, next to Abdu's restaurant (➤ 148) and even better **Siwa Traditional Handicraft** around the corner on the main market square (tel: 010-304 1191), which has embroidered clothes.

Where to...
Be Entertained

ALEXANDRIA

Alexandria's efforts to sustain a cultural life on a par with Cairo are slowly paying off. The old Sayyid Darwish Theatre (22 Sharia al Hurriya; tel: 03-486 5106) has been beautifully restored, and now houses the small *bijou* **Alexandrian Opera House** with performances of opera and classical concerts. The **Bibliotheca Alexandrina** (▶ 137) is the most important cultural venue in town, hosting international festivals of music, art and culture, as well as major international concerts. **The Alexandria Centre of Arts** (1 Sharia al Hurriya; tel 03-495 6633) has regular exhibitions and weekly concerts. **L'Atelier** (8 Sharia Victor Bassili; tel: 03-482 0526) has regular films, lectures

and exhibitions, as does the British Council (11 Sharia Mahmoud Abou al Ela, Kafr Abdu, Rushdi; tel: 03-545 6512) and the **Centre Culturel Français** (30 Sharia Nabi Danyal; tel: 03-391 8952). For listings of events and exhibitions check the monthly *Egypt Today*.

Beyond that, nightlife is pretty minimal, although it does perk up in summer. Several hotels offer a belly dance show, the best and most lively being at the **Helnan Palestine** or the nearby **Muntazah Sheraton**.

Most Alexandrian families hang out in one of the city's shopping malls, which offer cafés, restaurants, cinemas and other entertainments. For the more active, the **Delta Hash House Harriers** organise weekly runs and walks in the countryside around Alexandria on

Fridays at 2pm from September to June. Everybody is welcome and the meeting point is at the Portuguese Cultural Centre, Sharia Kafr Abdu, Rushdi. You can get more information about the walks and runs from www.geocities.com/ deltahhh and Howard Wellman (tel: 03-545 4364).

THE OASES

Nights are long in the oases, but if you're lucky you may find a cool beer on a café terrace, a water pipe to smoke in the company of locals or a light bright enough to read by. The only daytime entertainment, apart from quiet walks in the palm groves and outings to the desert, is bathing in the hot springs. But springs in town should be avoided, especially by women, as they're too public. More isolated springs are often delightful, but women are not advised to visit these alone. To get to some springs you'll need your own transport or you can join

a trip organised by local restaurants or hotels, on which you'll see some spectacular desert scenery as well. Most will also offer overnight stays in the desert, which are recommended.

If you want to see more of the desert, you'll need careful planning, an experienced desert guide and a four-wheel drive vehicle. Reliable and experienced guides have set up to travel companies: Ahmed al Mestekawi used to conduct desert patrols and now runs **Zarzora Expedition** (tel: 02-761 8105; www.zarzora.com) with expeditions to the Great Sand Sea, the oases and the Gilf al Kebir. **Egypt Off Road** (tel: 010-147 5462; www.egyptoffroad.com) is a reputable desert operator. The owner Peter Gaballa has taught many expat desert fans how to drive in the desert, and he organises the most fabulous desert tours, including a two-week trip to the Gilf al Kebir. The experienced rally driver **Hisham Nessin** (tel: 012-780 7999; www.raid4x4egypt.com) arranges some great desert tours of up to two weeks into the Western Desert.

Red Sea and Sinai

Getting Your Bearings

The main attractions of the Red Sea and Sinai are underwater: whatever their experience, there isn't a diver in the world who wouldn't want to explore these crystal waters. The Red Sea is home to some of the world's most amazing coral reefs, with about 1,500 different fish species and 150 types of coral. Much of the coastline of Sinai and the mainland is being developed, partly to exploit the diving possibilities, but also because of the area's year-round sunshine and beautiful beaches. Most resorts have a wide range of accommodation, and internationally accredited dive clubs.

In contrast to the hedonism along its coast, Sinai also has its spiritual side and is holy to Jews, Christians and Muslims. This was where Moses received the Ten Commandments and led the Hebrews across the parted Red Sea. The Holy Family also passed this way after fleeing Herod's wrath. For millennia Christian hermits have settled near Wadi Feiran and Muslim pilgrims have passed by on their way to Mecca.

A wild, rugged shoreline borders the Red Sea at Ras Muhammad

Surrounding the deep blue waters of the Red Sea is the harsh desert and barren, rugged mountains that inspired Egypt's early Christians to build the first monasteries – St Anthony's and St Paul's. Since ancient times people have also come in search of the gold that is found around Wadi Hammamat, turquoise from mines around Serabit al Khadem and more recently phosphates, which are mined in the Eastern Desert.

The Suez Canal separates Africa and Asia and, although the canal cities have lost most of their lustre, historic Ismailiya and Port Said still make a pleasant change from the rest of the coast.

★ Don't Miss

At Your Leisure

The Red Sea provides some of the best diving sites in the world

In Five Days

If you're not quite sure where to begin your travels, this itinerary recommends a practical and enjoyable five days in Red Sea and Sinai, taking in some of the best places to see using the Getting Your Bearings map on the previous page. For more information see the main entries.

Day One

Morning
From your base in **8 Sharm al Sheikh** (➤ 166–167), hire a car or book a taxi for the day and make the 30-minute drive to **3 Ras Muhammad National Park** (➤ 163). Stop at the Visitors' Centre for a video show of the park's highlights. Divers can take a boat to the Shark Reefs or The Mushroom, while others can snorkel at Anemone City or the Mangrove Channel. You can have lunch at the Visitors' Centre, but the park also has some great beaches to picnic.

Afternoon
Late afternoon, return to Naama Bay in Sharm al Sheikh for a stroll along the beach walkway and then dinner at the Hilton's fish restaurant.

Day Two

Morning
Once again arrange a car and start with a 90-minute or so drive to **9 Dahab** (➤ 167–168) where you can stop for a swim or snorkel at the **Canyon** (➤ 157) a bit farther up the coast. Have lunch at one of the numerous beach restaurants that line the bay of Asilah in Dahab.

Afternoon
After lunch drive inland for about two hours to the St Catherine area and start your ascent of **2 Mount Moses** (right, ➤ 160, also known as Mount Sinai) at around 5pm (earlier in winter) in time to watch the spectacular sunset over the desert mountains. Take the long and easy route up the

camel path (about three hours) and descend by the muscle-wrenching Steps of Repentance, which will take about 90 minutes. Stay at the monastery's auberge (➤ 171).

Day Three

Morning
If you missed the sunset, you can see the even more spectacular sunrise by rising very early (check with the monastery for exact times). Later visit **2 St Catherine's Monastery** (right, ➤ 160), and admire its amazing icon collection.

Afternoon
Drive back to Sharm al Sheikh for a late lunch and a swim, then catch the 6pm ferry to Hurghada in time for dinner and an overnight stop.

Day Four

Morning
Spend the morning diving in the area (➤ 156–159), or visit **6 Hurghada's** Red Sea Aquarium (➤ 166) and take a trip in the **Sindbad Submarine** (➤ 166). Have lunch in Hurghada Town, perhaps swapping stories with divers in Papa's Bar (➤ 174).

Afternoon
After lunch drive to al Gouna (about 20km/12 miles north of Hurghada) for a swim and dinner later in Gouna Town. Stay overnight in al Gouna.

Day Five

Morning
Pack a picnic for lunch and get a car or taxi for the two-hour drive into the desert to **4 St Paul's Monastery** (right, ➤ 164–165), around 200km (125 miles) north. It's then another 82km (51 miles) from there to **St Anthony's Monastery**.

Afternoon
After lunch it's a six-hour drive to Cairo so that you can arrive there in time for dinner.

⓪ Red Sea Diving

For many divers and snorkellers the Red Sea is sheer paradise. Its easily accessible coral reefs are among the most fascinating in the world, with deep coral walls, lagoons and submerged gardens teeming with a variety of sealife. The sun shines most of the year, the sparkling waters are warm and the visibility is generally crystal clear.

The Red Sea lies along the northern section of the Great Rift Valley, which runs from the Jordan Valley, through the Dead Sea, across Kenya and Tanzania and down to Mozambique. The Red Sea is about 1,930km (1,200 miles) long and can reach a depth of 1,850m (6,070 feet).

A school of Red Sea bannerfish, observed by a scuba diver

The Nature of Coral

The sea's tropical reefs are built from corals – primitive animals closely related to sea anemones. Each coral is made

PROTECTING THE REEFS

Egypt's coral reefs have suffered both at the hands of hotel builders and the tourists, so it's extremely important to protect them:

- Don't touch the corals and certainly never stand on them.
- Avoid kicking up sand, as it smothers the corals.
- Don't fish or feed the fish.
- Don't collect or buy any shells, corals or other marine souvenirs.

Clownfish are one of the many species thriving in the Red Sea

up of a mass of minute polyps that grow together in a colony. When a colony dies, another one grows on top of its skeleton, so only the outermost layer of the reef is alive. Corals grow very slowly, around 1–10cm (0.5–4 inches) a year, but the size of a colony can vary from a few centimetres to a few metres. Some are hundreds of years old. The most prolific coral growths are found in shallow, well-lit waters that are warm enough (at least 18.5°C/65°F) to allow zooxanthellae (microscopic plants on which corals depend) to thrive.

Three types of reef are found in Egypt. Fringing reefs lie in shallow water near land. Barrier reefs grow along the edges of islands and continental shelves and tend to be separated from the shore by a lagoon. Patch reefs are mounds of coral that grow out of the seabed. Between the shore and the seaward reef is the back reef, a mixture of sand, coral and rubble.

Spectacular Sealife

Even on the patchiest corals you might find small gobi, snappers, triggerfish, emperors and sea urchins, as well as bottom-dwelling species burrowing in the sand. In protected lagoons you might see wonderful varieties of seaweed and seagrasses. Most divers head straight for the reef fronts, with their spectacular features and variety of marine life. The top

SINAI'S TOP FIVE DIVING AND SNORKELLING SITES

- **Blue Hole** (a few kilometres north of Dahab). This large lagoon on top of a 300m (984-foot) vertical shaft features hard corals and a variety of fish on the outer reef. Beware that diving deep down is extremely dangerous and has claimed many lives.
- **The Canyon** (near the Blue Hole, Dahab). This narrow, extremely beautiful canyon has plenty of corals and a range of reef fish that can even be seen by new divers. But only experienced divers should attempt the deep exit out of the canyon.
- **The Islands** (near the Laguna Hotel, Dahab). A magnificent seascape covered with the most diverse and well-preserved corals in the area, with an amazing variety of fish. The added attraction here is a large amphitheatre, halfway along the reef, where schools of barracudas are common. It's also excellent for snorkelling.
- **End of the Road Reef** (north of Sharm al Sheikh). This submerged island has some of the best corals in Egypt and an abundance of fish.
- **Ras Ghozlani** (Ras Muhammad, ▶ 163). the most beautiful spot on the south coast features plenty of small reef species and well-preserved corals.

TOP MAINLAND SPOTS FOR DIVING AND SNORKELLING

■ **Shaab Abu Ramada** (The Aquarium), about 15km (9 miles) south of Hurghada. This shallow reef is home to the tiniest reef fish, stingrays, barracuda, tuna and grey sharks.

■ **Carless (Careless) Reef**, 5km (3 miles) north of Giftun Island. Divers from all over the world come to see the population of semi-tame moray eels, untamed sharks and jacks.

■ **Green Hole**, 59km (37 miles) north of al Quseyr. Excellent for both snorkelling and diving, this stunning coral growth is home to dolphins and blue-eagle rays.

■ **Beit Goha**, 20km (12 miles) north of al Quseyr. An exceptional and very shallow coral labyrinth harbours elaborate canyons and exquisite coral gardens.

■ **Sirena Beach Home Reef**, Mövenpick Sirena Beach Hotel, al Quseyr. Off the hotel's jetty is a fantastic reef with a variety of corals and fish (➤ 171).

20m (65 feet) attracts many of the most brightly coloured species, including damselfish, butterflyfish, clownfish and snappers. Even sharks are known to thrive here.

Racoon butterflyfish live among the coral reef

Try a Dive

Most hotels in Sinai and along the coast have a diving centre (or arrangements with one), with boats, equipment and experienced instructors and snorkelling equipment for rent or to buy (➤ 159). Egypt's diving centres are a relatively inexpensive way to learn open-water diving and earn a PADI (Professional Association of Diving Instructors) or CMAS (Confédération Mondiale des Activités Subaquatiques/World Underwater Federation) certificate, which enables you to dive anywhere in the world.

Around Sharm al Sheikh and along most of the mainland coast diving is done offshore from a boat. But beyond Dahab and Nuweiba you can easily swim out to the reefs, and Sinai in particular offers some interesting snorkelling opportunities along almost the entire coast. In Hurghada, most snorkelling and diving sites are accessible only by boat. The most popular day trip is to Giftun Island with opportunities for snorkelling before and after lunch.

Ras Muhammad National Park has some good spots for a picnic, and Hurghada and Dahab have plenty of eating places and watering holes.

The following are among the better-established and more reputable diving centres.

Sharm al Sheikh
✛ 201 E3
Camel Dive Club ✉ Naama Bay ☎ 069-360 0700; www.cameldive.com
Oonas Diving Centre ✉ Naama Bay ☎ 069-360 0581; www.oonasdivers.com
Red Sea Diving College ✉ Naama Bay ☎ 063-360 0145; www.redseacollege.com
Sinai Divers ✉ Ghazala Hotel ☎ 069-360 0697; www.sinaidivers.com

Dahab
✛ 201 F3
Fish & Friends ✉ Masbat ☎ 069-364 0720; www.fishandfriends.com
Nesima Diving Center ✉ Nesima Hotel ☎ 069-364 0320; www.nesima-resort.com

Hurghada
✛ 201 E2
Aquanaut ✉ Corniche, al Dahar ☎ 065-354 9891; www.aquanaut.net
Easy Divers ✉ Corniche, al Dahar ☎ 065-354 7816; www.easydivers-redsea.com
Jasmin Diving ✉ Jasmin Village ☎ 065-346 0475; www.jasmin-diving.com

Marsa Allam
Red Sea Diving Safari ✉ Marsa Shagra ☎ 02-337 1833/065-338 0021; www.redsea-divingsafari.com

---

RED SEA DIVING: INSIDE INFO

Top tip The best time to dive is spring or autumn. In summer, temperatures below the surface are pleasant, but out of the water it can be unbearably hot. From March to June, the *khamsin*, a hot desert wind bringing dust and sand, may blow. During the winter the water can be too cold for snorkelling without a wetsuit.

Hidden gems The hundreds of kilometres of coast south of al Quseyr are still mostly untouched, with spectacular unpolluted reefs, but many are accessible only to experienced divers.

2 Mount Moses and St Catherine's Monastery

For centuries pilgrims have climbed Gebel Musa (Mount Moses or Mount Sinai) to visit the site where Moses is believed to have received the Ten Commandments. Some make the ascent for the spectacular mountain views, while others search for a more spiritual experience.

Mount Moses rises 2,285m (7,500 feet) above sea level and can be climbed via two routes. The easiest (and longest) route follows a camel path and takes about three hours. The other path, known as Sikkat Sayyidna Musa (Path of our Lord Moses), takes around 90 minutes but is far more exhausting because it leads up the 3,750 steep Steps of Repentance, hewn by monks.

Deir Sant Katarin (St Catherine's Monastery)

At the foot of Mount Moses is the remarkable 6th-century Greek Orthodox monastery of Christian martyr St Catherine of Alexandria, built on the supposed site of the Burning Bush. In AD 337 the Byzantine Empress Helena built a chapel over the Burning Bush, which had already attracted many pilgrims and hermits. Emperor Justinian then enlarged and fortified it in the 6th century. About 20 monks, mostly from Mount Athos in Greece, now live at the monastery. However, the rapid expansion of tourism along the coast and the many day trippers threaten the peace of the monastery.

The entrance to the monastery is a small gate in the massive granite walls, near Kléber's Tower. To the right is Moses' Well, where the prophet met his future wife Zippora, while a left turn leads to an enclosure with a thorny bush, a cutting from the Burning Bush – the original is inside the chapel.

Right: The basilica of St Catherine dominates the monastery compound

---

THE TEN COMMANDMENTS

According to the scriptures (Exodus 3), God revealed himself to Moses as a flame of fire in the Burning Bush (also associated with Sinai), and told the prophet to lead the people of Israel out of Egypt to escape hardship under the pharaoh. The people fled to Sinai and Moses spent 40 days on the mountain, where God communicated the Ten Commandments to him, which were written on two stone tablets. Sinai is sacred to the Jewish community, Christians and Muslims because the Ten Commandments became the basis of Christian and Jewish religion, and the incident is also recounted in the Quran.

A CHRISTIAN MARTYR
Born in AD 294 to an Alexandrian family, St Catherine was tortured for her faith on a spiked wheel, which broke and beheaded her. This later inspired the Catherine wheel firework and heraldry symbol. Her remains are said to have been taken to Sinai by angels.

The granite Basilica of St Catherine, entered through original cedar doors, has 12 magnificent pillars, one for each month of the year, decorated with a saint's icon. The iconostasis (altar screen) is 17th century, but the sanctuary beyond it houses the Mosaic of the Transfiguration (AD 550–600), a masterpiece of Byzantine art. The icon collection is unique and covers 1,400 years, including the period between 746 and 842 when the monks in this isolated monastery were unaware of the injunction banning Christians from painting the Holy Family or saints. The precious collection of early manuscripts is not on public display.

TAKING A BREAK

Bedouins often sell tea at the top of the mountain, but don't count on it – take your own food and drink. Al Milga village has restaurants and little shops where you can stock up for a picnic. Simple meals are included if you're staying at the monastery's hostel.

A 6th-century Byzantine mosaic of the Transfiguration

✚ 201 E3
✉ Sinai interior, 450km (280 miles) from Cairo, 140km (90 miles) west of Dahab ☎ 02-2402 8513 (Cairo) ◷ Mon–Wed, Fri and Sun 9–noon; closed public holidays; check in advance 🍴 Café/restaurant (£) 🚌 Buses from Cairo, Sharm al Sheikh, Dahab and Nuweiba to St Catherine village (al Milga), 2km (1 mile) from the monastery ✈ Egypt Air flights to Sharm al Sheikh
🎫 Free

MOUNT MOSES AND ST CATHERINE'S MONASTERY: INSIDE INFO

Top tips The **climb up Mount Moses** is spectacular, both at dawn and dusk, and you can take in both by bringing a sleeping bag and staying outdoors in Elijah's Basin, near the summit. You can leave your luggage in the monastery's storeroom.
■ **Take lots of water** for the intense heat, but also come prepared with suitable gear, as it can snow here in winter. **Temperatures drop dramatically** at night, even in summer.
■ **Dress modestly** when visiting the monastery.

In more depth You need to obtain **special permission** to see the Chapel of the Burning Bush.
■ The St Catherine Protectorate publishes a good **guide to the monastery**, as well as some excellent walking guides to the surrounding area (tel: 069-347 0032; www.st-katherine.net).
■ Visitors to the mountains **must be accompanied by a Bedouin guide**, which can be organised through Mountain Tours' office at al Milga, Sheikh Mousa (tel: 010-641 3575; www.sheikhmousa.com).

3 Ras Muhammad National Park

Egypt's first national park was created in 1988. Only 12 per cent of it is open to the public, and it can get crowded with day trippers from nearby Sharm al Sheikh. Nevertheless, so far the project has been extremely successful in protecting the area's outstanding ecosystem.

Spectacular scenery of Ras Muhammad is home to a plethora of wildlife

The park's underwater area has some of the Red Sea's most remarkable coral reefs, including the spectacular Anemone City. On land there's a lot of wildlife, including foxes, gazelles and ibexes, and the mangroves are a valuable breeding ground for migratory birds. Children love the warm shallow waters of Mangrove Channel and the Crevice Pools. The Visitor Centre has free telescopes, wildlife videos and details of park trails.

✚ 201 E2
✉ 30km (19 miles) northwest of Sharm al Sheikh ⏰ Daily 8–5
🍴 Restaurant at Visitor Centre (£–££). Sat–Thu 10–5 💰 Moderate, camping permits from the Visitor Centre (tel: 069-366 0668; www.rasmohamed.com)

RAS MUHAMMAD NATIONAL PARK: INSIDE INFO

Top tips You need a passport with an Egyptian visa to **enter the park**. Visitors on a Sinai-only permit can go by boat to Ras Muhammad (check with the dive company) but are not allowed to travel overland beyond Sharm al Sheikh.

■ If you want to **dive** you need to arrive on a boat tour in Ras Muhammad. If you come by car you can go snorkelling in some amazing spots, but you need to bring your own equipment.

4 St Anthony's and St Paul's Monasteries

The monasteries of Deir Anba Antunius and Deir Anba Bulos (St Anthony and St Paul), hidden in the barren Red Sea mountains, are the oldest Christian monasteries in Egypt. Monastic rituals were more or less invented here, where the life of the Coptic monks has barely changed in 1,600 years.

St Anthony's Monastery

St Anthony (➤ 24) moved to the desert in AD 294, settling first in a spot with palm trees. But when things became too crowded he moved to a cave in the mountain, where he lived for 25 years until his death at the age of 105. The monastery dedicated to him was founded around AD 361 by his disciples, who lived an ascetic life in a community. Surrounded by 12m-high (40-foot) walls, the monastery compound is dramatically located beneath a ridge of cliffs in the Wadi Araba, at the foot of St Anthony's Cave, covered in centuries of graffiti and supplications left by pilgrims. The views from the top are fantastic, and well worth the steep climb up 1,200

The peaceful Monastery of St Anthony is at the foot of the mountain where the saint went into retreat

steps. The monastery itself is home to about 65 monks and looks similar to an Egyptian village, with houses, churches and gardens. The oldest building is the Church of St Anthony, which contains the saint's tomb and beautiful 13th-century murals, the most impressive in Egypt.

St Paul's Monastery

St Paul the Ascetic (not to be confused with the apostle) settled here before St Anthony, and lived in his cave for 90 years until his death at the age of 113. He met St Anthony at the end of his life and recognised his spiritual superiority. The dilapidated monastery, built around his cave by St

St Anthony, depicted on an embroidery, retreated to a mountain cave at the age of 80

Paul's followers, is overshadowed by its larger neighbour. The Church of St Paul, filled with candles and murals, encloses the saint's cave. The 17th-century Church of St Michael has an icon of the Virgin attributed to St Luke (AD 40).

TAKING A BREAK

Both monasteries have cafés and St Paul's also has a grocery, but consider taking a picnic.

✚ 200 C4 ✉ St Anthony's: 50km (30 miles) west of Zafarana; St Paul's: 40km (25 miles) south of Zafarana ☎ St Paul's: 02-2590 0218; St Anthony's: 02-2590 6025 ◉ St Anthony's: daily 7–5; St Paul's: daily 8–3. Dec and Lent: Fri, Sat and Sun. Closed Holy Week 🚍 Take a taxi or tour (► below). Buses from Suez to Hurghada stop 26km (16 miles) south of Zafarana; then walk 13km (8 miles) to St Anthony's. To get to St Paul's stop at the turn off on the Suez–Hurghada road, near Zafarana lighthouse, then walk for 14km (9 miles).

ST ANTHONY'S AND ST PAUL'S MONASTERIES: INSIDE INFO

Top tips The easiest, although perhaps not the most satisfying, way to visit both monasteries is by taking an organised tour from Cairo or Hurghada.

- At both monasteries there is an English-speaking monk who can give a guided tour (free, but donations welcome).
- The guesthouse at St Paul's only accommodates pilgrims (tel: 02-2590 0218), but both monasteries have a small cafeteria serving a selection of drinks and snacks.
- Take plenty of water while visiting the monasteries and the mountains.

In more depth Experienced walkers can hike along a trail in the hills between the two monasteries in about two days. Maps are available from St Anthony's.

At Your Leisure

5 Al Quseyr

You can enjoy some of the best snorkelling along the coast at this sleepy fishing town. The beaches here are beautiful, and the peace and quiet make this an agreeable alternative to Hurghada. Until the 10th century al Quseyr was the largest port on the coast and even in the 19th century there was regular traffic. The remains of a 16th-century fort, built by Sultan Selim, are a reminder of the town's former significance.

🛟 200 E1 ✉ 80km (50 miles) south of Hurghada 🍴 Al Quseir Hotel (£; ➤ 171) 🚌 Daily buses from Cairo, Qena, Suez, Hurghada and Marsa Alam

6 Hurghada

Since about 1980 al Ghardaqa (Hurghada) has grown from a tiny fishing village into Egypt's largest resort, and it's still expanding along the coast. The sprawling town and *souk* have little character, but the offshore reefs are a diver's delight and the beaches, with a warm sea for most of the year, offer all manner of watersports. The Sindbad Submarine (to book tel: 065-344 4688;

www.sinbad-group.com) and the small Red Sea Aquarium (6 Sharia al Corniche, ad-Dahar; tel: 065-354 8557) give an enjoyable insight into reef life.

🛟 201 E2 ✉ 529km (330 miles) southeast of Cairo, 299km (185 miles) northeast of Luxor ☎ 065-344 4420 (tourist office) 🍴 Several 🚌 Regular buses from Cairo, Luxor, Aswan and Suez ✈ Flights daily from Cairo, three per week from Luxor, and weekly from Sharm al Sheikh and St Catherine ⛴ Ferry from Sharm al Sheikh several times a week (tel: 065-344 7571; www.intlfastferries.com)

7 Al Gouna

The mainland's most stylish resort is built on a series of islands and lagoons. Wealthy Cairenes own villas here, while tourists stay at the beautiful luxury hotels. The complex also includes an 18-hole golf course, a private airport (➤ 37), aquarium and a small museum with replicas of ancient Egyptian treasures.

🛟 201 D2 ✉ 30km (19 miles) north of Hurghada 🚕 Taxis from Hurghada ✈ Flights to Cairo with SunAir (tel: 02-2267 5379; www.sunair-eg.com)

8 Sharm al Sheikh

The Israelis developed Sharm al Sheikh during their occupation of

The beach resort of Hurghada

Naama Bay at Sharm al Sheikh

Sinai (1967–82), both for military purposes and as a holiday resort. But since the Egyptians returned Sharm has become one of the Red Sea's most popular and high-quality resorts. The highest concentration of hotels and restaurants is at Naama Bay, which is known for its excellent watersports facilities, but hotels have now also spread into the neighbouring bays. On the cliff north of Naama Bay is Sharm's residential area, with villas and condominiums mostly inhabited by staff working at the hotels. Here also is the first Ritz hotel in Africa. Most of Sharm's treasures are under water – the only sight on land is Ras

Kennedy, a rock vaguely resembling the face of former US president John F Kennedy.

🚗 201 E3 ✉ 470km (290 miles) from Cairo 🍴 Several 🚌 Buses from Cairo, Dahab, Nuweiba, Suez and Taba ✈ Domestic flights from Cairo, Luxor and Hurghada 🚢 Ferry from Hurghada several times a week (tel: 069-260 0190; www.intlfastferries.com)

9 Dahab

Dahab, which means "gold" in Arabic, has superb beaches and some of Sinai's best dive sites near by (➤ 157), although the town itself is a bit of a mess. It's divided into three distinct parts: the Bedouin settlement of Asilah; the hotel area of al Mashraba; and al Masbat, which is made up of cheap campsites and hotels, where old hippies and young backpackers rave and hang out. The strip of seafront bars and restaurants serve typical backpacker staples such as spaghetti, milkshakes and banana pancakes. Young Egyptians associate Dahab with drug culture but, although things may appear relaxed, the Egyptian police are taking a tougher line and penalties are severe. The real attractions here as elsewhere along the coast are underwater,

Dahab is a traditional Bedouin settlement that has embraced tourism

particularly the dangerous Blue Hole, the Canyon and other nearby reefs. Alternatively, Bedouin organise camel treks into the spectacular desert interior.

➕ 201 F3 ✉ 100km (60 miles) northwest of Sharm al Sheikh 🍴 Bars, restaurants in the bay of Asilah (££) 🚌 Buses from Sharm al Sheikh, Taba, Nuweiba, Cairo and St Catherine

🔟 Ismailiya

Ismailiya's renovated and tree-shaded old town, built at the same time as the Suez Canal, makes for a pleasant walk. Start on Muhammad Ali Quay at the Swiss-style house of Ferdinand de Lesseps, the canal's French architect. Near by is the Ismailiya Museum's collection of ancient artefacts. Around Lake Timsah (Crocodile Lake) are several good beaches and restaurants. One of the best views of the canal is from Nemra Setta, a lovely garden suburb with colonial villas.

➕ 199 F4 ✉ 120km (75 miles) east of Cairo, 85km (53 miles) from Port Said ☎ 064-332 1078 (tourist office in Governorate Building, Sharia Sheikh Zayeed) 🎫 Ismailiya Museum daily 8–4, closed Fri 11:30–1:30; to visit de Lesseps House check with the tourist office 🍴 George's (££; ➤ 174) 🚌 Buses from Cairo, Hurghada and Port Said, Sinai

🔟 Suez Canal

Before the 167km (104-mile) Suez Canal opened in 1869, linking the Mediterranean to the Red Sea, European ships had to sail around southern Africa to reach the East, so it halved the distance between Europe and Asia.

The concept wasn't new. The idea of a canal cutting through the desert had already occurred to the 7th-century BC pharaoh Necho II, but an oracle dissuaded him from

---

SIX THINGS FOR THE CHILDREN

■ See the corals and fish from the **Sindbad submarine** in Hurghada (➤ 166).
■ **Red Sea Aquarium**, Hurghada, with colourful local fish and corals (➤ 166).
■ **Camel rides** in Naama Bay, al Gouna or Hurghada beach.
■ **Fun Town Amusement Park**, Naama Bay (tel: 069-360 2556).
■ Most 5-star PADI centres in Sinai and Red Sea offer a **PADI "Bubble Maker"** course for children between the ages of 8 and 10, for a 2m (6 feet) dive.
■ **Ghibli go-karting** centre in Sharm has a 220m (240 yards) track and small cadet go-karts designed for children.

completing the project. A century later the Persians dug a small canal, but it fell out of use over the centuries.

Work on the Suez Canal began in 1859, under the supervision of Frenchman Ferdinand de Lesseps. It took 10 years and 25,000 workers to finish and is still one of the world's greatest feats of engineering. When President Nasser (▶ 26) nationalised the Suez Canal in 1956 in response to the West's refusal to help finance the Aswan High Dam, Britain, France and Israel retaliated by bombing the area. The canal cities suffered further damage during the Arab-Israel wars (1948 to 1973), when the canal was closed and the city of Suez more or less levelled (it has yet to recover). Since the canal reopened in 1975, it has been Egypt's second-largest source of revenue, after tourism.

✚ 199 F5 ✉ Between Bur Said (Port Said) and Ismailiya 🚌 Buses from Cairo, Hurghada, Port Said and Ismailiya

🖩 Port Said

Brothels and hashish dens have long disappeared from the free port of Bur Said (Port Said), once dubbed "the wickedest town in the East", but a hint of its former seedy atmosphere lingers in the back streets. This relaxed town is a popular, cheap shopping destination for Egyptians as its bazaar sells international brands. It's also a stopover for Mediterranean cruise liners, but there are few sights apart from the Suez Canal, which is best viewed from the free ferry across to Port Fuad. In the early evening the locals stroll along the Corniche to watch the vessels on the canal. A new Suez Canal Museum is being constructed on Sharia Safia Zaghloul. The Military Museum (Sharia 23 July) illustrates the Suez Canal's troubled history.

✚ 199 F5 ✉ 225km (140 miles) from Cairo, 85km (53 miles) north of Ismailiya ☎ 066-323 4657 (tourist office) 🕐 Military Museum Sat–Thu 9–4 🚌 Buses from Cairo, Suez, Ismailiya and Hurghada

Port Said's harbour at the entrance of the Suez Canal

THE STATUE OF LIBERTY
New York's most famous landmark was originally intended to stand at the entrance to the Suez Canal, at Port Said. Inspired by the colossi of Ramses II (▶ 100), the French sculptor Bartholdi (1834–1904) designed a huge woman representing "Egypt carrying the light of Asia". Khedive Ismail (viceroy of Egypt 1863–79) loved this grand idea, but later decided it was too expensive, so the statue was presented to the United States.

Where to... Stay

Prices
The prices are for a double room per night.

£ under 400LE	££ 400–900LE
£££ over 900LE	

Since the late 1980s Sinai's coast has developed rapidly. Sharm al Sheikh in particular has seen a boom in hotels, most resembling small villages and part of international chains for package tourists. Budget options are rare, but there's a range of inexpensive hotels up the coast in Dahab.

SHARM AL SHEIKH

Camel Hotel ££

This lovely hotel is built in local style with pleasant and clean rooms, and is close to the beach. The hotel is attached to a well-established diving centre.

➕ 201 E3 ⌨ King of Bahrein Street, Naama Bay ☎ 069-360 0700; www.cameldive.com

Four Seasons Sharm al Sheikh £££

The Four Seasons Sharm al Sheikh is the most stunning five-star hotel in town with unequalled levels of service and comfort. Built in a Moorish style overlooking the Straits of Tiran, the Four Seasons offers large suite-size rooms with fabulous views. The hotel has a pool and watersports are available.

➕ 201 E3 ⌨ North of Naama Bay ☎ 069-360 3555; www.fourseasons.com/sharmelsheikh

Sanafir ££

One of the older hotels in town, the Sanafir has white domed rooms, decorated in traditional Egyptian style, set on several levels around a lagoon-shaped pool. There's also a waterfall and several lounge terraces with Bedouin sofas. Service is particularly friendly, attracting a young crowd that likes the nightlife and does not mind the noise. The diving centre is renowned.

➕ 201 E3 ⌨ Naama Bay ☎ 069-360 0197; www.sanafirhotel.com

Shark's Bay Bedouin Home £

One of the few budget options in Sharm, this is a Bedouin-owned camp on the beach and has simple but clean huts with or without bathroom. The restaurant is good.

➕ 201 E3 ⌨ Shark's Bay, 3km (2 miles) south of Sharm ☎ 069-360 0942; www.sharksbay.com

DAHAB

Nesima ££

This stylish and wonderfully relaxed hotel is one of the few in Sinai to be specifically aimed at the individual traveller. The very comfortable, well-designed domed rooms overlook a beautiful swimming pool. The hotel is popular with divers of all levels and has an excellent diving centre offering equipment and tuition.

➕ 201 F3 ⌨ Al Mashraba ☎ 069-364 0320; www.nesima-resort.com

ST CATHERINE

Al-Karm Ecolodge £–££

Al-Karm is a small eco-hotel built with European Union funding but owned by the Bedouin, under the supervision of St Catherine's Protectorate. Built in local stone and with no electricity, this place is all about simplicity and being in tune with the amazing surroundings of St Catherine.

🚏 201 E3 ⌂ Sheikh Awaad, 20km (12 miles) from St Catherine ☎ 069-347 0032; www.parksegypt.org/en/node/109

Auberge St Catherine £–££

The obvious place to stay in St Catherine is this refurbished hostel at the monastery, which offers 150 beds in single, double or triple accommodation, with breakfast and evening meal included. Rooms overlook an orchard. You can leave your luggage here while you climb Mount Moses.

🚏 201 E3 ⌂ St Catherine's Monastery ☎ 069-347 0353

AL GOUNA

Dawar al Omda ££

The Dawar al Omda (Mayor's House), built on a man-made island in a lagoon, is an inventive mix of modern architecture and traditional Egyptian features. The stylish interior is simply decorated with regional antiques and locally made furniture. The pool is small but there's good swimming near by in the lagoons.

🚏 201 D2 ⌂ Kafr al Gouna, Al Gouna ☎ 065-358 0063; www.dawarelomda-elgouna.com

HURGHADA

Giftun Beach Resort ££

One of the oldest resorts in town, Giftun is popular with divers and windsurfers for its excellent facilities, friendly staff and whitewashed beach chalets. At the lively bar divers exchange the stories of the day.

🚏 201 E2 ⌂ Resort strip, Hurghada ☎ 065-346 3040; www.giftunbeachresort.com

MARSA ALAM

Shaqra Ecolodge £

This delightful ecolodge run by the environmentalist Hossam Helmi offers simply furnished but comfortable rooms, total peace and quiet, and excellent diving or snorkelling opportunities. The same owner has several similar camps farther south.

🚏 201 E3 ⌂ Marsa Shagra ☎ 02-2337 1833; www.redsea-divingsafari.com

NUWEIBA

Basata £

Farther north on Sinai's eastern coast is a place like no other in Egypt. Basata is extremely popular with Europeans, Egyptians and Israelis who come to enjoy a relaxed and peaceful stay in this camp of simple beach huts and bungalows. Facilities are generally basic, but there is a desalination plant. The owner cares about the environment, so the preservation of the coral reef is a much-discussed topic at the simple, healthy communal meals. Drugs, alcohol and loud music are not allowed.

🚏 201 F4 ⌂ Ras al Burg on the Taba–Nuweiba road, 42km (26 miles) south of Taba ☎ 069-350 0480; www.basata.com

AL QUSEYR

Al Quseyr Hotel £

A charming hotel in a 1920s house on the seafront, the al Quseyr has just six rooms. The front rooms have the benefit of sea views, but all the rooms are atmospheric and comfortable, offering great value for money. Dinner is available upon request.

🚏 201 E1 ⌂ Sharia Port Said ☎ 065-333 2301

Mövenpick Sirena Beach £££

Inspired by traditional village architecture, the simple, comfortable domed rooms are in a pleasant garden. This resort is perfect for a peaceful holiday, with excellent service, good food and a large pool. It has some of Egypt's best snorkelling and diving from its private beach, and there's also a dive centre.

🚏 199 E1 ⌂ Al Quadim Bay, al Quseyr ☎ 065-333 2100; www.movenpick-quseir.com

Where to...
Eat and Drink

Prices
Expect to pay per person for a meal, excluding drinks and tips.
£ under 100LE **££** 100–150LE **£££** over 150LE

ST CATHERINE

Places to eat in St Catherine are rare, but the best option is probably the **Auberge St Catherine**. In the nearest village of al Milga there are a few basic eateries, including **Katrien Rest House** and **Ihlas**. Your best bet is to visit the bakery and local shops and enjoy a picnic in this wonderful landscape.

SHARM AL SHEIKH

Sharm al Sheikh, and particularly Naama Bay have no shortage of restaurants and bars, but most are in hotels, so food is expensive. However, in Sharm itself you can find cheaper places popular with Egyptians. As the majority of tourists in Sharm al Sheikh are Italian, you should have no problem finding good pizza or excellent pasta, although you can just about eat your way around the world here now. Even the Hard Rock Café has arrived, as have McDonald's, KFC and Pizza Hut.

Abu el Sid £££

Sister restaurant of the hip Egyptian restaurant in Cairo, this establishment serves the classic Egyptian *mezze* and other dishes in a trendy contemporary Egyptian setting, and with good Egyptian music. This place is very popular so book ahead.

➕ 201 E3 ⊠ Naama Bay, Sharm al Sheikh ☎ 069-360 3910; http://www.deyafa.net ⓒ Daily dinner

Al Fanar £££

Al Fanar is a delightful upmarket Italian restaurant on the waterfront serving delicious pizzas, the freshest fish and seafood. There are calming views over the sea.

➕ 201 E3 ⊠ Ras Um Sid ☎ 069-366 2218 ⓒ Daily 10am–10:30pm

The Fish ££–£££

One of the older restaurants in Sharm and just off the beach, it serves a good selection of fresh fish and seafood from its shrimp pond. The restaurant occupies a covered terrace, with nets and marine paraphernalia draped over pillars and walls. The cooking is excellent, but the service can be very slow.

Il Frantoio £££

This excellent and refined Italian restaurant has a lovely alfresco dining area, perfect on a warm evening. The food is inventive, using only the best ingredients – try the fresh raviolis, or grilled stuffed sea bass.

➕ 201 E3 ⊠ Hilton Fayrouz ☎ 069-360 0136 ⓒ Daily lunch and dinner

Little Buddha £££

The sister venue of the famous Paris Buddha Bar, this is definitely one of the places to be seen in Sharm. The massive lit up sweeping bar, the dark red walls, the classic Buddha Bar sounds, and a giant gold Buddha all set the tone, but the food is equally impressive. Sit at the bar and watch the delicious sushi being prepared, or dine at one of the tables and taste the inventive French-Asian fusion cuisine. Later

➕ 201 E3 ⊠ Four Seasons Hotel, north of Naama Bay ☎ 069-360 3555 ⓒ Daily lunch and dinner

in the night when the beat gets turned up, there is room to dance, or hang out on the Japanese futons.

➕ 201 E3 ⊠ Naama Bay Hotel, Naama Bay ☎ 069-360 1030; www.littlebuddha-sharm. com ⏰ Daily 6pm–3am

On Deck ££

This romantic restaurant is set on a platform on the sea. The sea is lit up at night so you can see the fish swim under your feet. Very good pastas and fresh seafood are the specialities here.

➕ 201 E3 ⊠ Lido Hotel, Centre of Naama Bay ☎ 069-360 2603 ⏰ Daily lunch and dinner

Pomodoro ££

A lovely Italian restaurant with indoor seating, Pomodoro has a great lively terrace to watch people walk by on the main strip. The hotel-diving centre and a popular bar. Indian restaurant and a popular bar.

➕ 201 E3 ⊠ Centre of Naama Bay ☎ 069-360 0700; www.cameldive.com/camel-restaurants.htm ⏰ Daily lunch and dinner

La Rustichella ££–£££

Sharm's many Italian residents and tourists love this charming Italian restaurant, where you can eat pasta almost as *la mamma* cooks it. Besides fresh pasta there is also plenty of fresh fish and seafood on the menu.

➕ 201 E3 ⊠ Behind Naama Bay ☎ 067-360 1154 ⏰ Daily lunch and dinner

Safsafa £–££

The original Safsafa in Sharm town is old and has only eight tables, but the new family-run restaurant is a much more upmarket eatery. The accent is still on fresh fish and seafood but, although stylish, it is low on atmosphere.

➕ 201 E3 ⊠ Naama Centre, Naama Bay ☎ 069-360 0150 ⏰ Daily lunch and dinner

Sala Thai £££

If you are looking for something special, other than the all available Egyptian or Italian food, then this is the place to head for. The classical Thai/Asian food at the Hyatt's

restaurant is exquisite and the interior is peacefully Asian with lots of teak wood and a pleasant terrace overlooking the sea.

➕ 201 E3 ⊠ Hyatt Regency Hotel ☎ 069-360 1234 ⏰ Daily lunch and dinner

TamTam ££

In this popular café and restaurant serving traditional Egyptian dishes such as *mezze*, salads, *meloukhiya* (soup made from a spinach-like vegetable, served with chicken or rabbit), *kushari* (macaroni, rice, onions, chickpeas and lentils topped with tomato sauce) and meat grills, the atmosphere is laid-back and joyous. Digest your food as the Egyptians do, with a strong mint tea and a water pipe.

➕ 201 E3 ⊠ Ghazala Hotel, Naama Bay ☎ 069-360 0150 ⏰ Daily lunch and dinner

DAHAB

Carm Inn £

One of the better waterfront places with freshly prepared Western,

Egyptian and Indian dishes, this is favoured by the local expats.

➕ 201 F3 ⊠ Masbat ☎ 069-364 1300 ⏰ 9am–10pm

Lakhbatita ££

Lakhbatita (Three Fishes Restaurant) is located between Penguin Village and the Inmo Hotel, and overlooks the Gulf of Aqaba. Run by an Egyptian chef and his Italian wife, the restaurant offers a gourmet menu with dishes from both their countries, as well as great seafood. No alcohol is served.

➕ 201 F3 ⊠ Mashraba ☎ 069-364 1306; www.lakhbatita.com ⏰ Daily 11am–midnight

Nirvana Restaurant £–££

Arguably the best in Dahab, this beach-side restaurant has tables literally on the beach. It serves excellent Indian food, and a wide selection of vegetarian dishes.

➕ 201 E3 ⊠ At the Lighthouse on the boardwalk, Masbat ☎ 069-364 1261; www. nirvanadivers.com ⏰ Daily lunch and dinner

ISMAILIYA

George's ££

Cairenes have been known to cross the desert just to eat at this pleasant Greek-run fish restaurant. The atmosphere is agreeable and intimate, while the owner's fresh seafood is famous. There is also a well-stocked bar.

🚹 199 F4 ☒ Sharia Sultan Hussein ☎ 064-391 7327 ⓦ Daily lunch and dinner

AL GOUNA

Sayadeen Fish Restaurant ££

Fresh seafood is an obvious speciality of this beach restaurant situated in a pavilion built over the sea with fantastic views. The menu focuses on a different national cuisine each month, so you can have your fish simply grilled or cooked the way it's done somewhere else in the world. Oriental dishes are also served.

🚹 201 D2 ☒ Mövenpick Hotel, beach ☎ 065-354 4501 ⓦ Daily lunch and dinner

Le Tabasco ££

Imported from the capital, Cairo's hottest bar/bistro in the heart of Kafr al Gouna, is just as trendy and lively. It has three terraces, the same relaxed atmosphere, cool tastefully designed interiors, excellent music and great food. The bar is on the second floor.

🚹 201 D2 ☒ Between the museum building and El Khan hotel, Kafr al Gouna ☎ 012-345 9263 ext. 5515 ⓦ Daily late afternoon–2am

HURGHADA

Abu Khadigah £

A very Egyptian down-to-earth place, Abu Khadigah is popular with local Egyptian workers, in this otherwise international beach resort. On the menu are straightforward Egyptian dishes such as stuffed cabbage leaves, *kofta*, hearty stews and other reminders of mama's kitchen back home in the Nile Valley.

🚹 201 E2 ☒ Sharia Sheraton ⓦ Daily 11–11

Felfela £–££

Part of the popular Cairene chain (▲ 75), this atmospheric restaurant is in a cliff-top location overlooking the Red Sea and harbour. It serves Egyptian dishes, from a variety of *mezze* to delicious roast pigeon stuffed with *firekh*.

🚹 201 E2 ☒ Sharia Sheraton ☎ 065-344 2410 ⓦ Daily 8:30am–midnight

Liquid Lounge £–££

This popular and ultra-relaxed beach bar serves snacks, good Western dishes and a slightly more elaborate dinner menu.

🚹 201 E2 ☒ Sharia Sheraton ☎ 010-512 9051 ⓦ 9am–3am

Da Nanni ££

The chefs, a couple, are Italian and they know how to make a delicious pizza. Da Nanni is considered by many to make the best pizzas in town. Home-made pasta is also on the menu.

🚹 201 E2 ☒ Sharia al Hadaba, Sigala ☎ 065-344 7018 ⓦ Daily lunch and dinner

Papa's Bar £

This lively bar is particularly popular with dive instructors and other temporary residents in Hurghada. Some nights the music gets turned up and the party is on.

🚹 201 E2 ☒ Next door to Pizza Rossi, Sigala ☎ 010-512 9051; www.papasbar.com ⓦ Daily all day until late

Portofino ££

Fresh Italian fish and seafood dishes are a speciality and the home-made pasta is the best in town. Fondues are also popular. There's an enjoyable atmosphere and the service is friendly: the owner likes to chat to guests in the evening.

🚹 201 E2 ☒ Sharia Sayed al Qorayem, al Dahar ☎ 065-354 6250 ⓦ Daily lunch and dinner

Rossi Restaurant ££

Good thin-crust crispy pizzas and comforting pasta dishes are served at this popular Italian restaurant.

🚹 201 E2 ☒ Sharia Sheraton ⓦ Daily 10am–midnight

Where to...
Shop

Most resorts on the Red Sea and in Sinai were tiny fishing hamlets or Bedouin settlements until recently, so there are no authentic *souks* or bazaars. The American-style shopping malls here have no local flavour. Most shops sell cheap tourist souvenirs but a minority sell better quality produce such as Bedouin embroidery, locally woven products and pottery.

It is alarming to see the corals, shells, starfish and even stuffed sharks on sale. Avoid buying these as it's damaging to the coral reefs.

The Red Sea Coast

The sprawling bazaar area in Hurghada's **al Dahar** has hundreds of shops and street vendors selling the tourist tat. The quality of merchandise is poor, but prices are reasonable if you're prepared to haggle. As Hurghada has become popular with Russian and Eastern European tourists, you may also find products from these countries.

Tax-free goods are available at the **Egypt Free Shop** opposite the Egypt Air office or at the pyramid-shaped shopping mall in Sigala.

Al Gouna has several top-quality shops. The boutique **Queeny** sells the best of European fashion labels. For something more ethnic head for **Malaika** with Egyptian cotton embroidered *galabeyas*. **Al Nol** makes Bedouin-style *galabeyas* and scarves in bold ethnic colours. The **Egyptian Women's Handicrafts** supports fairtrade projects all over the country: Moqattam's recycled paper and notebooks from Cairo, Bedouin embroidered pillows and purses from Sinai, and other handicrafts. All these stores are in Abu Tig Marina.

Sinai

Sharm al Sheikh's bazaar sells tourist souvenirs, including silver jewellery, papyri, copies of ancient statues and cotton T-shirts printed with Red Sea fish. A few shops stand out, however. **Aladin**, at the Falcon al Diar Hotel in Naama Bay (tel: 069-360 0828), sells Egyptian glass, Bedouin textiles, woodwork and beads. **Baraka Carpets**, in front of the Sanafir Hotel (tel: 012-218 1597/227 2363) has a great selection of woollen and silk carpets, Bedouin rugs and patchwork carpets, as well as other handicrafts. The best bookshop in Sharm is the **al Ahram Bookshop**, on the road to Sharm in Naama Bay, with a good selection of English-language books, papers and magazines.

Every Thursday a Bedouin market is held in the old part of al Arish on the north coast of Sinai, where veiled Bedouin women sell beadwork, silver jewellery and embroidered dresses. The market is mostly geared towards tourism, as their best pieces probably go directly to the shops in Cairo, but it's still a colourful sight.

Most hotels have their own shopping malls. The best places for Egyptian cotton clothes are **Mobaco** at the Sanafir, **Hilton Fayrouz** in Naama Bay, and **Pyramisa Hotel** at Shark Bay in Sharm al Sheikh; the **Shirt Shop** (Mövenpick Jolie Ville) has men's shirts, as has the franchised **New Man** (Sanafir and Pyramisa hotels).

Suez Canal

Port Said is a duty-free port and therefore popular with Egyptians looking for a bargain; you can buy almost anything here. Most shops selling brand names, electronics and designer jeans are on and around Sharia al Gumhuriya.

Where to...
Be Entertained

Listings of what's on in Sinai are in the monthly *Sinai Today* and *Egypt Today*, (check the websites www.sharm-el-sheikh.com and www.elgouna.com). For the Red Sea there's *Hurghada Bulletin* and *Red Sea Life*.

Scuba-diving/Snorkelling

All Red Sea and Sinai resorts have excellent dive centres offering equipment rental, boat excursions and diving courses (▶ 156–159).

Glass-bottom Boats/Submarines

Most resorts offer trips by glass-bottom boats, exploring the coral reefs. Contact **Sindbad Submarines** (tel: 065-344 4688; www.sindbad-group.com) in Hurghada; **Aquascope** is at the Hoi Palace in Hurghada (tel: 065-344 3710) and at the al Kheima Resort in Sharm al Moya (tel: 065-344 3710).

Nightlife

Sharm al Sheikh is lively at night around the bars and nightclubs of hotels, especially **Bus Stop** and **Pacha** at the Sanafir Hotel (▶ 170) and **Little Buddha Bar** (▶ 172–173) at Naama Bay Hotel. **Pirates Bar** (Hilton Fayrouz; tel 069-360 0136) is popular in the early evening when there's a happy hour. Naama Bay has a **Hard Rock Café** (tel: 069-360 2665), with the usual rock 'n' roll memorabilia. The **Camel Roof Bar** (Camel Hotel; tel: 069-360 0700) is the bar where divers and instructors meet, with great views over the sea. **Al Fanar** (▶ 172) turns into an open-air nightclub later on,

and is the place to be seen. In high season several music bars along the beach can also be good for a dance.

In Hurghada most of the larger hotels have nightclubs, also open to non-residents, with the **Dome** at the InterContinental a favourite. **Papa's Beach Club** (tel: 065-344 4146) often has wild parties with DJs from abroad. **Liquid Lounge** (▶ 174) is the most popular beach bar, with dance parties on Thursday, Friday and Saturday nights. **Black Out Disco** in the Ali Baba Palace on Sharia al Hadaba (tel: 012-221 7734) hosts parties with smoke and foam.

Alternatively, you can try your luck at the **Casino Royale** in the Mövenpick Jolie Ville in Naama Bay (tel: 069-360 0100). The **InterContinental** in Hurghada has a casino for late-night gambling.

Sports

All the Red Sea resorts offer watersports, including sailing, banana boats, windsurfing and parasailing. The best windsurfing places in Hurghada are **Three Corners**, **Giftun** and **Jasmin Village**. In Sinai: **Moon Beach Hotel** (Ras Sudr; tel: 02-336 5103; www.moonbeachretreat.com) is renowned for its windsurfing facilities.

Most resorts also offer horse-riding in the desert, camel rides on the beach or longer trips into the mountains with Bedouin guides.

Hot-air Balloons

German-run **Cast Ballooning** in Hurghada organises spectacular one-hour trips over the desert, returning by four-wheel-drive. There's also breakfast at a Bedouin camp (for more information tel: 065-344 4929).

Jeep Safaris in the Desert

Both the Red Sea Mountains and Sinai offer spectacular landscapes, as well as Bedouin camps. In Sinai there are trips from Dahab, Nuweiba and St Catherine's Monastery to picturesque wadis like the Coloured Canyon and Ras Abu Gallum.

Walks and Tours

MEDIEVAL CAIRO
Walk

The only way to discover the splendours of Cairo's medieval city is to walk its streets and alleys, lined with stunning mosques, amazing palaces and intriguing *wikalas* (merchants' houses). Many ancient monuments are still intact, but others have collapsed. The backdrop seems medieval, but the modern world is close by.

DISTANCE 4km (2.5 miles) **TIME** 3 hours to look at buildings, but a day to visit the major sights **START POINT** Ibn Tulun Mosque, Sharia Saliba (minibus 54 from Midan Tahrir to Sayyida Zeinab, but a taxi is easier) ✚ 197 D3 **END POINT** Sharia al Azhar ✚ 197 E4

Early morning or late afternoon is the best time to go. On Sundays the bazaar is closed and things are much quieter, so it's a good time to take a closer look at the architecture.

1–2
Turn left out of the mosque of

Many mosques have beautifully decorated interiors

Ibn Tulun (▶ 68) towards the main street, Sharia Saliba, then turn right. Sharia Saliba follows the medieval main street known as the Qasaba, lined with palaces and mosques most of which have been restored after the earthquakes in the 1990s. On the left is the 15th-century late Mameluke mosque-*madrasa* of **Amir Tagri Bardi**, followed by the very ornate but lovely 19th-century *sabil* (public fountain) of **Umm Abbas**. Farther on, facing each other, are the tall walls of a *khanqah* (Sufi convent) to the right and a mosque to the left, both built by **Amir Shaykhu** in the 14th century. Note the unusual pharaonic cornice above the entrance gate and the beautiful ceiling of the sanctuary *iwan*.

Outside turn right and walk about 150m (165 yards) to the impressive

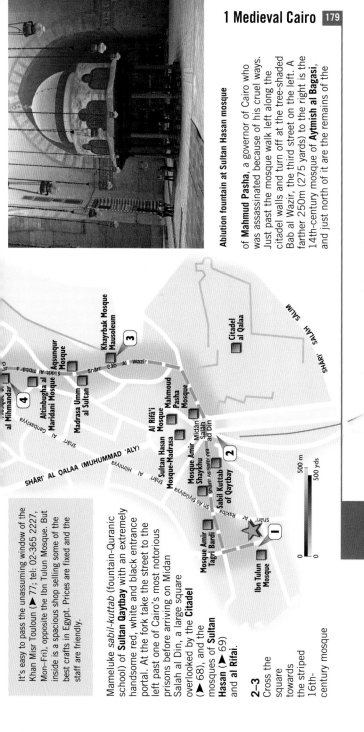

It's easy to pass the unassuming window of the Khan Misr Touloun (▶ 77; tel: 02-365 2227, Mon–Fri), opposite the Ibn Tulun Mosque. But inside is a spacious shop selling some of the best crafts in Egypt. Prices are fixed and the staff are friendly.

Mameluke *sabil-kuttab* (fountain-Quranic school) of **Sultan Qaytbay** with an extremely handsome red, white and black entrance portal. At the fork take the street to the left past one of Cairo's most notorious prisons before arriving on Midan Salah al Din, a large square overlooked by the **Citadel** (▶ 68), and the mosques of **Sultan Hasan** (▶ 69) and **al Rifai**.

2–3

Cross the square towards the striped 16th-century mosque

Ablution fountain at Sultan Hasan mosque

of **Mahmud Pasha**, a governor of Cairo who was assassinated because of his cruel ways. Just past the mosque walk left along the citadel walls and turn off at the tree-shaded Bab al Wazir, the third street on the left. A farther 250m (275 yards) to the right is the 14th-century mosque of **Aytmish al Bagasi**, and just north of it are the remains of the mausoleum and *sabil-kuttab* of **Tarabay al Sharifi** from the late Mameluke period. Farther along Sharia Bab al Wazir on the right is the entrance to the ruins of the once-impressive **palace of Alin Aq** and the early 14th-century mosque-mausoleum built for **Khayrbak**, a Mameluke *amir* who became the first Ottoman viceroy of Egypt.

3–4

Farther on the right is the mosque of **Aqsunqur**, which is also known as the **Blue Mosque** because of the beautiful turquoise Iznik (that is, ancient Nicaea, in northwest Turkey) tiles lining its interior. The street here is known as Sharia Tabbana. About 70m (75 yards) farther along on the left is the grand entrance to the 14th-century *madrasa* **Umm al Sultan**, and next door the huge but rambling 15th-century palace of **Katkhuda al Razzaz**. Farther along the street on the left is one of the very finest monuments in the area, the 14th-century mosque of **Altinbugha al Maridani** – with a beautifully carved *qibla* (showing the direction of Mecca) behind a stunning *mashrabiya* (wooden lattice) screen. Still on the left is the 14th-century mosque of **al Mihmandar**, decorated with lovely calligraphic verses of the Quran, which adjoins a much later Ottoman *sabil-kuttab* of Katkhuda Mustahfizan.

4–5

Where the street bends, its name changes to Darb al Ahmar. At the intersection the mosque of **Qajmas al Ishaqi** has fine marble decoration. On the left, just before Bab Zuwayla is the late Fatimid mosque of **Salih Talai** and beyond it the covered **Tentmakers' Bazaar** (al Khiyamiya ➤ 77).

5–6

Walk through the splendid restored **Bab Zuwayla** gate next to the Sultan al Muayyad Mosque, and along the market street of **Sharia al Muizz li Din Allah** (➤ 56–58) until you reach Sharia al Azhar. At the end are the beautifully restored mosque and mausoleum of al Ghuri. Turn right along Sharia al Azhar to the **al Azhar Mosque** (➤ 70). Use the underpass to Midan al Husayn and at the mosque of the same name take the small alley to the left into **Khan al Khalili** (➤ 71). The first alley left again brings you to **al Fishawi Café** (➤ 75).

6–7

After a stroll in the bazaar return to the mosque of **al Husayn** (closed to non-Muslims),

Elaborate designs decorate a window of the Sultan Qaytbay Sabil-Kuttab

of **Gamal ad Din al Ustadar**, built at great cost by the powerful prince who gave his name to this area, **al Gamaliya**. On the opposite corner stands the handsome 17th-century *sabil-kuttab* of **Oda Bashi** with lovely tiled panels, and next door is his *wikala* (merchant's hostel) which was one of Cairo's main trade centres for coffee and spices in the 18th century. Farther to the right is the *madrasa* of **Amir Qarasunqur** who was polo master to Sultan Qalawun; two polo mallets can be seen above the window of the mausoleum. On the next corner is Cairo's oldest surviving *khanqah*, built in 1306 by Sultan Baybars II. It has superb marble panelling in the mausoleum and a typical early Mameluke minaret. There are several more *wikalas*, in various states of

A bustling street market near al Ghuri mosque and mausoleum

and turn left along its western wall into a street lined with vendors selling prayer beads and incense. To the left is the 19th-century **Sabil-Kuttab of Ahmad Pasha**, now partly occupied by a sweet vendor. Turn left where the street bends, then immediately right and continue along Sharia Habs al Rahaba. To the left is the 15th-century mosque-*madrasa*

decay, along the street. Most are commercial centres for spices and coffee, but a few of them are still lived in.

7–8

Just before you reach the gate of Bab an Nasr, on your left is the large *wikala* of **Qaytbey**, built in 1481, with the typical plan of a large central courtyard surrounded by shops and storerooms on the ground floor and rooms for the traders upstairs. **Bab an Nasr** (Gate of Victory) with the two square towers is part of the Fatimid fortifications. Walk outside the gate left to **Bab al Futuh** (➤ 56) and walk back through the gate along Sharia al Muizz li Din Allah to Sharia al Azhar where you can pick up a taxi.

TAKING A BREAK
Stop in Khan al Khalili (➤ 71) and smoke a water pipe or have a drink at the café al Fishawi (➤ 75), or in the Naguib Mahfouz Café (➤ 76) on the main street of the bazaar. The restaurant part of the Naguib Mahfouz also serves good *mezze* and Oriental dishes. There are also several cafés along Sharia Bab al Wazir.

2 AROUND THE THEBAN NECROPOLIS

Cycling Tour

DISTANCE 16km (10 miles) **TIME** 1 day (start early, particularly in summer when it's too hot to ride in the midday sun) **START POINT/END POINT** Ferry terminal on the West Bank, Luxor (either ride round and cross over the bridge south of Luxor, or put the bike on the local ferry opposite Luxor Temple) ✚ 202 B4

Cycling is the best way to explore the amazing tombs and mortuary temples of the Theban necropolis and you'll also get a stronger sense of the Egyptian countryside. This tour passes beautiful villages where life is still traditional, many of the houses painted with motifs marking a pilgrimage to Mecca. You'll see people working in the field or children going to school, who might wave or give you a big smile. Take it easy and enjoy a rhythm very much in tune with the region.

You can rent bikes from several shops along Sharia al Mahatta (Station Street) on the East Bank, but better, more expensive ones are available from hotels, including the Sheraton, Mercure Inn and Windsor. Make sure you check the bike before renting it and always insist on a pump as the standards of the roads and tracks aren't always high.

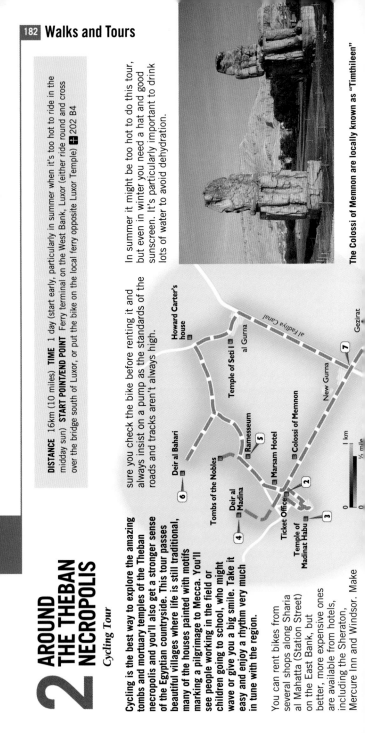

In summer it might be too hot to do this tour, but even in winter you need a hat and good sunscreen. It's particularly important to drink lots of water to avoid dehydration.

The Colossi of Memnon are locally known as "Timthileen"

1–2

Once on the West Bank cycle straight ahead for 10–15 minutes to the ticket booth on the crossroads before Deir al Madina. On the way, immediately past the al Fadliya canal to the right, note the village of **New Gurna**. This beautiful village, built by the Egyptian architect Hasan Fathy, was a failed attempt to relocate the villagers from Old Gurna, whose houses sit on top of the ancient tombs. Farther to the right are the **Memnon Colossi** staring across the sugarcane fields. These gigantic 14th-century BC statues of Amenhotep III are all that's left of his mortuary temple.

At the ticket kiosk, left at the crossroads, buy tickets for the places you intend to visit that don't sell tickets at the entrance.

2–3

Return towards the colossi, take the first road to the right along a little canal, then right again to the entrance of **Temple of Madinat Habu** (▶ 98).

3–4

Turn left on leaving the temple and, after 100m (110 yards), continue along the dirt track towards the ticket office and main crossroads. Follow the signpost for **Deir al Madina** (▶ 99–100).

4–5

Cycle back to the crossroads and turn left to visit the **Tombs of the Nobles** (▶ 96–97). Leave the bike in the site's car-park, opposite the Ramesseum. Walk back across the road towards the **Ramesseum** (▶ 100–101), where you can relax and picnic under the trees, or

have a simple Egyptian lunch at the Marsam Hotel, just past the temple.

5–6

Turn right (north) on to the road and then take the first road on the left towards the **Deir al Bahari** (▶ 94–95).

6–7

Back on the main road, turn left to the next crossroads then turn right. The domed house on top of the hill belonged to Howard Carter who found the treasures of Tutankhamun. Temple enthusiasts can stop at the mortuary temple of Seti I, which has exquisite wall carvings, or take a look at the cemetery across the road. Continue along the same road until the canal then turn right. At the New Gurna crossroads turn left back to the ferry.

Luxor

▪ Luxor Temple

TAKING A BREAK

Stop for a drink at the Maratonga café opposite Madinat Habu temple, or at the café near the Tombs of the Nobles.

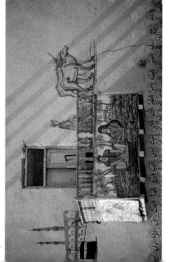

Vividly coloured pilgrimage paintings decorate a wall in Old Gurna

3 ACROSS THE DESERT IN SINAI

Driving Tour

DISTANCE About 492km (305 miles) **TIME** Preferably two days to stop over at St Catherine's Monastery to see the sunrise at Mount Moses **START POINT/END POINT** Sharm al Sheikh, but you could also start in Dahab or Nuweiba ➕ 201 E3

Bedouin and their camels settle in their encampment as evening falls

The road across the mountains of the Sinai peninsula is one of the most beautiful in Egypt, perhaps even in Africa. There are plenty of tours from Sharm al Sheikh, but they tend to be rushed and don't allow you to stop where you like, to take in a view or walk in the desert. It's a long drive, best done over two days, and a highlight of any trip to Egypt.

Although this tour follows a regularly used route, you are crossing a desert so make sure you have enough petrol and water. Be careful when leaving the main road, as there are still thousands of unexploded mines in Sinai, a legacy of the Arab–Israeli wars – do not enter any fenced-off areas. Keep a watch out for camels that sometimes wander across the road in front of vehicles.

Renting a car can be something of a lottery, so inspect the vehicle thoroughly before you agree to take it and make sure you know who to call if you have a problem.

1–2

Leave Sharm al Sheikh by the road, heading north to the airport and Dahab. After about 8km (5 miles) the road splits; take the left-hand fork to Dahab. From here the road then cuts farther into the mountains, which are coloured in many places with veins of minerals. The desert here is mostly rock and scrub, the defining features being the bare mountains and the valleys and plains in between. Apart from the occasional car or bus, the chances are you will have the place to yourself, although, depending on the season, you might see Bedouin camps. The road drops down to the coast again as you come to a police post (87km/54 miles). From here you can drive into Dahab (8km/5 miles) for a swim and a drink, or keep travelling north into the desert towards Nuweiba. At the major intersection, about 130km (80 miles) from Sharm al Sheikh, take the left turn towards St Catherine's Monastery.

2–3

The drive through the Sinai desert to St Catherine's Monastery (122km/76 miles) follows a good road through beautiful if stark landscape. The driving is generally easy and there are plenty of places to stop and admire the great *wadis* (dry riverbeds) that cut through the peninsula. Wadi Ghazala, some 10km (6 miles) after the Dahab police post, is accessible and if you feel adventurous you could

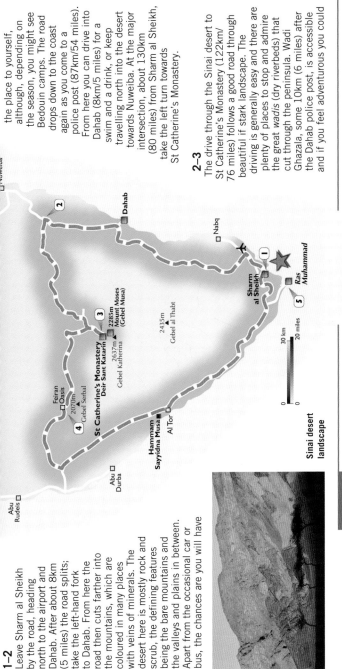

Sinai desert landscape

Members of a Bedouin family herding their sheep and goats in the Sinai desert

For more detailed itineraries in Sinai look for *The Red Sea Coasts of Egypt*, by Jenny Jobbins (AUC Press, available in Egypt).

TAKING A BREAK

Sharm al Sheikh, Dahab and the St Catherine area all have of options for eating and drinking and there are refreshments at Wadi Feiran.

follow it some way, though your car probably wouldn't like it. Also on this road is the MFO checkpoint, the multi-national force that observes the peace between Egypt and Israel.

There are several places to visit near St Catherine, starting with the monastery (▶ 160–162). The climb up to Mount Moses, where Moses is said to have obtained the Ten Commandments, is strenuous but worthwhile for its atmosphere and views over the mountains. The area around St Catherine is a protectorate where several walking trails have been laid out. The official office (by the monastery car-park) has details.

3–4

The road out of St Catherine continues through broad *wadis* for some 45km (28 miles), where the mountains close in again. This is the beginning of the palm-lined Wadi Feiran. Early Christians identified this with the exodus of Moses and it became sufficiently important to

warrant a bishop. The ruins of the cathedral and ancient settlement are being excavated at the oasis of Feiran. You can visit the small convent near by (ask if it's open at St Catherine's Monastery, or just ring the doorbell), and the mountains are dotted with the caves and shelters of hermits.

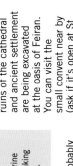

4–5

Having crossed the desert, 45km (28 miles) beyond Feiran is an intersection with the west Sinai coast road. Turn left here, following signs for Tor, along the road back to Sharm al Sheikh, some 160km (100 miles) away. Heading south, the road cuts through a wide, barren plain with 2,000m-high (6,600 feet) mountains to your left. Some 57km (35 miles) from the intersection a road leads right, through a small oasis, to the **Hammam Sayyidna Musa** ("Bath of Our Lord Moses"), a hot spring that's long been used for its healing properties. The farm here produces food for

St Catherine's Monastery. Farther on is Tor, once the gulf's main port for pilgrims returning from Mecca. **Ras Muhammad National Park** (▶ 163) is a further 87km (54 miles), and Sharm al Sheikh 27km (17 miles) from there.

Practicalities

BEFORE YOU GO

WHAT YOU NEED

		UK	Germany	USA	Canada	Australia	Ireland	Netherlands	Spain
●	Required								
○	Suggested								
▲	Not required								
△	Not applicable								
Passport/National Identity Card		●	●	●	●	●	●	●	●
Visa (tourist visa – available from airport on arrival)		●	●	●	●	●	●	●	●
Onward or Return Ticket		▲	▲	▲	▲	▲	▲	▲	▲
Health Inoculations (tetanus and polio)		○	○	○	○	○	○	○	○
Health Documentation		▲	▲	▲	▲	▲	▲	▲	▲
Travel Insurance		○	○	○	○	○	○	○	○
Driver's Licence (national)		●	●	●	●	●	●	●	●
Car Insurance Certificate (if own car)		●	●	●	●	●	●	●	●
Car Registration Document (if own car)		●	●	●	●	●	●	●	●

Entry requirements differ depending on your nationality and are also subject to change without notice. Check prior to a visit and follow news events that may affect your situation.

WHEN TO GO

Cairo

High season   Low season

JAN	FEB	MAR	APR	MAY	JUN	JUL	AUG	SEP	OCT	NOV	DEC
18°C	21°C	23°C	27°C	32°C	34°C	35°C	35°C	32°C	30°C	23°C	18°C
64°F	70°F	73°F	81°F	90°F	93°F	95°F	95°F	90°F	86°F	73°F	64°F

Sun

Sun/Showers

Temperatures are the **average daily maximum** for each month but differ greatly between night and day, and over the country. The Mediterranean coast is always cooler, while Cairo is extremely hot from June to September. The air becomes drier towards the south, but although Upper Egypt is always hot, the nights can be cold. March and April can bring the *khamseen*, a strong, hot wind that carries sand from the Sahara. The winter months can be quite cold, often with rain around Christmas. The tourist season is from November to February but Cairo and Luxor are chilly then, and hotels are overbooked. The best time to visit is May, or in October or November after the long, hot summer has ended.

GETTING ADVANCE INFORMATION

Websites

■ www.touregypt.net
Official site of Egypt's Ministry of Tourism.
■ www.sis.gov.eg
Site providing general information on Egypt,
including tourism and culture.
■ www.yallabina.com
What's on in Cairo, including entertainment, restaurants and nightlife.

In the UK and Ireland

Egyptian House
3rd Floor, 170 Piccadilly
London W1
☎ 020 7493 5283

GETTING THERE

By air There are direct scheduled flights to Cairo from New York and Los Angeles, and from many European capitals. You can also fly there from the Middle East and most of the adjacent African countries. Some international scheduled flights also land in Luxor, Alexandria and Aswan. Charter flights are available to Luxor, Hurghada and Sinai. When leaving Egypt, remember to reconfirm your flight 48 hours beforehand.

By sea There are twice weekly ferries May–November from Port Said to Limassol in Cyprus. Tickets and info are available from Canal Tours in Port Said (tel: 066-332 1874/ 012-798 6338; canaltours@bec.com.eg). Also in Port Said is Mena Tours (tel: 066-322 5742/323 3376) which sells tickets for the erratic ferries between Port Said and Beirut or Antalya (Turkey). There are excellent fast ferries between Nuweiba in Sinai and Aqaba in Jordan, tickets are sold at the Nuweiba harbour on the day of departure. Several ferry companies operate boats from Hurghada to various ports in Saudi Arabia.

By bus Buses from Tel Aviv, Jerusalem and Eilat in Israel go to Sinai and Cairo, crossing the border at Rafah or Taba, but at the time of writing the border crossing at Rafah was closed. Frequent buses also connect Cairo with Tripoli and Benghazi in Libya. You cannot obtain a visa at the Egyptian border if you enter by land, and there are likely to be long delays at border crossings.

By car Complicated bureaucracy means that entering Egypt by car is one of the least popular options. You should be allowed to bring a car into Egypt for three months if you can show an *international triptyque* or a *carnet de passage de douane* issued by the automobile club in the country where the car is registered.

TIME

Egypt is 2 hours ahead of GMT, or 3 hours ahead from the start of May to the start of October. But remember that time is a loose concept in Egypt.

CURRENCY AND FOREIGN EXCHANGE

Currency The basic unit of currency is the Egyptian pound (LE, *guineh* in Arabic). This is divided into 100 piastres (PT, *irsh* in Arabic). There are **notes** for 5, 10, 20, 25 and 50 piastres and 1, 5, 10, 20, 50, 100 and 200 pounds, as well as **coins** of 10, 20 and 25 piastres. Small denominations are useful for *baksheesh*. Egypt is still generally a cash economy, so ensure that you carry sufficient money for your needs.

Travellers' cheques, preferably in US$, can be changed in all banks and exchange bureaux but it can be complicated and there is a transaction charge.

Credit cards are widely accepted at banks, hotels and some restaurants, but it is wise to check first. Smaller establishments and shops are likely to prefer cash.

ATMs More and more five-star hotels and banks in tourist resorts have automatic cash dispensing machines. In most cities there are several ATM cash machines that will dispense cash to most Western-issued cards, with PIN.

In New York
630 Fifth Avenue
Suite 1706, New York NY
10111
☎ 212/332-2570

In Los Angeles
8383 Wiltshire Blvd
Suite 215
Beverly Hills CA 90211
☎ 323/653-8815

In Canada
1253 McGill College Av,
Suite 250, Montreal
Quebec H3B 2Y5
☎ 514/861-4420

WHEN YOU ARE THERE

CLOTHING SIZES

UK	International	USA	
36	46	36	
38	48	38	
40	50	40	Suits
42	52	42	
44	54	44	
46	56	46	
7	41	8	
7.5	42	8.5	
8.5	43	9.5	Shoes
9.5	44	10.5	
10.5	45	11.5	
11	46	12	
14.5	37	14.5	
15	38	15	
15.5	39/40	15.5	Shirts
16	41	16	
16.5	42	16.5	
17	43	17	
8	34	6	
10	36	8	
12	38	10	Dresses
14	40	12	
16	42	14	
18	44	16	
4.5	38	6	
5	38	6.5	
5.5	39	7	Shoes
6	39	7.5	
6.5	40	8	
7	41	8.5	

NATIONAL HOLIDAYS

1 Jan	New Year's Day
7 Jan	Coptic Christmas
Mar/Apr	Sham al Nessim
25 Apr	Liberation Day
1 May	Labour Day
18 Jun	Liberation Day
23 Jul	Revolution Day
6 Oct	Armed Forces Day
24 Oct	Suez Victory Day

Egypt also observes Muslim feast days and the month of fasting, Ramadan. Dates follow the lunar calendar and move back by 11 days a year.

OPENING HOURS

○ Shops   ● Post Offices
● Offices   ◐ Museums/Monuments
◐ Banks   ◐ Pharmacies

8am 9am 10am noon 1pm 2pm 4pm 5pm 7pm

☐ Day   ☐ Midday   ☐ Evening

All times given may vary. In tourist areas shops tend to remain open all day until late at night, especially in high season.

Banks in tourist areas often stay open all day until late at night. Banks at Cairo airport and the Marriott and Nile Hilton hotels in Cairo are open 24 hours. Museums and monuments close between 11 and 1 on Friday for prayers. Post offices are open from Saturday until Thursday. Pharmacies are often open until 9pm or later.

During Ramadan, everything tends to open an hour later and close an hour or two earlier, but shops and some offices generally reopen from 8 to 10pm.

TIME DIFFERENCES

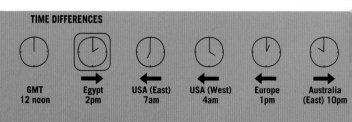

GMT 12 noon	Egypt 2pm	USA (East) 7am	USA (West) 4am	Europe 1pm	Australia (East) 10pm

PERSONAL SAFETY

Petty crime is rare in Egypt but like everywhere else you should watch your belongings in busy tourist areas and on full buses.

- Leave valuables in the hotel safe. Carry only what you need.
- There is a crackdown on drugs, with fines for possession, and life imprisonment or hanging for anyone convicted of dealing or smuggling.
- Foreigners travelling between cities in Middle and Upper Egypt usually have to move in a police-protected convoy.

Tourist Police assistance:
 126

TELEPHONES

Until recently, international calls could only be made from specified Telephone and Telegraph offices but Egypt now has an extensive network of payphones, operated by Menatel and Nile Communications. These can be used for local, national and international calls. Phonecards, available in values of LE10, 20 and 30, can be bought from telephone exchanges as well as shops and kiosks displaying stickers with the Menatel logo. It is still possible to make local calls from coin-operated phone boxes, shops, hotels and kiosks, but these tend to be more expensive than calls made on Menatel phones.

POST

Buy stamps at post offices, souvenir shops and hotel newsagents. Airmail letters take about a week to arrive: post them at your hotel or at a post office; avoid street letterboxes. Cairo's main post office (open 24 hours) is on Midan al Ataba.

ELECTRICITY

The power supply is 220 volts. Sockets take two-round-pin plugs. British and US visitors will need an adaptor. North American visitors should check whether appliances need a voltage transformer.

TIPS/GRATUITIES

Tips are expected and may be a person's sole or main source of income. As a general guide:

Restaurants	✓	8–10% (if no service included)
Cafés / Bars	✓	10%
Tour guides	✓	LE20–50
Car parking	✓	LE5–10
Taxis	✓	Agree price first, 5–10%
Hotel workers	✓	LE20
Lavatories	✓	PT50–LE2

POLICE 122

TOURIST POLICE 126/02-395 9116 (CAIRO)

FIRE 180

AMBULANCE 123

ANGLO-AMERICAN HOSPITAL IN CAIRO 02-735 6162

HEALTH

 Insurance Egypt has well-qualified doctors and good hospitals, particularly in Cairo and Alexandria. Taking out travel insurance which covers medical care is a must. Keep all receipts and medical bills for a refund back home.

 Dental Services In an emergency contact your embassy for a list of English-speaking dentists. Make sure you are covered by medical insurance. English-speaking dentist in Cairo: Dr Sabri Karnouk, Sharia Talaat Harb, opposite Cinema Metro, tel: 02-575 8392.

 Weather Use a high-factor sunblock, cover up with light cotton clothes, and wear sunglasses and hat when in the sun. Coffee and alcohol are dehydrating; instead drink at least 3 litres (6 pints) of water a day.

 Drugs Pharmacists *(saydaliya* in Arabic) usually speak English and can recommend treatment for minor ailments. A wide range of drugs is available over the counter and they are cheap. Check the expiry date and the leaflet to see if it is what you need. Most main cities or resorts have an all-night pharmacy.

 Water It is fairly safe to drink tap water in cities but buy bottles of mineral water elsewhere. Avoid ice cubes in drinks.

CONCESSIONS

Students and Youths
Museums and sights offer a 50 per cent reduction on tickets and there are also reductions on rail and airline tickets for students who have an official student card. An ISIC Student Card can be issued at the Egyptian Student Travel Services, 23 Sharia al Manyal, Roda Island, Cairo (tel: 02-531 0330; www.estsegypt.com). You need to bring one passport photo and proof that you are a student.

Senior Citizens
There are no concessions for senior citizens.

TRAVELLING WITH A DISABILITY

There are no special facilities for visitors with disabilities. Visiting the major sites can be quite a challenge although Egyptians will be ready to help. **Egypt for All** (tel: 02-311 3988; www.egyptforall.com) specialises in making travel arrangements for visitors with mobility problems.

CHILDREN

Children are welcome everywhere, and often attract a great deal of admiring attention. Some of the better hotels organise high chairs, cots and babysitters, but don't expect much in the way of baby-changing facilities.

LAVATORIES

Public lavatories vary between sitting, squatting and standing-up types, but they are often filthy. Instead of paper, a bucket of water or squirter is provided. For a more comfortable experience, use lavatories in quality hotels and restaurants.

WILDLIFE SOUVENIRS

Importing wildlife souvenirs sourced from rare or endangered species may be illegal or require a special permit. Before purchase you should check your home country's customs regulations.

CONSULATES AND EMBASSIES

UK
☎ 02-794 0850

USA
☎ 02-797 3300

Ireland
☎ 02-735 8547

Australia
☎ 02-575 0444

New Zealand
☎ 02-574 9360

The official language in Egypt is Arabic, but English is taught in schools. People are always happy, and proud, to practise their foreign languages, but even if you only speak a few words in Arabic you will generally meet with an enthusiastic response. The following is a phonetic transliteration from the Arabic script. Words or letters in brackets indicate the different form that is required when addressing, or speaking as, a woman.

GREETINGS AND COMMON WORDS

Yes **Aywa, na'am**
No **Laa**
Please **Min fadlak (fadlik)**
Thank you **Shukran**
You're welcome **Afwan**
Hello *to Muslims* **As salaamu alaykum**
Response **Wa alaykum as salaam**
Hello *to Copts* **Saeeda**
Welcome **Ahlan wa sahlan**
Response **Ahlan bik(i)**
Goodbye **Ma'a salaama**
Good morning **Sabaah al kheer**
Response **Sabaah en nu**r
Good evening **Masaa al kheer**
Response **Masaa en nur**
How are you? **Izzayak (Izzayik)**
Fine, thank you **Kwayyis(a) il hamdulillaah**
God Willing **Inshallah**
No problem **Ma feesh mushkila**
Sorry **Ana aasif (asfa)**
Excuse me **An iznak (iznik)**
My name is… **Ismee…**
Do you speak English? **Bititkallim(i) ingileezi**
I don't understand **Ana mish faahem (fahma)**
I understand **Faahem (Fahma)**
I don't speak Arabic **Ana mish aarif (arfa) arabi**

NUMBERS

0	**sifr**	14	**arbahtaashar**
1	**wahid**	15	**khamastaashar**
2	**itnayn**	16	**sittaashar**
3	**talaata**	17	**sabahtaashar**
4	**arbah**	18	**tamantaashar**
5	**khamsa**	19	**tisahtaashar**
6	**sitta**	20	**ashreen**
7	**sabaa**	21	**wahid wa-ashreen**
8	**tamanya**		
9	**tesah**	30	**talaateen**
10	**ashara**	40	**arbaeen**
11	**hidaashar**	50	**khamseen**
12	**itnaashar**	100	**miyya**
13	**talataashar**	1000	**alf**

EMERGENCY! Taari!

Help! **el ha'nee!**
Thief! **Haraami!**
Police **Shurta; bulees**
Fire **Hareea**
Hospital **Mustashfa**
Go away **Imshee**
Leave me alone! **Bass kifaaya!**
Where is the lavatory? **Feyn it twalet?**
I'm sick **Ana ayyaan(a)**
We want a doctor **Ayzeen duktoor**

SHOPPING

Shop **dukkan**
I would like… **Ayyiz (Ayza)**
I'm just looking **Batfarrag bass**
How much…? **Bi kaam?**
That's my last offer **Aakhir kalaam**
That's too expensive **Da ghali awi**
I'll take this one **Aakhud da**
Good / bad **Kwayyis / mish kwayyis**
Cheap **Rakhees**
Big / small **Kabeer(a) / sughayyar**
Open / closed **Maftooh / makfool**

DIRECTIONS AND TRAVELLING

I'm lost **Mush aarif ana feen**
Where is…? **Feyn…?**
Airport **Mataar**

DAYS

Today	**innaharda**
Tomorrow	**bukra**
Yesterday	**imbaarih**
Tonight	**innaharda bileel**
Morning	**issubh**
Evening	**massa**
Later	**bahdeen**
Monday	**youm al itnayn**
Tuesday	**youm at talaat**
Wednesday	**youm al arbah**
Thursday	**youm al khamees**
Friday	**youm al gumah**
Saturday	**youm is sabt**
Sunday	**youm al hadd**

Boat **Markab**
Bus station **Mahattat al autobees**
Church **Kineesa**
Embassy **Sifaara**
Market **Souk**
Mosque **Gaama; masgid**
Museum **Mathaf**
Square **Midaan**
Street **Shaari**
Taxi rank **Mahattat at taxiyat**
Train station **Mahattat al atr**
Is it near / far? **Da urayyib / baeed?**
How many kilometres? **Kaam keelu?**
Here / there **Hinna / hinnaak**
Left / right **Shimaal / yimeen**
Straight on **Ala toul**
When does the bus leave / arrive?
　Al autubees yisaafir / yiwsal emta?
I want a taxi **Ayyiz / ayza taks**
Stop here **Hina kwayyis**
Return ticket **Tazkara raayih gayy**
Passport **Basbuur**
Bus **Autubees**
Car **Arabiya**
Train **Atr**

RESTAURANT: **Al matam**

I would like to eat… **Ana ayyiz aakal…**
What's this? **Eeh da (di)?**
Alcohol / beer **Khamra / beera**
Bread **Aysh**
Coffee / tea **Qahwa / shay**
Meat **Lahma**
Mineral water **Mayya madaniya**
Milk **Halib**
Salt and pepper **Malh wa filfil**
Wine red / white **Nabit ahmar / abyad**
Breakfast **Fitaar**
Lunch **Ghada**
Dinner **Asha**
Table **Tarabeeza**
Waiter **Raees**
Menu **Cart / menu**
Bill **Al hisab**
Bon appetit **Bi l hana wa shiffa**

MONEY: **Filoos**

Where is the bank? **Feen al bank?**
Egyptian pound **Guineh masri**
Half a pound **Nuss guineh**
Piastre **Irsh**
Small change **Fakka**
Post office **Bosta**
Mail **Barid**
Travellers' cheque **Travellers' cheque**
Credit card **cart**

GLOSSARY

Ahwa café, coffee house
Amir military leader of the Mamelukes
Baksheesh alms, tip or bribe
Barque a ship with three masts
Beejou estate car communal taxi
Cartouche a group of hieroglyphs
　representing the name of a leader, often
　carved into a wall or tablet
Calèche horse-drawn carriage
Caliph leader during the Islamic Fatimid
　Dynasty (10th–12th centuries)
Caravanserai lodgings for travellers and
　animals, around a courtyard
Corniche coastal road
Faience ceramic glaze, sometimes on a
　minaret
Felucca Egyptian sailing boat
Fuul ubiquitous fava bean stew
Hypostyle part of the temple supported
　by pillars
Iwan vaulted space around a courtyard of
　a mosque or madrasa
Khanqah Sufi monastery
Khedive the viceroy of Egypt under
　19th-century Turkish rule
Kushari spicy mix of pulses, pasta and
　rice
Kuttab Quranic school for boys
Madrasa Quranic school
Mamelukes slave-soldiers who
　established a Muslim dynasty from
　13th–16th centuries
Maristan (Islamic) hospital
Mastaba grave, burial place
Mezze small plates of food, appetisers
Midan square
Mina ferry terminal
Moulid religious festival, often on the
　anniversary of a holy figure's birth
Ptolemics rulers of Egypt, 323–30 BC
Pylon temple gateway formed by two
　truncated pyramidal towers
Sabil public water fountain
Sahn courtyard
Sharia street
Shawarma meat roasted on a spit
Sheesha water pipe i.e. pipe for smoking
　(flavoured) tobacco that draws smoke
　over water to cool it
Souk market
Taamiya deep-fried, spiced ground fava
　beans
Tarboush fez, a traditional red, conical
　flat-topped hat with a black tassel, worn
　by some Islamic men
Vizier governor

Marsa Matruh

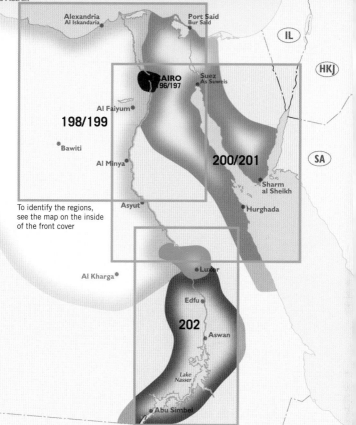

Alexandria
Al Iskandaria

Port Said
Bur Said

IL

HKJ

CAIRO
196/197

Suez
As Suweis

Al Faiyum

198/199

Bawiti

Al Minya

200/201

SA

Sharm
al Sheikh

To identify the regions,
see the map on the inside
of the front cover

Asyut

Hurghada

Al Kharga

Luxor

Edfu

202

Aswan

Lake
Nasser

Abu Simbel

Streetplan

Motorway
Main road
Other road
Railway
City wall
Important building

196/197 0 ———— 500 metres
0 ———— 500 yards

Park/garden/cemetery
Featured place of interest
Metro station

Regional Maps

Dual carriageway
Main road
Secondary road
Railway
Depression
Built up area

□ Town/village
✈ Airport
Featured place of interest
▲ Height in metres

198–202 0 ———— 40 km
0 ———— 20 miles

Atlas

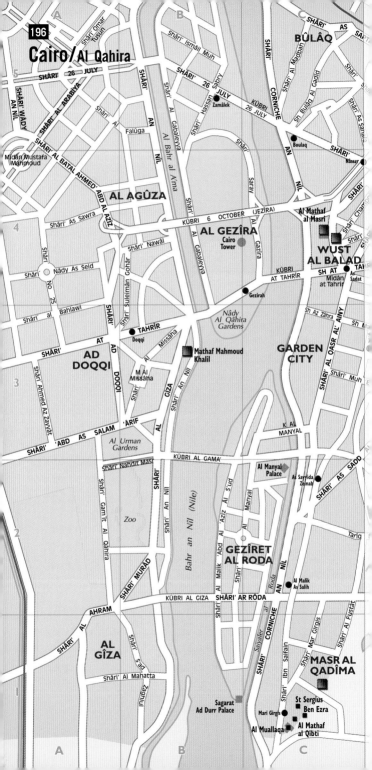

Cairo/Al Qahira

BÛLÂQ

SHÂRI' 26 JULY

Shâri' Omar Tusûn

SHÂRI' 26 JULY

Shâri' Ismaîl Muh

SHÂRI' AL ARABIYA

AN NIL

SHÂRI' WADY AN NIL

SHÂRI' AL BATAL AHMED

ABD AL AZIZ

Shâri' Al

Falûga

KÛBRI 26 JULY

SHÂRI'

Sabry

Hassan

Zamâlek

AN NIL

Shâri' Al

Shâri' Al Gabaleyya

Shâri' Al Bahr al A'ma

Boulaq

SHÂRI'

CORNICHE

Shâri' Al Maqdbâh

Shâri' Al Bulâq Al Gadîd

Shâri' As Sahira

Nâsser

Midân Mustafa Mahmoud

AL AGÛZA

Shâri' As Sawra

Shâri' No 25

Nâdy As Seid

Shâri' al Bahlawi

SHÂRI' AT

AD DOQQI

Shâri' Ahmed Az Zayyât

Shâri' 'ABD AS SALAM

Shâri' Nawâl

Shâri' Suleimân Gohâr

Saray

KÛBRI 6 OCTOBER (JEZIRA)

Shâri' Al Gabaleyya

AL GEZÎRA

Cairo Tower ●

Gazira

KÛBRI AT TAHRÎR

SH AT

Midân at Tahrir

As Sadat

WUST AL BALAD

Al Mathaf al Masri ■

Shâri' Chama

AS

SHÂRI'

● Gezirah

TAHRÎR

● Doqqi

AT MISSAHA

M Al Missâha

Al Urman Gardens

Shâri' Nahdit Masri

GIZA AN NIL

'ARIF

AL DOQQI

SHÂRI' AN NIL

■ Mathaf Mahmoud Khalil

Nâdy Al Qâhira Gardens

SH AZ ZÂHRA

SHÂRI' AL OASR AL' AINY

GARDEN CITY

Sh Muh

K AL MANYAL

KÛBRI AL GAMA'

Al Manyal Palace □

As Sayyida Zeinab ●

SHÂRI' AS SADD

Sh M

Gam'it Al Qahira

SHÂRI' MURÂD

Zoo

Bahr an Nîl (Nile)

AZIZ AL SUD

Manyal

'ABD AL MALIK

AN NIL

GEZÎRET AL RODA

Roda

▲

Tariq

Al Malik As Salih ●

KÛBRI AL GIZA

SHÂRI' AR RODA

SHÂRI' AL AHRAM

SHÂRI' Al Sad

Shâri' Al Mahatta

Zeprin

AL GÎZA

Al Malik 'Abd AN NIL

Salvater al

SHÂRI'

CORNICHE

Shâri' ibn Saifaîn

Shâri' Mar Girgis

SHÂRI' Al Fustât

MASR AL QADÎMA ■

Sagarat Ad Durr Palace ■

Mari Girgis ●

St Sergius ■ Ben Ezra

Al Muallaqa ■

Al Mathaf al Qibti

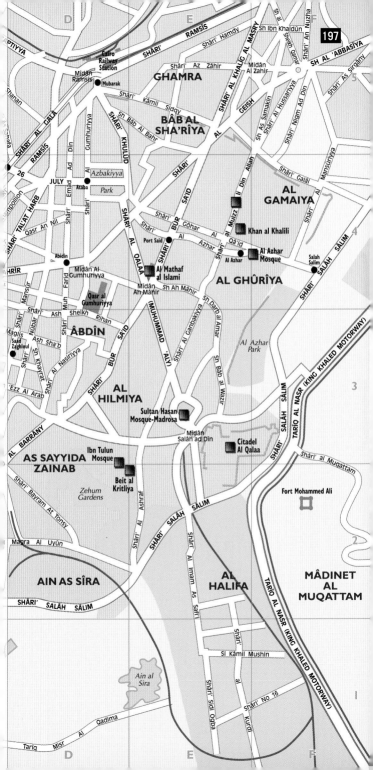

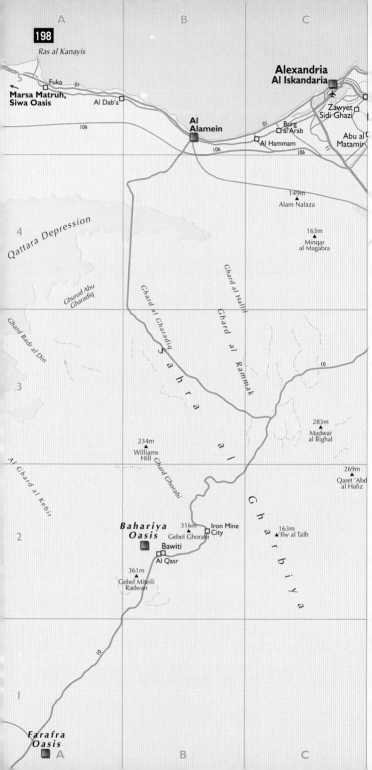

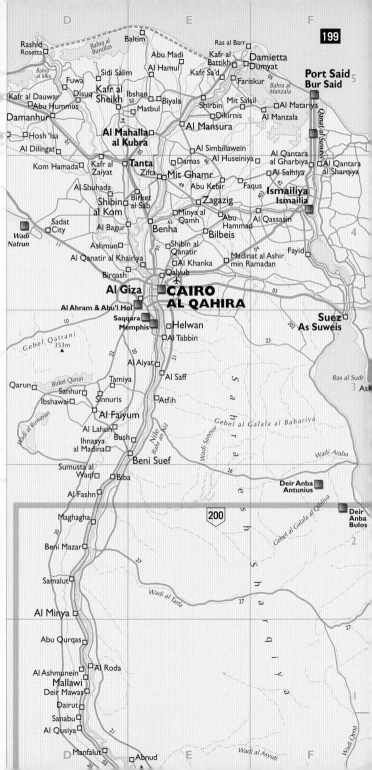

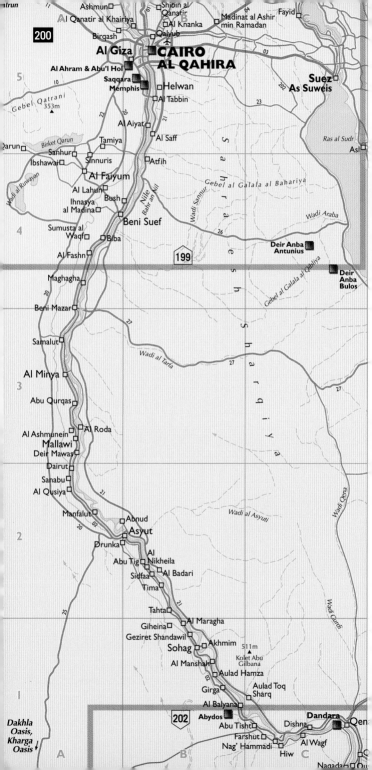

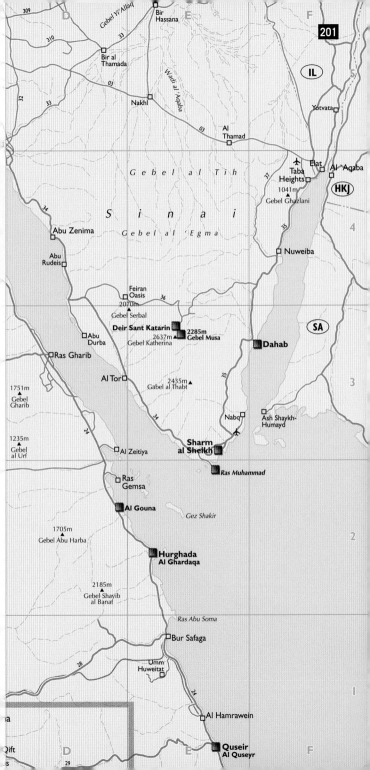

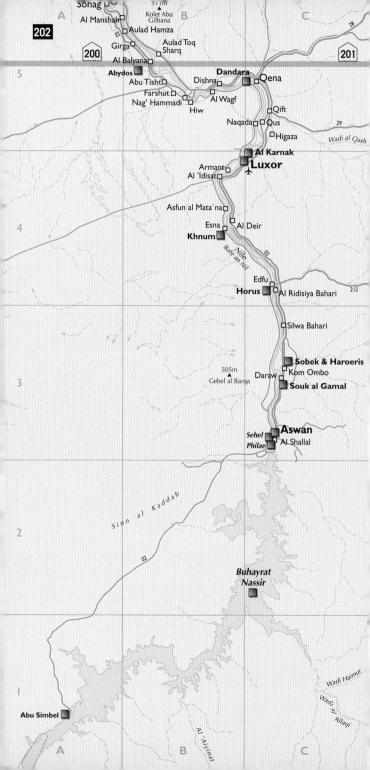

Picture credits

Abbreviations for terms appearing below: (t) top; (b) bottom; (l) left; (r) right; (c) centre.
The Automobile Association wishes to thank the following photographers and libraries for their assistance with the preparation of this book.
2(i) The Bridgeman Art Library/Getty Images; 2(ii) AA/C Coe; 2(iii) AA/C Sawyer; 2(iv) AA/R Strange; 3(i) AA/C Coe; 3(ii) AA/R Strange; 3(iii) AA/R Strange; 3(iv) AA/C Coe; 5l The Bridgeman Art Library/Getty Images; 5c Photolibrary Group; 5r © Images of Africa Photobank/Alamy; 6/7 Photolibrary Group; 9 Photolibrary Group; 10 The Bridgeman Art Library/ Getty Images; 11 Mary Evans Picture Library; 12 The Art Archive; 13 Patrick Landmann/Getty Images; 14 AA/C Coe; 15 Marc Deville/Getty Images; 16 AA/C Coe; 17 AA/C Coe; 18 AA/C Coe; 19 AA/R Strange; 20 AA/C Coe; 21t Sophie Bassouls/Sygma/Corbis; 21b Richard Gardner/Rex Features; 22 Mary Evans Picture Library; 23t The Art Archive/ Staatliche Glyptothek Munich/Alfredo Dagli Orti; 23b Mary Evans Picture Library; 24 Mary Evans Picture Library; 25 © Christie's Images/The Bridgeman Art Library; 26/27 The Art Archive/Musée du Château de Versailles/Alfredo Dagli Orti ; 27t Pascal Sebah/Getty Images; 27b Times Newspapers/Rex Features; 28 AA/R Strange; 29 AA/C Sawyer; 30 © Travelshots.com/Alamy; 31 Marwan Naamani/AFP/Getty Images; 32 AA/C Coe; 33l AA/C Coe; 33c AA/C Sawyer; 33r AA/C Sawyer; 45l AA/C Sawyer; 45c AA/C Sawyer; 45r AA/C Sawyer; 46c AA/C Coe; 46b AA/R Strange; 48t AA/C Sawyer; 48b AA/C Sawyer; 49 AA/C Sawyer; 50 AA/C Sawyer; 51 AA/C Coe; 52 AA/C Coe; 53 AA/C Sawyer; 54 AA/C Sawyer; 55 AA/R Strange; 56/57 AA/C Sawyer; 58 AA/C Sawyer; 59 AA/C Sawyer; 60 AA/C Sawyer; 61 AA/C Sawyer; 62/63 AA/R Strange; 63 AA/R Strange; 64/65 AA/C Sawyer; 66 AA/C Sawyer; 67 AA/C Sawyer; 68t AA/H Alexander; 68b AA/R Strange; 69 AA/C Sawyer; 70 AA/C Sawyer; 71 © Eddie Gerald/Alamy; 79l AA/R Strange; 79c AA/R Strange; 79r AA/H Alexander; 80 AA/C Coe; 81 AA/C Coe; 82 AA/C Coe; 83 © Ariadne Van Zandbergen/Alamy; 84 AA/R Strange; 85 AA/C Coe; 86 © Jon Arnold Images Ltd/Alamy; 88 AA/H Alexander; 89 © Art Kowalsky/Alamy; 91 AA/R Strange; 92/93 Pictures Colour Library; 93 © Aladin Abdel Naby/Reuters/Corbis; 94/95 AA/R Strange; 96 © Jim Henderson/Alamy; 97 © Ariadne Van Zandbergen/ Alamy; 98 AA/R Strange; 99t AA/C Coe; 99b AA/R Strange; 100 AA/C Coe; 101 AA/R Strange; 102t Upperhall Ltd/Robert Harding; 102b © Elvele Images Ltd/Alamy; 107l AA/C Coe; 107c © carolyn clarke/Alamy; 107r AA/R Strange; 108 AA/R Strange; 109t AA/R Strange; 109b AA/R Strange; 110 AA/C Coe; 111t Photolibrary Group; 111b AA/C Coe; 112 © Geoffrey Morgan/Alamy; 113 AA/C Coe; 114 AA/R Strange; 115 © Travelshots.com/Alamy; 116 © Harry Papas/Alamy; 117 AA/C Coe; 118 AA/C Coe; 119 AA/R Strange; 120 AA/R Strange; 121 AA/R Strange; 122 AA/R Strange; 123 Photolibrary Group; 129l AA/R Strange; 129c Pictures Colour Library; 129b AA/R Strange; 130 AA/C Coe; 131 AA/C Coe; 132 AA/C Coe; 133 © Jon Arnold Images Ltd/Alamy; 134 AA/C Coe; 134/135 © Worldwide Picture Library/Alamy; 136/137 AA/C Coe; 138/139 © Ariadne Van Zandbergen/Alamy; 139 © Robert Estall photo agency/Alamy; 140 © Pete M. Wilson/ Alamy; 141t AA/R Strange; 141b AA/R Strange; 142 AA/C Coe; 143 © Miamnuk Images/Alamy; 144 Tony Waltham/ Robert Harding; 151l AA/R Strange; 151c AA/C Strange; 151r AA/R Strange; 152 © Maximilian Weinzierl/Alamy; 153 © Wolfgang Pölzer/Alamy; 154 AA/R Strange; 155t AA/R Strange; 155b AA/R Strange; 156 © Wolfgang Pölzer/Alamy; 157 © Gavin Hellier/Alamy; 158/159 © Maximilian Weinzierl/Alamy; 161 AA/R Strange; 162 AA/C Coe; 163 © Maximilian Weinzierl/Alamy; 164 AA/R Strange; 165 AA/C Coe; 166 © Arco Images GmbH/Alamy; 167 © Jon Arnold Images Ltd/Alamy; 168 © Alan Copson City Pictures/Alamy; 169 AA/C Coe; 177l AA/C Coe; 177c AA/R Strange; 177r AA/C Sawyer; 178 AA/C Sawyer; 179 AA/C Sawyer; 180 AA/C Sawyer; 181 AA/C Sawyer; 182 AA/C Coe; 183 AA/C Coe; 184 AA/C Coe; 185 Jochen Schlenker/Robert Harding; 186 AA/R Strange; 187l AA/C Sawyer; 187c AA/C Sawyer; 187r AA/C Sawyer; 191cl AA/C Coe; 191tr AA/C Sawyer; 191cr AA/C Sawyer

Every effort has been made to trace the copyright holders, and we apologise in advance for any accidental errors. We would be happy to apply the corrections in the following edition of this publication.

SPIRALGUIDE
Questionnaire

Dear Traveller

Your comments, opinions and recommendations are very important to us. Please help us to improve our travel guides by taking a few minutes to complete this simple questionnaire.

You do not need a stamp (unless posted outside the UK). If you do not want to remove this page from your guide, then photocopy it or write your answers on a plain sheet of paper.

Send to: The Editor, Spiral Guides, AA World Travel Guides, FREEPOST SCE 4598, Basingstoke RG21 4GY.

Your recommendations...

We always encourage readers' recommendations for restaurants, night-life or shopping – if your recommendation is used in the next edition of the guide, we will send you a FREE AA Spiral Guide of your choice. Please state below the establishment name, location and your reasons for recommending it.

_____

_____

_____

_____

_____

Please send me AA Spiral _____
(see list of titles inside the back cover)

About this guide...

Which title did you buy?

_____ **AA Spiral**

Where did you buy it? _____

When? m m / y y

Why did you choose an AA Spiral Guide? _____

_____

_____

_____

_____

Did this guide meet your expectations?

Exceeded ☐   Met all ☐   Met most ☐   Fell below ☐

Please give your reasons _____

_____

_____

_____

_____

continued on next page...

Were there any aspects of this guide that you particularly liked?

_____

_____

_____

_____

_____

Is there anything we could have done better?

_____

_____

_____

_____

About you...

Name (Mr/Mrs/Ms) _____

Address _____

_____ **Postcode** _____

Daytime tel no _____ **email** _____

Please _only_ give us your email address and mobile phone number if you wish to hear from us about other products and services from the AA and partners by email or text or mms.

Which age group are you in?

Under 25 ☐   25–34 ☐   35–44 ☐   45–54 ☐   55–64 ☐   65+ ☐

How many trips do you make a year?

Less than one ☐   One ☐   Two ☐   Three or more ☐

Are you an AA member? Yes ☐   **No** ☐

About your trip...

When did you book? m m / y y   **When did you travel?** m m / y y

How long did you stay? _____

Was it for business or leisure? _____

Did you buy any other travel guides for your trip? ☐ Yes ☐ No

If yes, which ones? _____

_____

Thank you for taking the time to complete this questionnaire. Please send it to us as soon as possible, and remember, you do not need a stamp (unless posted outside the UK).